The combination c
nothing new, but for those of you who are a trifle uncomfortable advising clients, or for those who are seeking an alternative healing method, this book provides expert guidance and a fresh approach to the ever-developing art and science of astrology.

Counseling comes in many forms and encompasses various disciplines. One astrologer comes to grips with *codependency and the ACA syndrome*, so prevalent in our society. Another chapter explains the special difficulties and opportunities in the world of *medical astrology counseling*. Counseling also applies to the *business* world, as one of our authors proves in style.

Many people are grappling with *life issues* or recurrent crises that have never been resolved. Learn how to get to the bottom of these issues by recognizing certain symptoms of each of the 12 signs and strengthening their key qualities, eventually healing the spirit.

Adolescent rebellion is viewed in terms of the letters of the astrological alphabet. Explore the work of *Wilhelm Reich and Alexander Lowen* regarding body structure in association with planetary placements. These body types include schizoid, oral, masochistic, psychopathic and rigid.

But the bottom line in any science, art, or discipline is the basic understanding of what can and cannot be accomplished. The contributors of *Astrological Counseling: The Path to Self-Actualization* emphasize the importance of *listening* to clients to meet their needs and educating them as to the vast potential of astrology, as well as its limits. For those just starting out in this field, a straightforward discussion of delineating a natal chart with asteroids and secondary progressions is explained step by step.

Learn more about this service-oriented profession, and you just may learn about yourself, too.

Joan McEvers

Author of *12 Times 12* and co-author with Marion March of the highly acclaimed teaching series *The Only Way to . . . Learn Astrology*, Joan McEvers is a busy practicing astrologer in Coeur d'Alene, Idaho.

Born and raised in Chicago where she majored in art and worked as a model and illustrator for an art studio, she moved to the Los Angeles area in 1948 and continued her professional career in the sales field. This is where she met her husband Dean and raised their children.

Self-taught, Joan began her serious study of astrology in 1965 and in 1969 studied with Ruth Hale Oliver. About this time she started to counsel and teach astrology. She has since achieved an international reputation as a teacher and lecturer, speaking for many groups in the U.S. and Canada. An AFAN coordinator and member of NCGR, her articles have been published in several national and international astrological magazines.

In 1975 Joan and Marion founded Aquarius Workshops, Inc. with Joan as President. She also helped establish its quarterly publication *Aspects*, which is widely recognized for the wealth of astrological information packed in each issue. She continues to contribute to this periodical.

12 Times 12 details each of the 144 possible Sun/Ascendant combinations. Each description includes information about personality, appearance, health, likely vocational areas, interests and attitudes. Having always been intrigued with astrological/vocational potential, Joan and Marion presently are conducting a "Vocational Probe," seeking to establish a computer program which can be given to schools to assist young people in selecting work and career fields. They are collecting myriad types of vocational data for this program.

Co-winner with Marion March of the Regulus Award for contribution to Astrological Education, Joan also has been presented a Special Commemorative Bicentennial Award for the excellence of her published works from the *Astrological Monthly Review*.

Currently, she is editing a series of anthologies comprising The New World Astrology Series of Llewellyn Publications, working on a Horary Astrology book, and preparing for the fifth book in the March/McEvers ongoing series. She also reviews books and cassettes for Astro-Analytics Publications and writes their bi-monthly newsletter.

A double Aquarius with Moon in Leo, when she isn't preoccupied with astrological activities, Joan enjoys spending time with her husband, four children and five grandchildren, quilting and playing bridge.

THE NEW WORLD ASTROLOGY SERIES

This series is designed to give all people who are interested and involved in astrology the latest information on a variety of subjects. Llewellyn has given much thought to the prevailing trends and to the topics that would be most important to our readers.

Future books will include such topics as vocational astrology, various relationships and astrology, electional astrology, astrology and past lives, and many other subjects of interest to a wide range of people. This project has evolved because of the lack of information on these subjects and because we wanted to offer our readers the viewpoints of the best experts in each field in one volume.

We anticipate publishing approximately four books per year on varying topics and updating previous editions when new material becomes available. We know this series will fill a gap in your astrological library. We look for only the best writers and article topics when planning the new books and appreciate any feedback from our readers on subjects you would like to see covered.

Llewellyn's New World Astrology Series will be a welcome addition to the novice, student and professional alike. It will provide introductory as well as advanced information on all the topics listed above—and more.

Enjoy, and feel free to write to Llewellyn with your suggestions or comments.

Other Books in This Series

Forthcoming Books

Llewellyn's New World Astrology Series

ASTROLOGICAL COUNSELING

The Path to Self-Actualization

Edited by
Joan McEvers

1990
Llewellyn Publications
St. Paul, Minnesota 55164-0383, U.S.A.

FIRST EDITION

Cover and Book Design: Terry Buske
Original cover painting *Crystal Ship* © **1990 Melissa Ireland.**
Courtesy of Spirit Art, 7800 Computer Ave. S., Bloomington, MN
55435.

Computer-generated charts calculated and printed utilizing Matrix Blue Star Software, copyright© 1989 Matrix Software.

Library of Congress Cataloging-in-Publication Data

Astrological counseling: the path to self-actualization / edited by Joan McEvers.
       p.   cm. -- (Llewellyn's new world astrology series)
       Includes bibliographical references.
       ISBN 0–87542–385–X
       1. Astrology. 2. Counseling—Miscellanea. 3. Self-actualization (Psychology)—Miscellanea. I. McEvers, Joan.
       II. Series.
BF1729.C67A88   1990
133.5′81583—dc20   90–46437
                                             CIP

90 91 92 93 94   10 9 8 7 6 5 4 3 2 1

Llewellyn Publications
A Division of Llewellyn Worldwide, Ltd.
P.O. Box 64383, St. Paul, MN 55164–0383

Contents

INTRODUCTION

The very beginnings of astrology are shrouded in history. According to some accounts, it all began with Chaldean shepherds turning their eyes to the sky as they sat on the hillsides tending their sheep. They noted that certain stars appeared to make constant, variable patterns and that they could judge earthly events with the corresponding heavenly phenomena. The grandiose spectacle of the changing, shifting heavens prompted them and other ancient sky-viewers to figure out correlations to events happening on Earth. Over centuries, viewers in all parts of the world added to the lore that "as above, so below," realizing that the phenomena in the heavens reflected life on Earth.

In ancient times, astrology and astronomy were inseparable, and every astronomer/astrologer practiced both as a matter of course. Over the centuries as astrology fell into disfavor, astronomy gained ascendance, disavowed astrology, and became a science of measurement... dealing with magnitudes, distances, motions, physical conditions and mutual relations of the celestial bodies.

The first known astrology was mundane astrology, concerned only with the welfare of the king and State. Astrologer-priests advised the leaders of such large-scale events as wars, floods, famines and plagues. Counseling, as we know it, was unheard of. The stars dictated the fates, and the astrologers were all-powerful, convincing their rulers that all events were predestined and fated. The actual practice of "reading" individual horoscopes was a long, long distance in the future.

Around 100–30 B.C., the Egyptians practiced a mystical form of astrology which focused on the economic and religious activities of their civilization. The Nile was the source of all life, and its floods brought fertility to an otherwise barren region, just as in modern times we harness the power of the great rivers for electricity. The Egyptians knew and believed that the flood tides of the Nile were influenced by the Moon and the Sun.

According to prominent British astrologer, Michael Baigent, the earliest known astrological records date from the reign of Babylonian king Ammisaduqa around 1700 B.C. He further states that astrology is not the product of a vast antiquity reaching back into the past for hundreds and thousands of years as certain of the Greek writers believed. Rather, it began in the first dynasty of Babylon (1950–1651 B.C.).

By the 15th century, influences from Greece, Rome and the Orient had been combined, systematized and refined to give astrology a similar form to what it has currently. But long before that, Achilles Tatius (4th century) reported the existence of Egyptians mapping the heavens on their pillars. The royal library at Nineveh contained many documents that related to the astrology of the ancient Babylonians, who had borrowed their concepts from the Sumerian invaders. The Chaldeans, originally Assyrians and Babylonians, were known for their magical powers, many of which were related to the practice of astrology. Their empirical knowledge spread to Egypt, Greece and eventually Rome, where accounts of the influences of the signs and planets were preserved by astrologers, poets, scientists and physicians.

One of the first astrological works so preserved was a long poem by Marcus Manilus titled *Astronomica*. He developed a method of relating certain mundane events to the individual through a moveable circle of houses based on the Part of Fortune. The house which held the Part of Fortune was considered to be house one, with the rest of the houses following around counterclockwise.

It is most intriguing that astrology has disappeared from the pages of history for hundreds of years at a time, only to arise from the ashes like the Phoenix wherever learning and curiosity prevail. Around 180 A.D., astrology began to decline in Europe, mainly because the technical ability to make observations and calculations was lost. As the Roman Empire crumbled, astrology also crumbled into a superstitious melange. One significant comeback took place in Europe around the 10th century. Astrology had survived through translations of Greek, Hebrew and Latin into Arabic, and these translations began to appear in the libraries of learned men. From this time until the end of the 12th century, learning flowed from Spain and the Arabic world to northern Europe. There was great demand for Latin translations of Arabic manuscripts dealing with mathematics as well as astrology and astronomy.

In the medical and astronomical fields the Arabs showed great skill, and they set up centers of learning in Baghdad and Damascus, where the Caliph established a major observatory and library. Arab astronomical studies had a strong astrological orientation. As opposed to the Babylonians and Assyrians, they used a practical form of astrology to aid them in everyday life, such as mapping propitious times to undertake travel, to marry, to set up a business. Their charts were based on a form of what we know as horary astrology today, and their emphasis on favorable and unfavorable indications was to become a great help in the rehabilitation of astrology in the West during the Renaissance. The greatest Arab astrologer of the time was Albumasur, whose book *Introductoriu* was translated into Spanish in the Middle Ages, eventually making its way into Europe.

In the 2nd century, the great Greek mathematician and astronomer Claudius Ptolemy wrote two major works, the *Almagest* and the *Tetrabiblos,* or *Four Books on the Influence of the Stars*, which remained the leading treatise in the field for centuries. This book described a system (Ptolemaic) of astronomy and geography based on the theory that the Sun, planets and stars revolve around the Earth. This system was generally accepted until displaced by the Copernican system, which didn't come into being until 13 centuries later.

Astrology in the Middle Ages

As the Middle Ages began (approximately 476–1492), theologians were concerned as to whether astrology should be classed as a legitimate science or as a forbidden divinatory art. John of Salisbury decided that in its apparent denial of free will, astrology had pagan associations. St. Albertus Magnus first recognized the theological value of Greek and Arab philosophy and science; he initially publicized the teachings of Aristotle; and he concluded that while perhaps the stars could not influence the human soul, they could surely influence the body and human will. But astrology was still only used by the literati, and its influence was assumed to affect the affairs of heads of state rather than the average person.

Astrology began to enjoy a new respectability, and astrological studies acquired curricula in European universities. The University of Bologna, where Dante studied, had a chair of astrology as early as 1125. Astrologers were regarded with great respect, even reverence. Guido Bonatti, one of the most famous of 13th-century astrologers, chose times for the army to put on its armor, to mount, to charge. In 1327 Cecco d'Ascoli, Bologna's professor of astrology, was burned at the stake—not because he was an astrologer but because of his heretical views. He is one of astrology's few martyrs.

Astrological practice was still very much concerned with the prediction of wars, pestilences, revolutions and catastrophes, and only the ruling classes could afford to employ an astrologer. According to British astrologer Nicholas Campion, astrology in medieval Europe consisted of two major types: natural, regarded as the relationship between celestial phenomena and terrestial events; and judicial, used mostly for horaries and elections, but also for nativities.

Astrology during the Renaissance

During the Renaissance, some European writers asserted that astrology was modern and scientific and that religion was the residue of ancient superstitions. They were called heretics by their opponents, who felt they were seduced by Satan. Many factors must be taken into consideration to correctly assess the significance of astrology in Europe during the Middle Ages and the Renaissance. During this time, three distinct branches of astrology had been developed. *Judicial* astrology determined the individual's destiny according to a horoscope cast for the moment of birth. *Horary* answered questions of the hour by means of a chart cast for the exact moment the question was asked. *Mundane* astrology was used to forecast events of national significance.

The Italian poet Dante (13th century) wrote of these three branches of astrology, making reference to them in both *Paradiso* and *Purgatorio*. English poets Chaucer (14th century), Milton (17th century), Shakespeare and Spenser (both 16th century) all alluded to astrology in their works. Chaucer actually cast horoscopes for some of his *Canterbury Tales* characters. Finally, astrology was being used for and by those who were not royalty or warlords.

Astrology in the Orient

The earliest Indian astrological text was probably written about 2000 B.C., and today the sub-continent is the only one where astrology has a strong influence on daily life. Here astrology is strongly tied to the concept of Karma, which is broadly defined as the journey of the soul through successive incarnations to an ultimate union with the infinite. Behavior in each lifetime determines the starting point in the next. Astrology is used to help determine that next starting point.

The major difference between Oriental and Western astrology is the use of the *sidereal zodiac*. Although some Western astrologers have adopted this method, most use the tropical zodiac. The sidereal method views the planets against the background of the constellations rather than as they appear in equal fields of the ecliptic in the tropical method. The influence of astrology is observed in all areas of Indian life, from marriage to building a house, laying the cornerstone, etc. Though Indian astrologers cast charts for the average citizen, these charts were totally predictive, rather than referencing potential characteristics, traits and talents.

In China, astrology was most likely introduced along ancient trade routes, and over the centuries Chinese astrology developed a highly individualistic outlook. Emperors and warlords used their astrologers to determine auspicious times for campaigns and ceremonies. This type of astrology is based on a very complex system of five elements, five planets plus the Sun and Moon, yin and yang, and 12 signs of the zodiac represented by animals... rat, ox, tiger, hare, dragon, snake, horse, goat, monkey, cock, dog and boar... the signs, rather than dividing the sky, divide the equator.

Prominent Contributors to Astrology

The most renowned and controversial astrological forecaster was *Nostradamus* (Michel de Notre Dame), who was born in St. Remy in 1503 and served as astrologer and physician to three French kings. The great seer's quatrains are still consulted with the hope of finding the key to his accuracy. Many of his predictions came true in his lifetime, and some modern astrologers claim that others have come to pass since, including the rise of Oliver Cromwell, the Lord Protector of England; the birth of Napoleon; and the exact date of the end of World War II. His admirers feel that his quatrains predicted the rise and assassination of John F. Kennedy. However, because he felt that mankind was not ready for predictions of the future that would result in harmful effects, he made his verses so obscure that they are almost impossible to interpret.

Much of astrology's popularity during the Renaissance was due in part to the Church and the positive encouragement it received from several popes. It is said that Martin Luther, the German religious reformer, was so opposed to astrology because it was in such favor at the Vatican. Popes Sixtus IV and Julius II engaged actively in astrology, and Leo X employed astrologers throughout his reign. Their example was followed by the leading courts of Europe with many employing court astrologers. The Vatican is still said to have the greatest astrological library in the world.

Johannes Campanus, a 13th-century mathematician and chaplain and physician to Pope Urban IV, is given credit for inventing the 12-house horoscope similar to the ones currently in use. Johann Muller, better known as *Regiomontanus*, was a professor of astronomy at Venice. He printed books on trigonometry and was responsible for publishing some of the earliest ephemerides; he also translated Ptolemy's *Almagest*.

Regarded as the founder of modern astronomy in establishing that the Earth rotates daily on its axis and that the planets revolve in order around the Sun, Polish astronomer **Nicolaus Copernicus**, who was born in 1473, established the rules for modern astrologers. The printing of his famous treatise *De Revolutionibus Orbium Coelestium* was delayed because of religious and political conditions. It was published while Copernicus lay on his deathbed.

Sixteenth-century astronomer/astrologer **Tycho Brahe**, who worked in Denmark under the patronage of King Frederick II, studied Copernicus' tables and revised them into a more correct form. In his book *De Disciplinus Mathematicis,* Brahe stated: "Those who deny the influence of the planets violate clear evidence which for educated people of sane judgment it is not suitable to contradict." In his study of the motion of the planets he was assisted by **Johannes Kepler**, who based his discovery of the three laws of universal gravitation (planetary motion) on Brahe's research. Kepler also designed a telescope with two convex lenses and crosswires in the focus for use as a pointer to fix the positions of stars and planets. In an address given at the University of Copenhagen, he defended the practice of astrology, stating:

> We cannot deny the influence of the stars without disbelieving in the wisdom of God. Man is made from the elements, and absorbs them as much as food or drink, from which it follows that man must also, like the elements, be subject to the influence of the planets.

A contemporary of Kepler, **Galileo Galelei**, the great Italian astronomer, mathematician and physicist, investigated the natural laws that laid the foundations of modern experimental science. He constructed the first complete astronomical telescope in 1609, and through its use he discovered sunspots, craters on the Moon, Jupiter's moons, and Saturn's rings. His astronomical discoveries confirmed the Copernican theory of the solar system, but when he attempted to show that there was a scriptural confirmation, he was condemned as a heretic and was forced by the Inquisition to abjure his belief that the Earth moved around the Sun.

The most renowned 17th-century astrologer was Englishman **William Lilly**, author of *Christian Astrology*, the forerunner of modern horary astrology. Lilly was not an astronomer, but he was well able to understand astronomy/astrology books which had been translated from Latin into English. He predicted the beheading of King Charles I, as well as the Great Fire of London, and these predictions got him into trouble as he was suspected of complicity in the fire. He was tried and acquitted. Lilly also earned a license to practice medicine and is believed to have used astrological knowledge in treating patients.

Isaac Newton, whose book *Principia Mathematica*, which has been described as the greatest mental effort ever made by one man, had a solid astrological foundation, and though he pioneered modern astronomy, he never faltered in his respect for astrology.

Unfortunately, the popularity of astrology in the 16th and 17th centuries did little for its reputation. Penny almanacs and handbooks kept the common people happy with garbled prognostications (much like the horoscope columns in modern-day newspapers and magazines), and the whole subject was criticized accordingly. The question of free will versus predestination, or whether or not the soul was free of planetary influences while the body and mind remained subject to it, were debated and discussed by theologians, scholars and noblemen.

Noted thinkers have long endorsed the efficacy of astrology. Ralph Waldo Emerson stated: "Astrology is astronomy brought to Earth and applied to the affairs of men." The great German poet Goethe, in a letter written to Schiller in 1798, states:

> The superstition of astrology has its origin in our dim sense of some vast cosmic unity. Experience tells us that the heavenly bodies which are nearest us have a decisive influence on weather and plant life. We need only move higher, stage by stage, and who can say where this influence ceases? The astronomer observes that the heavenly bodies are subject to mutual disturbances; the philosopher is inclined, nay rather forced, to assume that action can take place even at the greatest distances; thus man, in his presentiment, needs only to go a stage further, and he will extend such influences to the moral life, to happiness and misfortune. Such fanciful ideas, and other of the same kind, I cannot even call superstition; they come naturally to us and are as tolerable and as questionable as any other faith.

Confucius said: "Heaven sends down its good or evil symbols and wise men act accordingly."

In the late 19th and early 20th centuries, astrology experienced a resurgence of interest, and astrologers combined all available knowledge to cast horoscopes based on the date, time and place of birth of the individual. The writings of Alan Leo, Charles Carter and Isabelle Pagan gained prominence in England, and astrologers Evangeline Adams, Walter Gorn Olds (Sepharial) and Elbert Benjamine (C.C. Zain), among others, assumed importance in the American astrological field. By this time astrologers were counseling clients in everyday affairs, pointing out potential career directions and advising them on investments, marital affairs and business.

Between World War I and II, the English and German schools of astrology came into much prominence, and a more psychological flavor was apparent in terms of astrological counseling. Witte and the Ebertins were the guiding forces in Germany.

Modern Astrology

Astrology has grown and prospered in the last 50 years, during which time astrological giants such as Grant Lewi, Llewellyn George, Marc Edmund Jones, Dane Rudhyar and Manly Palmer Hall pioneered humanistic and individualistic astrology based on philosophy and metaphysics. Instead of predestined fate read in the stars, modern astrologers now use psychological and humanistic approaches as they consult with their clients, who are not necessarily kings, princes and leaders, although U.S. President Reagan was advised by astrologer Joan Quigley. Now the astrologer's client is the layperson who wishes to know potentials, pitfalls and timing. Perhaps a better name for astrological services is "consulting" since the conscientious practitioner does not necessarily advise or predict fatalistic events, but rather offers options, suggests synchronization of thought and action, and points out efficacious times for moves, job changes, financial investment, etc. Modern astrologers tend to avoid terms like "reading" the chart, preferring to analyze, counsel, interpret or consult.

As you will discover in reading this book, there are many different kinds of astrological counseling now available to the public. People are searching for meaning in their lives and a purpose to their existence in our technological world. The ancient symbols and the mythology of astrology still appeal to erudite individuals not only as an excellent means of self-understanding but also as a link to ancient knowledge. The endurance of astrology through the annals of time proves its worth.

What This Book is About

The authors in this book discuss business, medical, psychological and spiritual approaches to astrological consultation. **David Pond**, from Port Angeles, Washington, is an outstanding astrologer whose expertise in metaphysical and spiritual concepts is well known and admired. He presents an excellent guideline for any astrological counselor. **Maritha Pottenger**, a Los Angeles resident who works as an astrological editor in San Diego and is the author of several astrological books, points out how to find the person in the horoscope as well as how to zero in on that particular person's reason for seeing the astrologer.

Gray Keen from Redwood City, California, reminds us of how Plato sat on a rock while dispensing advice and warns us to beware of stereotypical counseling practices. Many of you may be familiar with **Bill Herbst** from his fascinating book *Houses of the Horoscope*. Here, he discusses the difference between astrological counseling and psychotherapy. His clients in Minneapolis, Minnesota benefit from his psychological and therapeutic background.

When it comes to business consulting, **Doris A. Hebel** from Chicago has no peer. Her clientele consists mostly of businesspeople, and Doris is an authority on the astrology of investments, business operations and timing. **Susan Dearborn Jackson**, who hails from Eugene, Oregon, discusses how you can read the body from the chart, thus gaining insight into temperament and psychological attitudes, which help in guiding the client consultation.

With an exemplary background in psychology, astrology and healing, **Ginger Chalford** from Miami, Florida explains how the astrological counselor can help the client heal him/herself physically, mentally and psychologically. **Donna Cunningham**, another well-known astrological author (*Healing Pluto Problems*, among others), describes how to counsel codependent people. Her background is psychological and she has a degree in social work. Donna resides in Brooklyn, New York.

With a degree in clinical psychology, **Donald L. Weston** from Portland, Oregon explores the connection between astrology and psychology and makes a good case for using asteroids in astrological analysis and consultation. **Eileen Nauman** has recently moved from Ohio to Cottonwood, Arizona, where she continues to practice her MedScan techniques. Eileen details her approach to medical astrology and focuses on how to deal with the client who needs medical attention.

All of these astrologers are well known in the field and are responsible practitioners with many years of counseling experience. We know you will benefit from the information they present in this book.

Joan McEvers
Coeur d'Alene, Idaho
May 1990

Bibliography

Baigent, Campion and Harvey. *Mundane Astrology*. Wellingborough, Northamptonshire, England: The Aquarian Press, 1984.

The Columbia Viking Desk Encyclopedia. New York, NY: The Viking Press, Inc., 1953.

Lynch, John. *The Coffee Table Book of Astrology*. New York, NY: The Viking Press, Inc., 1962.

Parker, Derek and Julia Parker. *The Compleat Astrologer*. New York, NY: McGraw-Hill Book Company, 1971.

Webster's Biographical Dictionary. Springfield, MA: Merriam-Webster Inc., 1976.

David Pond

David holds a B.A. in Education and a Master of Science degree in Experimental Metaphysics from Central Washington University. The co-author of two books, *The Metaphysical Handbook* and *Crystals, Stones & Chakras*, he is currently completing work on the soon-to-be-published *The Art of Relationships*.

A practicing professional astrologer since 1975 along with maintaining his astrological practice, writing and conducting workshops, he is also a junior high school basketball coach. David complements his professional activities with a rich family life, joining his wife Laurie in raising their four sons.

ASTROLOGICAL COUNSELING

We are in the middle of a cultural/spiritual revolution that is sweeping the planet. An accelerated growth in consciousness is affecting every man, woman and child, snowballing so that the perceived sense of the pace of evolution is quickening.

We are waking up. This awakening is leading to an emerging new myth of a global consciousness where we are all but individual cells of consciousness within. This evolution/revolution has many people living in a reality that their previous cultural training has left them ill-prepared to understand. A hunger exists in the population to understand life from a larger perspective; thus, the role of astrological counselor is experiencing elevation to a higher status.

As the populace becomes increasingly dissatisfied with life lacking in meaning and significance, more and more individuals will turn to astrology to satisfy a need that has not been met by traditional systems. Astrologers are finding themselves in the unique situation of possessing a tool that can help people connect with the divine intent that brought them into this incarnation: the astrological birth chart. The birth chart is a *blueprint of the soul's intention* for this life and helps individuals to discover their purpose and unique niche in the larger reality of an evolving global consciousness.

This chapter explores what it takes to be an effective, helpful astrological counselor; the philosophical background of why to use astrology in the first place; the preparation and training necessary to become an astrological counselor; professional ethics to consider in one's practice; and the preparation and actual conducting of an astrological counseling session.

Astrologers themselves must evolve to keep up with evolutionary trends that are occurring within the larger population. A few years ago I was talking with a psychic friend about the accelerated pace of consciousness growth on the planet. His point of view was that astrology was going to fall by the wayside as a tool because people would soon evolve beyond its relevance. Being a professional astrologer who makes his entire living by astrology, I did not take this information lightly. I gave it considerable thought and ultimately rejected his notion, but it did give me cause to reflect. Astrology will not pass away as irrelevant, but it is likely that old worn-out interpretations will have to be discarded to keep up with people's actual experiences.

Yes, it is an exciting time to be an astrologer, but it is also a time when the needs of your clients will push you to continually grow in your understanding of the birth chart to aid others on their evolutionary journey.

Why Use Astrology?

Embarking on a career as an astrological counselor is entering into a sacred tradition of helping others discover their purpose in life. Astrology is unique among all of the helping professions in that it starts with a map constructed with the individual directly in the center of the universe. Most systems help individuals fit into their cultural norms, whereas astrology is tailored to one's distinctions. People are drawn to astrologers because something is missing in the traditional systems of counseling that typically focus on that which is unhealthy in the individual. *The beauty of astrology is that it allows individuals an in-depth exploration of their inner world without assuming something is wrong with them in the first place.* It helps people to reconnect with the cosmos by providing a bridge to a personal mythology that is intertwined with the collective mythology. This is a healing in itself in that it helps people discover the purpose and meaning of their lives in a larger context than traditional systems are able to provide.

Two important questions to ask yourself when considering this field are "Why do I want to be an astrological counselor?" and "What are my motivations?" But just as important as knowing what you have to offer is knowing your limitations. If you try to field every request, you ensure mediocrity in your sessions. There are likely to be some aspects of astrology that you simply are not as interested in as others; you cannot be everything for all people. The astrological birth chart is such a magical tool that many believe it can answer any and all questions. Perhaps it can, but can you? Do you want to? Are your interests more in line with careers? Relationships? Spiritual development? Financial concerns? Health? It is perfectly permissible to acknowledge that some areas are not your interest nor your forte. It will add integrity to your practice if you allow yourself to direct some clients to other astrologers who might have more of an interest and expertise in your clients' type of questions.

Qualities of a Good Astrological Counselor

1. A natural interest in helping others find their strengths and sense of purpose in life.

2. A love and compassion for the variety of the human experience.

3. A fascination with the use of astrology in your life.

4. A magical imagination that is drawn to the interconnectedness of all of life's experience and a belief that there is a spiritual meaning behind every experience.

5. A willingness to be a student of life forever as astrology will never be mastered, only delved into more deeply.

Astrology, Psychology and Mysticism

The use of astrology in counseling brings a session close to the practice of psychology. Although they have much in common, I resist the modern trend to marry astrology and psychology. Astrology is not just another language for describing the psychological processes of developmental stages and cause and effect. Astrologers who pursue the study of psychology gain considerably, just as psychologists can benefit by knowing the astrological make-up of their clients, but the two disciplines essentially come out of different traditions. Psychology was born out of the scientific tradition, where astrology's roots are in the mystical traditions.

Modern scientific inquiry is based on the assumption that you can isolate cause and effect. Astrology starts with the premise of the *interrelatedness of all life*. These two premises are mutually exclusive. To prove astrology to the scientific community, astrologers would have to relinquish much of the beauty astrology offers.

I once heard this saying: "Mystics learn all that they can about the knowable, and leave the rest as a source of wonder and awe." I like to think of that statement as a high-water mark for the practice of astrology as well. Much of life remains unexplainable, and rather than thinking that this disproves astrology, allow this to be a source of wonder and awe and the majesty of creation. I believe that astrologers should be proud of their roots in magic, mystery, alchemy and shamanism, rather than watering them down to become more palatable to the scientific community.

Ideally, the role that the astrological counselor plays for his or her clients is not that of the all-knowing sage with all the answers. Instead, I see astrologers as resource facilitators helping their clients ask the right questions to probe the mysteries and uncover the essential harmony that is their birthright. It is this deep questioning that is the search which helps clients discover their path—a path that leads to more penetrating questioning and the uncovering of still deeper levels of truth within the fathomless depths of the human psyche, the profound mystery that is life.

Preparation Necessary to Become an Astrological Counselor

Astrology is a vast wondrous study of human potential. One of the first issues to deal with in learning to be an effective astrological counselor is to realize that there is a major difference between astrological interpretation and astrological counseling. Knowing astrology is one thing, but to be able to help others better understand their lives and find greater meaning through the use of astrology is another.

The science of astrology consists of chart construction and learning the interpretations of the various placements. If this was all there is to astrology, computers would become the best astrologers. However, astrology is also an art that requires an intuitive sensitivity and an ability to synthesize all the hundreds of pieces of information to present a cohesive whole view of the chart, skills that only humans are able to perform.

How to convey the information in a meaningful, useful way to others deserves special attention and is presented later in this chapter. Counseling requires the development and application of a completely different set of skills, abilities and talents than the learning of astrology itself.

In the many years I've taught astrology classes, I have never encountered a student who became a professional without becoming obsessive and compulsive about the study for at least a few years. There are so many variables to put into perspective that it takes total immersion into one's study to ultimately see light at the end of the tunnel and make a coherent whole out of the language. Students who patiently keep plugging away never seem to break through and become adept in the use of the craft. It is important to realize that the study of astrology is inherently vast; you'll never come to a time when you feel that there is nothing more to learn. And only certain types of individuals are comfortable with this. I've been a professional for 14 years, and I still feel that I am just beginning; there is still so much to learn. For some people, this characteristic immensity of astrology is exactly the feature that attracts them to the study, and for others, it is that which keeps them away.

Since astrology is still outside the mainstream of our cultural education, there are rather few training programs available for the budding astrologer. One must be willing to read everything available, take workshops, attend lectures and conferences as they present themselves, and essentially seize every opportunity to develop understanding.

When I first became obsessed with the study of astrology, I drew up birth charts for all the important people in my life and put them on three-by-five-inch index cards. I kept these with me at all times so that I could refer to the charts when I noticed some significant feature of the person in my life. I would then attempt to see where this behavior was indicated. I even placed these cards on my car's dashboard near the speedometer so that I could contemplate these charts on long drives.

Astrology is essentially a language that *describes the human experience*, not the experience itself. To become a good astrologer, become well versed in the ways of humanity. Books are helpful in adding insights, but they cannot take the place of actual experience. I think astrologers who have a breadth of life experience are more able to relate to people and have empathy for what others are actually going through. The lessons that I've learned through raising children, being in relationships, gardening, undergoing successes and failures in business, winning and losing in sports, and paying bills have helped me as much as astrology books in my practice.

Not that studying astrology books is being discouraged—quite the contrary. A professional has the responsibility of staying well-informed. However, it is helpful to complement your astrological study with research in mythology, philosophy (both Eastern and Western), comparative religion, current world affairs, movies, the arts, and anything else that can broaden your base of knowledge.

Chart interpretations from other astrologers also can be of benefit. You not only see how another professional operates but also develop empathy for your clients' experiences with you. What is it like on the other side of the table? What works and doesn't work for you? What triggers your defenses? What helps you feel more at ease?

Another technique for becoming a better astrologer is the formation of a *study group* with astrologers to review each other's work. In the training for becoming a traditional counselor, there is considerable supervision and review of performance as one first begins to work with others. Astrologers, however, are often left to their own devices to develop their craft. You might make back-up tapes of your sessions with clients and invite a critique from other astrologers in a study group. This takes courage, but it is certainly worth the effort.

The bottom line is that it does not take a good teacher to learn astrology. It takes a good student!

Ethics

There are many questions regarding professional ethics that need to be considered before embarking on a career of astrological counseling. The astrological birth chart is a powerful tool that can give you insights into the inner dimensions of a person's life. The responsibility of using this information in ways that can be helpful, loving and uplifting is tremendous. Clients will ask questions concerning other people in their lives. Is it permissible to give information pertaining to another person who did not ask you to look into his/her life?

A good rule of thumb to follow is that it is not advisable to reveal information about someone's chart without permission, other than how it directly pertains to the person whom you are counseling. I also question clients as to their motivations and intentions for wanting the information. If I suspect it is not in the other person's best interest, or that somehow my client is trying to seek an advantage over the asked-about person, I always fall back on professional ethics, stating that I am not at liberty to reveal the information.

I've grown to believe that *permission* from the person whose chart you are interpreting is a necessary ingredient in giving a good analysis of the chart. This consent is an invitation at the higher-mind level to peer into the inner levels of the birth chart to see how it relates to the individual. Without permission, a chart is just a piece of paper with symbols that relates to thousands of potential interpretations. With such approval, the intuitive faculty is brought into play and the astrologer is essentially *led* to appropriate information to bring forth.

I also consider *confidentiality* to be an irrevocable rule. I like to believe that the integrity of my stand on this issue creates an invisible aura of trust that future clients will also be able to detect, and this will allow them the freedom to reveal their true process during our sessions. Conversely, I believe that we can never hide from our own subconscious, and when one violates professional ethics there will be an element of non-trustworthiness in the aura. In this case, clients will not be as inclined to reveal their true process to the counselor.

I was confronted with this issue when a client of mine was involved in a serious crime that the FBI was investigating. The FBI had seized this person's telephone bills and contacted me because my number showed up on a bill. The FBI suggested that I help apprehend this person by setting up an appointment and then informing the Bureau as to its time. They intended to capture this person before s/he got to my house. The crime was serious, and they pushed me with the concept of my civic duty to help.

Was it ethical to violate confidentiality? Was it ethical not to help the FBI? Ultimately, I came to the conclusion to protect the confidentiality of my relationship with the client. It was not just for the person in question; I felt that violation of this principle would taint my relationships with future clients. We all have our role to play in civic duty, and I felt that mine wasn't in the apprehending of criminals.

Another question of ethics in becoming an astrological counselor is learning how to *overcome personal biases* with some of the signs. It is quite natural and human to have an affinity with some zodiacal signs and to be less attracted, or even to dislike, some of the signs based on personal experiences and tendencies within our own charts. However, these biases should not be carried into the counseling session.

Learn to find the beauty in every sign, every chart, every client. Every sign has its positive and negative characteristics. If you have seen only the negative side of a particular sign, perhaps it is symbolic of an issue that you should face in *your* life. Look into your own chart to better understand your reactions to the sign in question. I think an ethical astrologer would not interpret a chart that s/he was biased against, for to do so the astrologer inadvertently would be giving the message to the client that "You would be fine if you just had another chart!"

Yet another ethical concern arises as a counselor deals with the issue of *how information is presented*. Are you helping to provide a more sophisticated "excuse" framework for your clients, or empowering them? "Saturn made me do it" is not much different than "The devil made me do it." I've grown to believe that every force in the universe is in a giant conspiracy for our ultimate evolution and well-being. From this perspective, it is important to honor the spiritual integrity of every individual and to understand that there are not good charts nor bad charts, not good signs nor bad signs, not good aspects nor bad aspects, only appropriate issues to deal with for the person born to the chart. Help your client move away from astrological excuses and on to accepting the appropriateness of every aspect of his/her chart as if it represented the learning curriculum that the soul chose to take on in this particular incarnation. Help clients accept what they have been given to work with, and then help them find a healthy way to express these factors in their lives. The astrological birth chart is a marvelous tool for helping your clients face themselves and take total responsibility for their situations in life.

A final point of ethics that every counselor ultimately must face is the issue of *transference*. It is not uncommon for clients to fall in love with their counselor. A typical scenario is the situation of a frustrated person whose marriage is faltering because of a lack of communication and understanding from his/her partner. The person begins seeing a counselor who offers compassion and understanding—the very features missing in the client's marriage. Love blossoms as the counselor becomes the projected view of the ideal understanding partner. It happens. An ethical astrologer would never take advantage of this in any way.

Can You Face Emotional Heavies?

An important issue to consider while embarking on a career in astrological counseling is how well you handle heavy emotional responses in others. An astrological session is often a cathartic experience for your clients. Long-forgotten emotional pain is frequently brought to the surface while you are exploring the birth chart. Be prepared for this—keep a box of tissues in your office! But just as important, ask yourself, "Can you allow others to emote without reacting yourself?" If you can, these emotional releases can be very healing for your clients. But if you resist these experiences, you will inadvertently be sending a message of disapproval to your clients, which can be quite counterproductive.

So many messages of our culture signal that it is not all right to experience emotional pain. We even label emotions up and down, implying that some are good and others bad. Sayings such as "Love is a risk, you might get hurt" also promote this notion of avoiding pain. But hurt happens; it is part of the human experience. Love is not a risk of getting hurt, it is a guarantee.

Astrologers are often put in the role of helping others to honor the truth of their experiences. When we can touch another's pain with compassion and mercy, it melts. People spend so much time resisting pain that they often run away from life trying to avoid this aspect of the human experience. When you can help your clients embrace their pain, this in and of itself is a healing, with resolution soon to follow. A wound can be healed, but first it has to be accepted.

Counseling Born in the Moment

Counseling that is born out of the needs of the moment is more helpful to your clients than a preset format that is imposed on the session. Be willing to respond to every clue and opportunity to connect with your clients that spontaneously presents itself.

The books on astrology always deal with the archetypal level, never with your clients. It is wise to realize ahead of time that 100 per cent of your interpretation is not going to be right on. Is that all right with you? Do you have enough humility to adjust your understanding of astrology based on your clients' first-hand experiences?

In your sessions, it is your opportunity to learn astrology from your clients. It is perfectly permissible to ask "How do you experience this?" Go ahead and offer your assumptions of what you think the part of the chart you are interpreting means, but be willing to learn from your clients. They are living it and can teach you a tremendous amount.

This *interactive type of counseling* is replenishing for you. I know certain counselors who can see only a few clients a day because they find themselves exhausted from giving all they can. It is their belief that they should be in complete control of the session, and their ethics dictate that if they are not exhausted at the end of the session they didn't give enough. Conversely, I know other counselors who see six or seven clients a day and are revitalized through each of the sessions. These are interactive counselors. They believe that there is some-thing to be learned from each and every client, just as there is something to teach. Through the interactions, they are learning and growing throughout the day. In my mind's eye I see that if there is a true need for my service, the need in the client will create a vortex of energy to which I can respond. The energy for the session is already there in the client's need for the service.

One thing that the chart does not show is the level of consciousness with which the client is operating. There are two truths about each of us: a *spiritual truth* and a *species truth*. The chart shows potentialities, but it does not show what level of spiritual awareness your client has attained. This will require your intuition and sensitivity to assess because the same aspect in a chart will manifest very differently in the person who has worked on developing his/her spirituality as opposed to the person who is still immersed in the species level of consciousness, with all of its attendant issues of territoriality, grudges, jealousies, greed, and so forth.

The saying "Walk a mile in their shoes before you judge them" is very important before you make your assessments of how to best guide your clients. First, understand their truth and see the appropriateness of their situations through their perspective. Remember that we all are doing the best we can, given the information and experiences with which we have to work. So before offering advice, first develop empathy so that you can truly understand others' choices from their perspective. Then, let your counseling be born out of the moment, and you will increase the likelihood of truly reaching them.

Most counselors in this field acknowledge a certain magic of synchronicity that occurs in the types of clients and questions they attract while going through a similar lesson in their own life. As you become aware of this, you will find that it is not unusual to hear yourself giving exactly the same advice to your clients that you need to hear.

In astrological counseling, communication is the key. Having the information at hand is one thing, but conveying it in a way that your clients can easily grasp is the real issue. This deals with the issue of *intention* and *effectiveness*. Knowing your intention of what you want to get across is part of communication, but the effectiveness of reaching your clients cannot be measured in you; you have to pay close attention to how they are receiving it.

The chart itself is a potent tool in learning about your clients, but there are many other tools you can use as well. As a counselor, draw on every clue you can. Your clients' body language, eye contact, voice control, etc., also will tell you much about how to best establish rapport. *Mirroring* is a powerful technique for facilitating rapport. Adjusting to your clients' body movements, rate of breath and speech, and so forth, is the mirroring process. You have to be subtle with this, however, or your clients will feel that you are mocking them rather than establishing rapport.

The Healing Connection

The listening described above helps to discern the explicit clues that can be perceived through the senses. There is another type of listening at a deeper level that also can be cultivated. It could be described as *listening to the essence of being* that is beyond the sensory level. It does not always occur, but when it does it is unmistakable. It rarely happens in the beginning of a session as a client's defenses are still operating. But as a session progresses and your client surrenders to the opportunity, the defenses drop to a point where you can feel this person with a profound sense of knowingness. If you allow this imprinting of the client's essence upon you, you will be able to describe things that your client is going through and experiencing, not by external observation, but rather by describing what you are going through in his/her presence. I describe it in terms of my client's experience, but in truth, I am describing what I am experiencing. If you are able to do this in a non-judgmental way of complete acceptance, a healing connection will be established.

Astrology speaks to many levels of a person's character. As you describe potential manifestations of certain aspects in the chart, a client is often entertained as s/he realizes that there is more to astrology than a simple parlor game. As this continues, more of the masks of protection melt away, and eventually you begin to speak the person's truth. Astrology at the most profound level goes beyond describing what type of career, mate and lifestyle would be best for your client. It most importantly speaks to the inner dimension of the person's life.

People often feel so lonely, isolated and alienated in the modern world that when one sees them beyond their mask they experience a sense of being known and accepted that can be healing beyond techniques and procedures. To cultivate this healing connection, you have to be able to set aside your agenda of what you think should happen and allow the magic of the moment to present itself. This is often scary territory for a counselor because you are not in control.

I think it takes a faith that every organism on the planet strives to be well and whole; a basic drive for wellness is inherent in all of us. To believe this is to believe that every person is doing the best s/he can, given the current circumstances of his/her life. To encourage a healing in the direction that it wants to take is to become a facilitator of the healing process rather than the all-knowing director. As you accept the innate drive for well-being within your clients, your interactions with the deeper level of their being becomes a catalyst that assists and gives permission for the healing to take place.

Helping Clients Deal with Their Past

There are so many situations in life that make absolutely no sense as they are occurring. But with time the meaning begins to unravel. Issues from the past often linger as haunting memories that block individuals from fully experiencing the present. I feel that every situation in life that each of us has faced has been brought by our souls and is perfectly tailored for our spiritual growth.

Astrology provides a wonderful vehicle for harvesting the meaning from past experiences that were not understood in the moment. The popular saying "No use in crying over spilt milk" implies that the past cannot be changed anyway, so why bother with it. Yet, the past is the foundation of the present and is a living reality from which much benefit can be experienced.

Instead of the attitude of "forgive and forget," I encourage the attitude of "forgive and *learn*." Spending time with clients helping them release the emotional energies locked in past painful experiences can be extremely fortuitous in showing them how to embrace present and future opportunities. If they are able to remember the date of the painful or confusing memory, I look up the transits they were going through at that time. This often gives them a handle to grasp the significance of the event. But even if they are not able to pinpoint the experience exactly, the birth chart itself also serves as a tool for revealing what they could have learned and why the experience was important for the actualization of their birth potential. The bottom line in dealing with the past of your clients is to help them remove the armor surrounding their hearts.

The Counseling Environment

The environment where you conduct your sessions also will have an impact on how your clients receive information. Give some thought as to how to create non-threatening surroundings that are conducive to contemplation. If your office is filled with symbols, totems and paraphernalia that reflect you, it will be a distraction for your clients. Joel Goldsmith, a healer in the '40s and '50s, believed it important to invite the spirit of God into his office before his clients came. He felt that this facilitated the healing process.

You needn't conduct your sessions in an ashram, but it helps to spend some time arranging the physical and spiritual environment.

What to Do Before the Client Comes

Being an effective counselor does not require that you be a master and have no personal problems in your life, but it does require the ability to *set your personal issues aside*. If you are not capable of this, you simply will read your own experiences into the chart before you.

I once heard a story about the tradition of worry baskets. Apparently, there is a tribe of Indians that has a tradition of placing baskets outside their tepees. When a visitor comes to call, he first gathers some sticks that represent his worries. He then sets these sticks in the basket, symbolically leaving his worries outside before entering his friend's home. After his visit, he then takes his sticks out of the basket and goes on his way.

This story can be a useful analogy in preparing to

work with a client. You can meditate before a session and acknowledge that you have your issues and worries to work through, but realize that you would like to place them in a worry basket while working with your client so as to be a clearer channel. Vow to yourself that you will gather your personal issues after the session so that you are not avoiding your personal work, just setting it aside for the time being. I also prefer to ask my higher mind to assist me in bringing forth the information that can be most helpful for the client at this point of his/her path.

Know the Main Themes of the Chart

It is always worthwhile to spend some private time studying the birth chart before a client arrives. When I first started interpreting charts for others, I read all my reference books on every planet, sign, house and aspect in the chart to feel adequately prepared. With experience, this is no longer necessary, but I still find it helpful to contemplate a chart before a session. Now, if I can close my eyes and recreate the chart in my mind, I'm ready.

In your preparation you should give some thought as to how a client receives information. What sign is *Mercury* in? What aspects are involved? This can give you clues as to the best way to present your information. Aspects to the *Sun* and *Moon* will give you clues as to the person's self-esteem and whether you should be bold or gentle in your approach. You can also study the *transits and progressions* to get a clue as to why this person is choosing to see you at this time. Take particular note of the transit of *Saturn* by house and aspect. This will help you understand what pressures your client is going through now. You should also look at the position of the *progressed Moon* as this will tell you where the personal emotional needs lie. Heed the transits of the outer planets to see where your client is being asked to evolve beyond a previously established view of the world.

One further source of knowledge is the interaction of your chart with the client's. Are there competitive or conflict-oriented aspects between the two charts so that you'll have to be careful not to elicit a defensive reaction to your presentation?

What to Do When the Client Comes

Try to empathize with what your clients are going through when they first meet you. They typically have invested considerable expectations and are often quite nervous when they first arrive.

It is vitally important to establish rapport before the session actually begins. I often offer a cup of tea or coffee initially and engage them in small talk. This is not simply hospitality—I've grown to believe that it takes at least seven minutes for our two auras to merge. Instead of jumping right into the session, I've learned that nothing is really heard in the first seven minutes anyway—they are busy checking everything out. So I simply spend the first moments indulging in this getting-acquainted process.

When you first sit down with clients, it is advisable to know their expectations. I often ask "Why did you choose to look into your astrology at this time?" Knowing their expectations can help you meet their needs. If you were a hair stylist and a client sat down in your chair, you would first ask what it was s/he wanted. It is a good place to start with astrology as well.

Next, you can inform them of your game plan—what you expect and what they can expect. Do you like interruptions and questions at the moment, or do you prefer that they save their questions until the end? How long will the session be? An hour to an hour and a half is optimum. Sessions longer than this tend to be exhausting, and there begins to be diminishing returns as your clients will begin to experience information overload.

You could use the first part of the session to explain your philosophical attitude concerning the use of astrology, but remember, you do not have to sell it to them, they are already here. You might discuss your point of view concerning destiny and free will, how you think astrology can be most helpful, your attitudes towards cycles, change and transformation. Perhaps you will address the concept of challenges leading to opportunities, and so forth.

Covering the Content

I find it best to develop a consistent game plan as to how to cover the chart. I like to start with the Sun and move outward to Pluto. Some astrologers start with the 1st House and then progress through the chart to the 12th House. Developing a consistent style can help you organize your information to ensure thoroughness, and it can also help with your sense of timing. You will know where you should be at different points throughout the session in order to complete the interpretation in a reasonable amount of time.

As the interpretation begins, you will soon find a path into the client's inner experience. Sometimes it takes longer than others, but you will always find this path. Once there, interpret the chart from within the client's perspective. This takes experience, but with time you will know when you actually have reached your client's inner experience. And once you are in, stay in.

Be attentive to the elasticity of the magnetic flow between you and your client. Pacing is very important. It is advisable to allow for peaks and valleys in the session. If you string a series of heavies together with your client, you will sense a resistance. If you are too condescending, you will sense hunger for deeper insights.

After interpreting a difficult aspect, such as a square

or opposition, offer a way out of the problem. Is there a mediating planet that provides a positive release for the planets locked in the tension? Notice the planets that rule the signs these tension planets are in: What houses are they in? What aspects do they make to other planets in the chart?

There are always resolutions to conflicts within the chart. Make sure that your clients do not feel that they are at the mercy of planetary aspects; always show a possible way out of the tension.

One of the benefits of astrological counseling over traditional forms is that the model itself is healing for individuals. It is not uncommon for people to tell me after their astrological interpretation that they wish they had come across this years ago; it could have saved them thousands of dollars in counseling fees. Simply stated, astrology works. Just describing the chart and how it relates to the person's life is a healing in itself. This is important to remember in your sessions: *You do not have to solve every problem—just describing it from an astrological perspective helps your clients accept the appropriateness of the issues they find confronting them.*

I think it is impossible to separate yourself from your biases and opinions concerning how your clients should live their lives. As an astrologer, you become a spokesperson for the cosmos to your clients. The impact of your statements on your clients' psyche can never be overestimated. Thus, I think it is important for astrologers to own up to their biases and opinions. I am a rather fiery person and prefer an upbeat approach to life. If current situations aren't working for a client, I believe it is worthwhile to change, but these are my biases. When I am interpreting a chart and notice my biases starting to influence what I am saying, I inform the client that this is my opinion, not necessarily cosmic truth.

I also try not to solve problems for people. Instead, I present the options and encourage them to make their own choices. I view this as empowering them, rather than creating dependency on my advice. I like to work with ongoing clients if they are using the information and then are ready for more. However, I do not encourage a clientele base that wants me to make decisions for them. The worst possible scenario for me is when a client becomes dependent on astrology to the degree that s/he has externalized his/her search for answers.

Sometimes you are asked as a counselor just to be empathetic to a client's situation. As a counselor, you want to be helpful; you want to solve the problems that your clients present to you. But there are some situations, particularly outer planet transits, where it is wise just to give your clients permission to experience a temporary feeling of disorientation. Outer planet transits to the natal chart essentially tear down a pre-existing structure so that the person can evolve to new structures. When clients are going through outer planet transits, I attempt to help them align with the uncertainty they are experiencing by encouraging the attitude that this is information being sent to them by their own soul. And while the new information is coming in, they may feel temporarily disoriented. This permission to feel confused is often very comforting, as this is the truth of their experience.

There are times when you *know* something to be true about a client that s/he is not able to acknowledge. These are the times when you can take refuge in your craft with such statements as "Well, this may or may not be true for you, but many people have experienced such and such with this astrological aspect."

It is important that you give people the time and space that it takes to digest the information. Numerous times I have heard from clients years after our session such statements as "You know, when I first received my reading years ago, I could not acknowledge many things that were brought out. I recently ran across the tape of the session, and upon listening to it again I can now see the truth of much of what I rejected earlier." This is not uncommon. Upon hearing information that is inconsistent with one's perceived sense of self, the new information is most often rejected as erroneous in the moment. Know that ahead of time, and give people the time to absorb the information at their own pace.

In conclusion, I feel an astrological session with a client is successful when the following conditions have been met: I have been able to present the material in the chart so that the client becomes fascinated and even enthralled with his/her growth process; the client becomes excited, even hopeful, about the prospect of taking on challenges by developing the resources revealed within the chart; the client is able to look at the past, not as a frozen sea of forgotten memories, but rather as a living reservoir of opportunities to learn from to improve present opportunities; the client leaves with a profound respect of life itself and his/her role within it. If I am able to instill these attitudes within my clients, then I feel that I have used this astrological tool as a valuable service.

Maritha Pottenger

Maritha learned astrology "at her mother's knee," attending classes with Dr. Zipporah Dobyns from age 12. She has an M.A. in Clinical Psychology as well as 15 years of experience as a professional astrologer. She has spoken for numerous conferences (AFA, UAC, SWAC, ISAR, NCGR, etc.) and lectured, counseled, taught, and led workshops across the United States, Canada and western Europe.

She is the author of three books—*Encounter Astrology, Healing with the Horoscope,* and *Complete Horoscope Interpretation*—as well as numerous computerized interpretation products for Astro Computing Services. She is Editorial Director for ACS Publications of San Diego and continues to teach, write and counsel in the field of astrology. She has a rising Uranus and a stellium in the 11th House.

POTENT, PERSONAL ASTROLOGICAL

COUNSELING

Webster's defines a counselor as "an advisor." The assumptions one has about people and about astrology, however, will affect the kind of advice one offers. In this essay, I will attempt to make my assumptions clear (rather than unconscious) and give examples of how I use astrology as a counseling tool.

My primary assumption is that the purpose of counseling is to *empower the client*, to be a catalyst for him/her to recognize more options, alternatives and possibilities in life and to realize that astrology can help us expand our choices.

A second assumption is that *life is meaningful, purposeful and follows patterns and cycles.* Astrology helps us to identify some of those patterns and cycles. However, astrology does NOT dictate the specifics of how we handle a given cycle. It lays out the framework, the issues. Each individual person decides for him/herself how to manifest the overall pattern. And, each individual can change—if desired.

For example, developmental psychologists (and parents) are aware that one of the tasks of adolescence is separating one's identity from the parental matrix. The paths which teenagers pursue in order to achieve this separation are many and varied. Some adolescents will overidentify with a peer group to seek a sense of belonging. Some will flee into an early marriage as a way to gain a separate space. Others will travel away from their home base to establish a sense of uniqueness. Some will become entrepreneurs to prove that they can do their own thing in the world. Some will study subjects far afield from their parents' interests. There are as many potential methods of separating from parents as there are adolescents in the world.

Adolescent Rebellion

The paths which teenagers can travel in seeking a sense of who they are and how they differ from their parents vary from extremely constructive to extremely destructive. The adolescent, however, retains the personal power and ability to make different choices. If the paths tried have resulted in painful consequences, the option exists for choosing differently in the future. Besides identifying the overall issues and themes for a given period, an astrologer can help the individual identify potential strengths, abilities and talents. The astrologer can also pinpoint possible weaknesses, along with offering ways to turn "liabilities" into "assets." One of the major qualities of our most renowned psychotherapists (e.g., Carl Jung, Fritz Perls, Virginia Satir) is this capacity to turn perceived negatives into positives.

Some basic principles which can help to transform "negatives" into "positives" include:

(1) There is usually MORE than one "right" answer.

(2) Our greatest strength can become a weakness if overused (so that we depend on it even when something else would be more appropriate and helpful).

(3) Our greatest weakness can become a strength if applied to the appropriate arena in life.

(4) Each of us has the power (and responsibility) to change our own lives.

(5) The basic thrust of life is toward health and happiness.

(6) Some conflict is a natural part of life and is no reflection on the worth of the person.

(7) Many people are nicer, more talented, more capable, more loving, more . . . than they think (i.e., most people are harder on themselves than they deserve).

(8) Many people fall into artificial dichotomies (e.g., "I must be perfect or I am nothing").

(9) Acceptance is a great healer.

A number of studies have correlated successful counseling with personality characteristics of the counselor. These include: empathy, respect, congruence, ability to be concrete and to hold similar expectations for the consultation as are held by the client. If the counselor has empathy, appreciation of and acceptance for those they counsel, the client is more likely to accept and like him/herself better. Shared goals and expectations means both counselor and client have a better chance of moving in the same direction in the consultation. The ability to be concrete allows us to get down to specifics and what really matters in the person's life. It also aids our clarity in noting when strengths may be overused to become weaknesses and how weaknesses can be turned into strengths by applying them in a different context.

Take the example of a teenager on drugs. Several different factors could contribute to this behavior. By identifying the factors and drives involved, alternatives (positive ways of channeling those human drives) can be perceived. Four likely candidates are: escapism, peer pressure, sensual gratification and rebellion.

Astrologically, escapism is particularly associated with "Letter 12" (Neptune, Pisces, 12th House) of the astrological alphabet. "Letter 9" (Jupiter, 9th House, Sagittarius), since it is connected to a quest for meaning, truth, and enlightenment, can also denote escapism—seeking one's dream the easy way. A central part of treatment would be to find other channels for the idealism and perfectionism involved. Religion is one potential focus; so is helping/healing work. Groups such as AA are ideal for people wrestling with this issue as such groups turn victims (one side of Letter 12) into saviors (another side of Letter 12). The creation of beauty could be very helpful— whether in song, dance, sketching, landscaping, hairdressing or myriad other forms. The individual needs an alternative, positive focus for the yearning toward something more, something higher, something inspirational in life.

If peer pressure is an issue, we would expect a strong focus on other people in the chart (perhaps "Letters 7"—Venus, Libra, 7th House, Pallas, Juno; "8"—Pluto, Scorpio, 8th House; and "11"—Uranus, Aquarius, 11th House strongly emphasized). Some potentially vulnerable placements include any rulers of the 1st (Mars, Ascendant ruler, ruler of signs in the 1st) placed in the 7th or 8th Houses. One form this can take is: "My power, my ability to act is in the hands of other people." Similarly, the Sun (or Leo to a lesser extent) in those houses might feel: "My ego is vulnerable to others; I need them to like and admire me." Those with planets in Air houses and signs in general are sociable, so need people to some extent. Water and Earth signs, however, are more inclined to insecurity than are Fire and Air. People who are prone to self-criticism (e.g., Virgo, Capricorn, Saturn or Vesta rising or in the 1st House, rulers of the 1st in the 6th or 10th, or rulers of the 6th or 10th in the 1st) may be more vulnerable to feedback from others if they are not achieving satisfaction and a sense of accomplishment in their work.

In such cases, we would look for ways to strengthen the individual's sense of self and personal power. Programs which encourage people to assert themselves in other ways could be appropriate. We might try affirmations, lists of positive qualities and other ways of getting in touch with what people like about themselves. Initially, a live-in residential situation might be helpful whereby the peer group becomes one which will support a drug-free environment. We would encourage others to be freely admiring and approving of any positive actions. The individual needs to be "a star" in healthy ways. Exposure to role models who are strong, assertive, vibrant and competent could be useful as well.

If self-indulgence is the issue, drugs being a form of sensual pleasure, we would expect a Fixed focus (especially "Letters 2 and 8"—Venus, Taurus, 2nd House and Pluto, Scorpio, 8th House). The individual could explore other avenues of material pleasure: spending more money; getting backrubs, massages or hugs on a regular basis; making love more often; using a Jacuzzi; collecting more possessions; getting involved in an aesthetic hobby, etc. The key is to substitute new, satisfying pleasures for the one (drugs) which is being given up.

If rebellion and experimentation is part of the issue, we would expect a focus on our risk-taking elements in the chart—"Letters 1, 5, 9 and 11"—especially Mars, Sun, Jupiter and Uranus. Parents and any "concerned others" need to be cool and avoid reacting with outrage as that is part of the pay-off for these teenagers. The youngster can be encouraged to channel the need for excitement, living on the edge, playing with danger, into other activities: hang gliding, mountain climbing, motorcycling, etc. An

Outward Bound course (where people test their physical limits) might be in order. Finding other ways to get an "adrenalin rush" or get "high" on life is the focus. We need risk-takers in this world. They are our pioneers, inventors, ground-breakers. However, they wreak havoc in their own lives (and those of people close to them) if they do not channel these risks into reasonably constructive activities.

Behavior Patterns

A third assumption I make is that *people have a basic human drive toward becoming more*, actualizing more potentials, being more of what they can be, *but no one is perfect*; we all have some inner conflicts, strengths and weaknesses with which to deal. (The astrological corollary to this is that there is no perfect chart. We are all working on something or we wouldn't be here.) Astrology can help to identify inner conflicts and offers perspective on alternative approaches, ways to be more complete, more self-actualizing.

Psychology presents the concept of "defense mechanisms"—locked-in patterns of behavior which may inhibit us from making the best of choices. The horoscope reflects potential defense mechanisms, and also indicates ways to overcome them.

Displacement

One danger in life is *displacement*, meaning doing the "right thing" in the "wrong place." Commonly, people are expressing a basic drive or need in an area of life where it is uncomfortable for themselves or other people. There is nothing wrong with the drive per se; it is *where they direct it* that makes the difference.

Consider, for example, the woman who has a Virgo stellium in the 5th House. She may turn her kids into her job. This can be constructive in the sense of being very dedicated and encouraging competence in her children. However, if the nit-picking, critical, analytical, flaw-finding lens of Virgo is turned too heavily toward the children (or toward herself as a parent), it could become a problem. She could be too faultfinding, judgmental and always focused on what is wrong—either with the kids or with herself as a mother.

If this is going on, we can say that the woman is displacing. She is expressing a natural human drive (the desire to find flaws in order to fix, repair and improve) in an arena where the results are less than positive. The solution *is not* to deny her critical side and say "That's bad." (She'd most likely just turn the criticism toward herself in excess.) Rather, the solution is to find other avenues and channels to direct her discriminating, methodical, painstaking side. She might, for example, take up carpentry—which involves exacting work and produces a useful, tangible result. She might adopt jigsaw puzzles or acrostics as a hobby—something which allows her to become absorbed by details and putting pieces together. She could take a course in auto mechanics or any kind of repair work. She may decide to teach others bookkeeping, computer programming, or anything which requires a disciplined mind and linear thinking. She might become a problem-solver or troubleshooter for a youth group, recreational facility or little theatre.

Her possibilities are endless. The point is, she should not try to deny a very real (and potentially positive) part of her nature. Rather, she must find a way to express it in her life where the results are positive rather than negative. Virgo represents the drive to work efficiently, but when dealing with relationships we have to focus on the positive as well as on the flaws, realize we cannot make anyone else change, and try to set a good example, while encouraging constructive action.

Dichotomizing

Another common human tendency is *dichotomizing*. People easily fall into a black-and-white approach to life. There is a tendency toward extremes, toward making forced choices: either I am right or wrong; good or bad; loving or distant. Astrology helps us to see that life is full of mixtures, that few things are "all or nothing," that often both sides of a polarity are present.

T-squares, Grand Crosses and oppositions point to the potential of identifying strongly with one (or more) positions, and not dealing with the other positions (or drives) represented. The "Cardinal dilemma" (Cardinal Grand Cross), for example, symbolizes the drive for freedom, dependency/nurturance, sharing as an equal, and control. It is a key to the need for personal hobbies and interests (Aries), home and family (Cancer), partnership (Libra), and career (Capricorn). People dealing with a Cardinal dilemma may be tempted to deny one corner or another, believing they "cannot fit it in." Yet the chart indicates that all parts are necessary for the person to be whole and happy. The challenge is to recognize the various options and to create space for each of them in life and expression. The astrologer can help clients explore various ways to act out the different needs and encourage them to acknowledge the fact that each can be useful.

People particularly tend to *polarize* (overdo one side and underdo another) with the six basic polarities of astrology. It may be helpful to the client to discuss more completely the full range of themes connected to each side of the polarity. Few people *totally* deny one side of a polarity. (For example, even the most dedicated of penny pinchers has something/someone on whom they spend money, and even the most extravagant individual is financially cautious in some realm.) Once a client realizes that both sides are present, and are potentially positive, s/he can find ways to be more moderate in his/her expression. S/he can figure out the best avenues to actualize the characterictics involved and to organize his/her life to make a time and a place for these different emphases and various ways of being, which are all important.

It is fairly common for people to establish *neurotic habit patterns* which they cannot seem to change. One definition of neurosis is: the process of defeating yourself by repeating yourself. The horoscope can offer clues regarding capacities that may be overused.

The Stellium

A *stellium* (by house or sign) often indicates a major talent. But talents, when overdone, can lead to problems. For example, a superbright person may try to use rational intellect at all times, even when an emotional reaction would be more helpful. In such a case, a useful talent becomes a liability. It may be helpful to the individual to explore other parts of the chart and acknowledge other sides of his/her being which can make a contribution to a whole life. Harmony aspects (trine and sextile, as well as the Grand Trine) are also warning signals that the person may indulge in "too much of a good thing." Harmony aspects indicate inner agreement, and when "all systems are go," it is easy to go too far! (An example is the person with intense Fire trines who believes "I have a right to what I want in the world, and if the world does not give it to me, I'll take it.") Here again, the individual may need to get in touch with other parts of his/her psyche (and horoscope) and allow the expression of other sides.

Another common issue with stellia is *the need for diversification*. People find it easy to get stuck in one channel of expression as, for example, the individual with a stellium in the 2nd House who meets all needs for pleasure through overeating. Such people can lose weight and eat less by developing other channels for satisfying the pleasure principle of the 2nd House. Similar to the teenager with the drug problem, s/he might spend more money, get regular backrubs or massages, make love more often, take up gardening, pottery, sculpture, weaving or some other artistic hobby which creates beauty (especially of a sensual/tactile sort), etc. S/he can satisfy his/her material/physical-oriented side through other means beyond food. (And s/he can exercise more to speed up his/her metabolism—balancing too much of the Venus principle with a little of the Mars principle.)

There are some occasions when stellia signify people who are "burned out" in the areas concerned or dysfunctional, trying to learn to handle that part of life (e.g., mongoloids often have stellia in the mental signs or houses such as the 3rd, 6th, 9th, 11th). The stellium points to an issue or a *focus*. Individuals need to do as much as they can to express the themes connected to the stellium, within the limits of what is possible. (A person with limited cognitive capacities could be very involved with relatives, exhibit nimbleness or flexibility, enjoy doing things with the hands, or like other forms of 3rd House action.) Whether stellia are a sign of great talent or "overload" (like a burned-out fuse), the individual still needs to balance these activities with other parts of life.

Repression

Repression is another potential defense mechanism. When we repress something, we bury it in the unconscious, forgetting we ever knew it. But it takes energy to keep something buried. Repression, if carried on for too long or too intensely, can lead to physical illness.

I do **not** recommend diagnosing from a horoscope. However, if a client has a physical block, ailment or illness, I am willing to examine the horoscope in terms of identifying the emotional/mental issues which may lie behind the physical problem. I believe in treating physical problems with physical solutions—if appropriate—as well as using meditation, prayer or relaxation for the spiritual side. However, by resolving the inner psychological (emotional/mental) conflict and making peace with the repressed urges, the person no longer is fighting him/herself. S/he can heal the self and the problem will not recur.

If illness is an issue, I may review the astrological associations for various body parts and physical problems. I can then consider the psychological drives represented by each body part or illness. A client can examine his/her life for positive, fulfilling and harmonious ways to express those inner needs.

For example, headaches are associated with Mars. If headaches are a problem for a client, I would look to standard physical approaches such as relaxation, biofeedback, lowered stress, etc. I would also note that Mars is associated with freedom needs, assertion, the desire to do one's own thing in the world. It is correlated with anger and irritation when blocked. I would explore with this client if s/he were forcing him/herself to do a lot of things s/he did not want to do, or if s/he were habitually stopping him/herself from what actually is desired. As an example, perhaps headaches commonly occur when someone is cooking dinner for the family and would rather be gardening. Perhaps headaches come up when a partner asks him/her to do something s/he would rather not do, etc. The person will have to find ways to satisfy the Martian side of his/her nature while still not denying other parts of who s/he is, such as his/her conscience, desire for intimacy, etc. Usually, just letting go of some unnecessary responsibilities, or allowing a bit more leeway to do what s/he *truly wants,* will do the trick.

The psychological principles of drives associated with each planet and keyed to various body parts will work fine without a horoscope. If you wish to examine the chart, any configurations which have conflict hold the *potential* of repression. (We may decide to allow one side of our nature and repress another side which seems to conflict with it.) Furthermore, anything connected to the Water element (Water planets, Water houses and Water signs) has the potential of being partly unconscious and easily repressed. The main point, however, is identifying the underlying needs and drives—of which the physical problem is symbolic—and finding constructive ways to satisfy those needs and drives.

Projection

Projection is another possible defense mechanism. My definition differs somewhat from Freud's original definition. I see projection as attracting someone into our lives who will *overdo* a potential which we are *underdoing.* Commonly, we project parts of our nature which do not seem to "fit" with the bulk of who we are. The problem arises in that the person who expresses characteristics which we deny in ourselves will often live them out in exaggerated form. Once projection is identified, the challenge is to plan, organize and actualize ways in which to express those characteristics *in moderation* with positive results.

Candidates for projection are any parts of the horoscope which are very different from the major emphases. For example, in a chart which is mostly Earth and Water by planetary, house and sign emphasis but has Mars in Leo in conflict aspect to much of the chart, Mars is a likely prospect for projection. The individual may unconsciously deny his/her need to be significant, admired, fiery, exciting and in charge, and instead attract a vibrant, charismatic, magnetic individual to "live out" the Mars in Leo themes for him/her.

If the Earth/Water individual learns from this example to allow his/her natural dynamism out, all will be well. If, however, the Earth/Water person continues to project, the person/people attracted will become more and more extreme. What was exciting and sexy becomes arrogant, self-centered and childish. The more a quality is denied on the inside, the more overdone it is on the outside. If, however, the Earth/Water person learns to allow that Martian side out, s/he can become a lively, fun-loving, on-stage personality—in some area of her/his life—while still keeping the Earth/Water stability, helpfulness, seriousness and dedication for the bulk of activities.

It is important to remember that projection is a two-way street. If the Earth/Water type unconsciously selects a fiery individual to live out that Mars, the fiery individual is also attracted to the Earth/Water person to express the grounded, disciplined side which the fiery person projects! If either moves more toward the middle, toward moderation, the other has a chance to change (or find someone else to play the game with). The goal is for each to teach the other how to actualize a less-developed part of his/her own nature.

Astrologically, we can project anywhere in the horoscope, although it is less likely in the 1st and 2nd Houses. Projection is *most likely* in the 7th and 8th—traditional houses of "other people." Planets and signs tenanting the 7th and 8th are commonly experienced initially through significant others (and projection) before we make them our own. If a client falls into projection, the likely targets are:

1st House: rare (usually we identify with these placements)

2nd House: rare (may project into possessions)

3rd House: siblings, neighbors, relatives, people near at hand

4th House: nurturing parent

5th House: lovers and children

6th House: coworkers and colleagues

7th House: anyone, but especially partners

8th House: anyone, but especially mates

9th House: religious leaders, moral authorities, teachers, grandchildren

10th House: rule-maker parent, boss, authorities

11th House: friends, groups, organizations

12th House: inspirational figures, victims, God

A fourth assumption which I make is that *the horoscope is a mirror of human drives, potentials and issues.* That is, the planets do not make things happen. The planets symbolize or reflect back human issues and needs. Character is destiny. People's attitudes and actions create or attract certain events and situations to them. This puts a heavy emphasis on the power (and responsibility) of the client. It also emphasizes that s/he has **choices**.

Let us look at the example of someone with Neptune in the 7th. Some traditional books or astrologers will warn the individual with Neptune in the 7th that s/he might marry an alcoholic. Certainly that is one option. But how helpful—as a counselor—is it to say, "You could marry an alcoholic"? How does that help the person in any way to deal with the issue?

So, what is happening when we mix the 7th House (our urge for partnership and sharing) with Neptune (our quest for cosmic consciousness/for infinite love and beauty)? We have the search for God mixed with human relationships. Logically, we can see a number of possibilities. Some people will literally marry God (go into the church). Some will search forever for the perfect partner, never finding him or her. No one will ever measure up to the impossibly high standard. Others will have multiple relationships, wanting *so much* to have the beautiful dream that they talk themselves into believing everything is ideal. When they wake up to the reality of a human relationship that is not perfect, they may give it up and try again with a new Prince or Princess Charming. Each time, they fall for the fantasy. Another option is attracting partners who believe they are perfect and ideal and expect to be placed on a pedestal!

Savior/victim relationships can also occur, where one party plays God to the other, trying to save him/her—whether from alcoholism, drug addiction, illness or some other form of escapism. The victim is avoiding facing an imperfect world. The savior has succumbed to the illusion that s/he can make everything perfect for another person.

Another option is to project the search for beauty and choose partners who are exceptionally attractive or artistically talented. If we select someone mostly on the basis of outside appearance, we are likely to be disappointed and disillusioned later. If we attract someone who is artistic with a talent for creating beauty, we also need to recognize our own aesthetic side, lest we fall into extremes in the relationship. (A typical division by projection, for example, is the spacey, talented, impractical artist and the hardworking, disciplined, critical realist.)

Some people will simply have incredibly high standards for relating and sharing—almost a spiritual sense where unless it is pure and ideal they do not want to be involved. Some people will make their relationships an ultimate value and constantly strive to create a more perfect environment, a more ideal sharing. Other people will seek God together. Rather than expecting one to provide the truth and meaning for the other, *together* they can study, read, take a spiritual path, travel or otherwise seek that sense of meaning and inspiration in life. This last couple is still blending Neptune and the 7th House—but in a very different way than the earlier examples!

If individuals can realize that their search for meaning and something higher in life is connected to their desire for a sharing, human relationship, they have the opportunity to make some choices. They can address their idealism and build a positive channel for it. Whether they choose to create beauty, adopt a healing role on a professional level, or seek a partner to share their religious/philosophical/spiritual quest does not matter. The key is that the client is now empowered. The client can learn to *share* the reach for the infinite with a partner—neither party expecting the other to do or be all or provide infinite love and beauty for him/her. By recognizing the underlying motivations, clients can develop satisfying channels for meeting their needs to replace old, frustrating conflicts. They have choices and they have options.

Dealing with Issues

My fifth assumption is that *people can and do change;* they are not set in stone. This means that the horoscope maps issues for us—not details. If exact specifics were defined in the chart, movement, change and personal power would not be possible. When we change the way we deal with various issues, we change the specifics, details and events of our lives.

Take the example of a Mars/Saturn conjunction. Some books will tell you that this means you will be blocked, inhibited, held back from personal action. (The world will get you.) Other books will accuse the person with such a conjunction of being hard, ruthless, ambitious, willing to step on people to get to the top. More modern texts may say that you are potentially very capable, have tremendous drive and endurance, and can achieve almost anything in life.

Who is right? *They all are.* (And they are all wrong, too!) *Some* people at *some* periods in their lives will feel blocked, inhibited and held back. At other times, they may be ruthless, ambitious and hard. And they are likely to have periods of great achievement. To limit any client to one form of the potential expressions of any Mars/Saturn combination is shortsighted and rarely helpful.

What are we combining? Mars symbolizes self-will—the drive, energy, vitality, physical health and strength to go after what you want in life. It indicates assertion and (potentially) aggression, the pursuit of one's own personal desires. The basic theme is "I want to do what I want to do, and I want to do it *now!*" Saturn symbolizes the rules of the game, the limits that are bigger than a single human being, the multiple restrictions placed by societal rules and regulations, physical laws (such as gravity) and social expectations (such as "appropriate" behavior). Saturn is a key to all the "shoulds" and "shouldn'ts" of life, including our internal monitor—the conscience.

So, what can happen when we put together self-will with the limits to self-will? Four general outcomes are possible, with many variations on a theme within each general group.

(1) The individual may overdo the limits side of life and give up. Such people are afraid to even try. They surrender, convinced they would just fail and fall short anyway. Expecting to be blocked, criticized, inhibited or otherwise limited in their endeavors, they stop before starting and do not even try for what they want. Dr. Dobyns calls them "self-blockers."

(2) The person may overdo the self-assertion side and be constantly pushing the world. Such people are trying to do more than is possible and continually hit the stone wall of reality, having to confront the fact that there are certain rules of the game of life; we cannot live solely on our own terms. Until they learn to live within the limits, such people may break the laws of society (criminals), the regulations of social behavior and expectations, the physical laws of the universe (e.g., endangering their health through Type-A behavior or other actions which ignore the basic limitations of a physical body), etc. Dr. Dobyns calls them "overdrivers."

(3) The individual may swing from one extreme to the other—pushing life and trying too hard, feeling impatient that they haven't "got it all"—and then falling into self-criticism and inadequacy feelings for not having achieved what they think they "should" have. They may bounce back and forth for a lifetime.

(4) The person may reach a reasonable compromise between assertion and reality. Such people accomplish a great deal, working voluntarily within the limits of the world. They figure out the rules of the game (what is possible and what is necessary) and do all that they can to get what they want from within a pragmatic framework.

Is there a way to make a judgment between these four general potentials? Yes and no. The first clue is that the planets are the strongest statement. So, all other things being equal, Saturn in the 1st House is more likely to indicate self-blocking, while Mars in the 10th is more likely to symbolize overdrive. (However, all other things are seldom equal.) Houses are also vital. A strongly occupied 10th House shows a strong inner focus on limits, rules and roles, regulations and doing things right. This can lead to self-blocking if carried too far. Generally, the more Fire in a chart (counting planets strongly aspected and occupied houses as well as occupied signs), the more potential overdrive. The more Water and often Earth, the more caution, conservatism and potential for self-blocking.

Cultural expectations are significant. Certain cultural groups (e.g., Japanese) are much less likely to express overdrive through criminal behavior (although they may do it in business). Women are traditionally socialized to be less in touch with the Martian side of their nature so are more prone to depression and potential self-blocking.

Herein lies the trap for the unwary astrologer who believes that astrology should be able to "predict" which path the client will take. If you see ten clients, each one containing a strong, repeated theme of Mars/Saturn in the horoscope, how do you decide which one is a criminal, which one is a successful business executive, which one is a frustrated, inhibited artist, which one is an unhappy, inadequate, unemployed individual, etc.?

I hope to God you don't!

Suppose you are right. Your psyche is right on that day and you tell a client (correctly) that she is a dynamite person, the president of her company, earning $800,000 a year, and already listed in several *Who's Who*s. What have you accomplished? Well, you probably feel great. Being "right" is a wonderful sensation; I love it myself. How does the client feel? She probably feels a sense of awe (though she may also wonder if you simply recognized her from those *Who's Who* articles). She is also likely to feel "Oh, I guess it had to be this way. I guess I was destined to be successful. After all, that's what the horoscope says and that is what happened." So, where does she go from here?

Let us suppose she is a fairly together person and she decides, "This is incredible and amazing that an astrologer could pick up all that about me, but I am still going to do my part regardless of what the stars say." She may continue on her road to the top. She could also decide, "The stars guarantee me success; I can do what I want!" and slip into overdrive, stepping on people and being too ruthless and self-centered in her drive for success. She might also decide, "Gee, if it's all foreordained anyway, there isn't much fun to it. Guess I'll just let life happen since it doesn't matter what I do; fate will determine it anyway" and fall into self-blocking.

The above example theorizes a client who has had a successful, productive life. How much more damage might be done with a client who feels naturally inadequate, unable to cope, who identifies himself as a failure if the astrologer were to "confirm" that "Yes, your horoscope indicates that you have had a hard life and are likely to encounter many roadblocks and much difficulty in this life. You have many challenges ahead!" In an extreme situation, such a client might even choose suicide rather than continue what he saw as an "inevitable" downward trend.

I'm not saying that astrologers are supposed to be Pollyannas and only seek the positive in the horoscope. Unremitting sweetness is as poisonous as unmitigated gloom. The point is that if we are successful in guessing the right details of a client's life we usually contribute to that client feeling "locked in"—it "had" to happen that way. As modern psychological research demonstrates, one of the most important factors in people handling their lives is a sense of personal responsibility and personal power. Accurate predictions of details take power and responsibility away from the client.

And what of the times when the astrologer is partially right and partially wrong? Take, for example, our successful lady executive. By concentrating on her current achievements, I may take the focus away from other options and other experiences. If I blow her away by predicting her exact salary or the precise field of business she occupies, we may never get around to discussing how inadequate she felt as a child, how she could never please her father and believed until age 30 that she would never amount to anything! I may never discover that she has experienced at least two of the different paths of blending Mars and Saturn in her chart and in her nature. Similarly, with a man who feels totally blocked, inadequate and unhappy, if I focus only on his current pain and lack of success (as he defines it), I may never discover that 10 years ago, he was a high achiever, the top of his field, pushing himself to the limit. Then, he overdid the stress and ended up in a serious accident with subsequent health problems that led to his current difficulties and feelings of failure. So, he has experienced overdrive and realistic accomplishments as well as self-blocking. If I reaffirm his self-blocking stance with "correct" predictions, there is little support for other options in his life!

When working with people, being "right" can also mean being very "wrong." The truth is many-sided and often not that simple. Any "information" or "truth" we convey is interpreted—first by us and then by the client in terms of the context of the consultation and his/her present life circumstances and past experiences. Suppose, for example, we notice an upcoming period has a major focus on reality issues, dealing with the physical world, figuring out what is possible and doing it, fulfilling reasonable responsibilities without overburdening the self or others, working hard and possibly feeling serious, under pressure, limited or extremely practical (a Saturn period). Consider the impact of such a description (or a much more specific one) on:

1) A 50-year-old housewife who has never worked outside the home and is being divorced by her husband for a younger woman

2) An 18-year-old young woman who has just been accepted by one of the most prestigious medical schools in the U.S.

3) A 45-year-old lawyer who is ready to chuck a promising career in the corporate world to pursue his life-long dream of being a painter

4) A 2-year-old child

5) An idealistic 20 year old who has just joined a "back to nature" farming commune

6) A 55-year-old male who has just been promoted to a Vice Presidency

7) A 33-year-old unemployed father of two who has held 30 different jobs and has only a high school education

8) An Army bride whose husband is being shipped abroad

9) A stonemason who loves his work

10) A 45 year old who has just been hired as the first woman to hold the position of high authority she has gained in her field

11) A woman undergoing shock treatments for severe, debilitating depression

12) A recent immigrant to this country who barely speaks English and will probably face prejudice due to her ethnic background

13) A parent involved in a child-custody battle

14) Someone who has just invested his life savings in a "get-rich-quick" offer through a magazine ad

15) Someone just accepted for training for the Olympic decathlon team

Clearly, *the way we present* our "pure" information is likely to affect the degree to which our clients focus on the positive or the negative aspects of their situations. It will affect the degree of choice our client sees available.

Astrologers who believe the planets are running the world will see fewer choices and possibilities for their clients. They will be more willing to make flat-out, no-nonsense, definitive predictions, e.g., "You are going to lose your job in the month of May," or "You will get married next spring," or "You will receive an important promotion at work within the next three months." Their language will tend to be deterministic and "lock people in" as far as options, using phrases such as "must," "have to," "cannot," "necessarily," "absolute(ly) final," "of course," "obvious(ly)," "no choice," "inevitab(ly)," "without fail," "it is."

Astrologers who believe that the planets are primarily (or entirely) symbolic will couch future trends in terms of possibilities and potentials, using phrases such as "possibly," "might," "may," "potential," "can likely," "somewhat," "could be," "tend to," "imply," "suggest," "lean in the direction of," "seems," "appears," "often." They assume that events are dependent upon the actions of the client—as in the previous Saturnian example. Hard work and much success is possible. Depression and feeling blocked is also possible. And certainly, both could be experienced together!

Sometimes, unilateral predictions are correct. Often, they are wrong. When wrong, they do our field a disservice. (Astrologers and astrology look silly.) When right, they help to lock a client into thinking things *had* to be that way. (The power of the self-fulfilling prophecy also ought to be considered.) The more an astrologer implies there is *only one* right answer, *only one* possibility, the more the client is encouraged to deny his/her personal responsibility and power in life.

In an increasingly complex world, seeing things in terms of black and white with only one "correct" response to a given situation tends to lock people into linear thinking. It encourages dichotomies. In today's world, *synthesizing* viewpoints can be much more valuable. One of the characteristics associated with psychological health is "tolerance of ambiguity"—including the ability to see more than one approach, more than one answer to problems. A global perspective is more likely to set up a win-win situation than a narrow "one option only" point of view.

All of us view the world through the interpretive lens of our experience. When I hear an astrologer predicting doom and gloom, I figure it is extremely likely that s/he is a very unhappy person. When I find an astrologer telling client after client that his/her relationship is in trouble, I wonder if that astrologer is having conflicts in relationships. If I meet an astrologer who foresees only the heart's desire of each and every client, I suspect that client is inclined to "make nice" in his/her own life and may try to avoid facing life's challenges or anything s/he defines as "unpleasant."

If a pattern emerges in the astrologer's counseling, there is a strong likelihood that the pattern is quite personally meaningful to that astrologer.

My definition of a professional astrologer is someone who utilizes the mirror of the stars to assist other people in seeing their options more clearly. When dealing with people face-to-face, I strive to continually ask myself, "What other options are there? What additional possibilities exist? What might I have overlooked?" Keeping a mental list of diverse people (as the examples above) helps. I can refer to the list and ask myself, "Would I say the same thing to a man/woman . . . older/younger person . . . someone at the top of his/her field/someone down and out vocationally. . .," etc. This not only stretches my thinking in terms of choices but also helps to cut down on stereotyping. It is important to think in terms of the client with whom we are dealing, but equally vital not to limit clients due to assumptions about their sex, age, or other variables.

If astrology is truly a Uranian field, it ought to be used to bring freedom, wider vistas, enlarged choices, open circulation of ideas and increased tolerance to people. That is the kind of astrology I try to practice. How about you?

For Further Reading

Dobyns, Zipporah. *Expanding Astrology's Universe.* San Diego: ACS Publications, 1983.

Pottenger, Maritha. *Complete Horoscope Interpretation.* San Diego: ACS Publications, 1986.

_____. *Healing with the Horoscope: A Guide to Counseling.* San Diego: ACS Publications, 1983.

Bill Herbst

Bill Herbst lives and works in Minneapolis, Minnesota. Since 1973, he has pursued what he calls "Intimate Dialogues" with a broad clientele of individuals and couples. His work draws on numerous sources, from psychology to metaphysics, and focuses on the delicate balances between individual life-purpose, universal mission, and the personal mountains of paradox that stand in our way.

He is the author of the critically acclaimed textbook on the psychological significance of astrology, *Houses of the Horoscope*. His second book, to be published in 1991, is entitled *The Oracle of Love*.

Seven thousand sessions have shown him that the languages we create to define ourselves and our world are important keys to the mystery of human life.

ASTROLOGY AND PSYCHOTHERAPY

A Comparison for Astrologers

There is some dispute in the world of astrology over the issue of counseling. In the most obvious sense, every working astrologer is a counselor. We provide information and perspectives for our clients, based on a system of symbolic information. We advise them. That makes us counselors, or at the very least, consultants.

But beyond this general definition, there are more specific issues concerning *psychological counseling* and its relation to astrological practice. Where does the astrological end and the psychological begin? Are there conflicts between the two? If we practice as psychological counselors, do we need traditional credentials to be on solid ground? Is astrology a good basis for what is generally termed "therapy," and beyond that, should astrologers be involved in practicing psychological therapy at all?

Astrology, like many disciplines, is remarkably diverse. Although the public expectation of an astrologer carries with it the presumption of expertise in every application of the system, this is rarely the case. Each person discovers a particular niche in using astrology. There are astrologers who specialize in financial counseling, using astrological cycles to forecast the ebb and flow of economic trends both in the marketplace and in the lives of individual clients. For a practitioner with these interests, the relationship of astrology to psychotherapy is hardly a burning issue.

But even such specialists are likely to have been drawn initially to astrology because of its psychological potentials. The rebirth of astrology in the 20th century was propelled by corresponding developments in the infant science of psychology. Most interpretive frameworks contemporary astrologers studied to learn their craft were written by men and women with a strong psychological orientation. The bulk of what is written about astrology—books, essays, articles, even the idiocy of Sun sign columns in newspapers and magazines—refers directly or indirectly to the psychology of individual life.

Demographics

I define three groups of people involved in astrology for whom the issue of psychology and its counseling dimensions are relevant.

1. Professionals

This first group includes the majority of full-time, working astrologers. "Professional" is defined here in the most common way, meaning that one's livelihood is associated with the ongoing practice of a discipline that requires specialized or advanced training. All or at least a part of this group's income is earned from the use of astrological tools and insights in formal sessions with individuals who are regarded as clients. To be considered part of my first group, one must conduct an arbitrary minimum of 50 to upwards of 500 sessions per year.

The content of these sessions involves analysis and discussion of clients' lives—experiences, circumstances, attitudes, or other contexts, especially as these correlate with symbolic patterns in natal charts, transits, etc.—with special emphasis on new information, insights, perspectives, strategies, options, or clarification.

This is the smallest of the three groups. Since astrology is not as well-organized as many other disciplines, accurate statistics on the number of professional astrologers are sketchy at best. Many do not belong to astrological organizations, nor do they state that they are astrologers on their income tax returns or census forms. Not all of them advertise. Many will not be found in the Yellow Pages of the telephone directory under "Astrologers." So coming up with accurate numbers for this first group is somewhat of a problem. My guess is that there are no more than 2,000 individuals in this country who belong in this category. This is, however, the group for which the issue of psychological counseling has most direct and obvious relevance.

2. Working Non-Professionals

The second group includes those who are not full-time or even part-time professionals who still use astrology in regular or sporadic interactions with other people. They may or may not be paid money for their services, but in either case they do not depend on astrological counseling as a significant source of income. They may or may not think of the people with whom they work as clients, but they do feel a serious and sincere responsibility about their role. They may or may not have the ambition to become professional astrologers, and they may or may not conduct formal sessions, but they are interested in talking to others about the events and meanings of their lives, and this general interest has become linked with the use of personalized astrological tools and insights as important components in that pursuit.

This second category is probably 20 times as large as the first. For every professional astrologer who maintains a regular clientele in an ongoing practice, there are probably 20 people who share the same interests and motivations and, to some extent, the same skills, but for one reason or another they do not create a livelihood built around astrology. Although the concerns of this group are not as direct as those in the professional category, the issues of psychological counseling are still relevant.

3. Almost Everyone Else in Astrology

Of the literally millions of people in this country who are interested in or actively studying astrology, the vast majority do not "practice" at all. That is to say, they do not use their astrological knowledge in formal or even informal sessions with other individuals. They may be interested in the astrological implications of others' lives, but they have not studied astrology in much depth or they lack confidence about their mental or verbal skills. They may balk at the ethical or moral responsibilities surrounding interpretation.

This is easily the largest group of the three categories. Although there are many people in this group whose knowledge extends only to the general idea of Sun signs, it also includes many others who are talented and insightful about astrology, who may have studied the philosophy and techniques of astrological interpretation in depth (they have read numerous astrological textbooks, taken classes, or attended seminars).

For this last group, the issue of psychological counseling in astrology would seem, at first glance, basically philosophical, or at least, merely hypothetical. But the very fact that so many people are interested in astrology belies this.

The Spiritual Element of Real Life

Once survival needs are established—air, food, shelter, and all the basic protections necessary to maintain life—human beings turn their attention to new levels.

Especially in a culture like ours where survival is fairly easy to maintain, other pursuits become attractive. We shift our focus away from base survival and toward the quest for greater satisfaction, greater happiness, greater fulfillment. The quest takes many forms: pleasure, wealth, personal or cultural power, aesthetics, sexual gratification, mastery of and excellence in any of a thousand endeavors, etc. But however much we may become obsessed with these relatively physical dimensions of satisfaction, our attention tends to stray from these levels alone.

Sooner or later, the mystery of being alive emerges. What is this life I am living? How did I get here, and where am I going? What is my relation to the world around me? Who am I? What is this self? Who is thinking these thoughts? What is permanent about me? What is temporary? How do I work? How does it ALL work? Even the most callously materialistic people wonder about the mystery of life, and for many of the rest of us this mystery becomes an ongoing inner dialogue. Some would maintain that these and the infinity of similar questions are strictly within the realm of the spiritual, part of religion and metaphysics. I would counter that while they certainly invoke the metaphysical, they also concern the psychological.

Modern psychology can be thought of as a specific orientation toward the investigation of Life's mysteries, especially those associated with individuality. Therapy, as it is most often currently practiced, involves numerous techniques and processes designed to help achieve more effective adjustment to those mysteries. I use the term *adjustment* because I cannot use the word *answers*. As far as I am aware, there are no answers to the mysteries of Life.

There are astrologers who believe strongly that our

discipline should be separated from counseling, that it is not therapy and must not be mixed with such work. I know that some astrologers are nearly rabid in their insistence that astrology should be safeguarded from association with "psychic" or otherwise intuitive processes, insisting instead that it be used in a purely "scientific" manner. I have heard well-known and expert astrologers advise students to avoid "esoteric readings" (sessions with metaphysical or spiritual content) with their clients, unless the client specifically requests such information. Although I can readily understand the concerns raised, I have a different point of view.

My question to these astrologers is this: *How do we distinguish?* How do we draw the line between astrological interpretation and psychological counseling, between rational and intuitive methods, or between "normal" and "esoteric" delineations? Astrological work may not be the same as classical psychotherapy, but does that mean it should not be practiced with sensitivity toward therapeutic effects? Many serious astrologers may not wish to be associated in the public mind with carnival psychics, but does that mean we should banish intuition from our discipline just because it can be abused? And what is the point of practicing astrology if we omit any reference to the spiritual dimension of life?

Each of us must choose for ourselves how we will use the astrological system in practice, and there is no reason to presume that any two of us will or should arrive at the same orientation. However, I would feel irresponsible to myself and my clientele if I adopted the view that astrological sessions must somehow be differentiated from psychological counseling sessions or that astrology could be practiced in a way that avoids the question of spirituality.

It's all a continuum. Practical living, psychology,

metaphysics, astrology—finally, they are all on the same scale. The neatly defined divisions that separate them are artificial, the product of human territoriality, possessiveness, and the tendency to clearly define a niche in order both to carve out turf for oneself and, more importantly, to avoid the overwhelming fact that Everything is Everything. Ministers often find themselves in the role of psychologist. Psychologists often find themselves in the role of minister. And astrologers often find themselves in the roles of both minister and psychologist.

But having made this point, I need to go further. If I treat "everything as everything," then I've got only a one-line statement—haiku instead of an essay—and the book of which this essay is one chapter wouldn't sell many copies. No, in the most practical sense there are many distinctions between the institutions of psychology and astrology, especially as they are understood and practiced in this culture. To some extent, the very future of astrology as a serious discipline depends on our recognizing and revising the distinctions that currently exist.

Therapy or Not?

Therapy has already been mentioned in this essay, but the term has not yet been defined. It's one of those words that's easy to throw around but difficult to pin down. Almost everyone has a feeling for what therapy is, but few people can define it precisely. I asked three of my friends who are certified, practicing psychological therapists to help me out by defining what therapy is. All I wanted was one paragraph—a nice, simple, general definition for my essay.

Weeks went by and not one of my friends called back. So I called them. As it turned out, each of them had spent considerable time thinking about my question. All of them thought it was important, and none of them had come up with anything approaching a simple answer. Remember, these are *therapists*, trained professionals. Yet not one of them had a simple definition of therapy.

A precise, clinical definition of the term probably does exist, perhaps in the bylaws of the American Psychological Association or the rulebooks of various State Certification Boards. But my point is that for most of us— including professionals—therapy is a lot like pornography: *We know it when we see it, but it's very hard to define in the abstract.*

Webster's defines *therapy* as "therapeutic nature or power." So looking up *therapeutic,* we find "serving to cure or heal; concerned in discovering and applying remedies for diseases." We check *psychotherapy* and discover "the application of various forms of mental treatment to nervous and mental disorders." What's common to all these definitions is the concept that psychotherapy involves treatment of mental diseases, which we can extend to include the realm of emotional disorders.

In other words, *psychotherapy is for people who are ill.* Now, I have no doubt that many traditionally trained psychotherapists would disagree. Psychological counseling has undergone a radical reformation over the past 30 years, and many formerly conservative therapists have altered their practices to embrace a larger world view.

The early standards of psychotherapy with its couch and silent, bearded psychiatrist may remain strong images in the collective mindset, but the world of psychology has virtually exploded beyond those narrow limits. Revolutionary seminar programs such as EST and LifeSpring shoved psychology off its comfortable couch. Approaches such as Rolfing and the Alexander Technique opened psychology to the benefits of the bodywork massage table. The development of transactional analysis and family systems revealed the power of relationship in most psychological issues. Chemical dependency, addiction therapy, and the huge success of the 12-step approach extended therapy into day-to-day living. Various forms of process therapy added elements of creative visualization and mythology to what was once seen as a largely rational framework.

And while the power centers of psychology may retain a certain stuffy conservatism, they are assailed by new research in various "outlaw" disciplines, including the science of psychoneuroimmunology and the neo-astrology movement that grew out of the Gauquelins' work.

"Therapy" may remain a technical term to describe a specific form of psychological counseling, and the institution of psychology may still jealously guard its copyright. However, the general context of therapy has broadened to include hundreds of different techniques that cover a wide range of approaches and philosophies. In that sense, astrology is a discipline ideally suited to the application of psychological counseling.

Disease, Diagnosis, and Stereotype

The myth that psychotherapy is for "sick people" has diminished, but it remains a social stigma under which traditional psychology still labors. No one likes to be thought of as mentally or emotionally ill (in spite of the undeniable fact that most of us are, to some extent), so vast numbers of people continue to believe that if you are in therapy there must be something *wrong* with you. This is furthered by the fact that many psychologists use a system of personality "diagnosis" that grew almost entirely out of the disease model used by Western medicine.

While consulting an astrologer may carry an image of being at least slightly weird, thankfully there is no "disease" stigma. My own astrological counseling is particularly suited to healthy individuals. In fact, the healthier a person is, the more s/he can benefit from working with me. My work is aimed at furthering the ineffable process of maturation by pinpointing the particular paradoxes and dilemmas contained within an individual life, while also revealing the overall direction and purpose of that individual's life-development.

Psychological diagnosis should help a therapist retain clarity on a client's condition through the often confusing puzzle of interaction. But diagnosis is no replacement for authentic recognition of the client's identity as a whole person. Shorthand categories for pigeonholing people are very seductive. Sometimes the diagnosis becomes the primary vehicle through which the psychotherapist interacts with his patient. No doubt most psychologists strive to avoid this pitfall, but it is there nonetheless.

I don't engage in diagnosis of my clients' personalities or lives. Since psychology was my original orientation, my first love, and because my formal education was in that field, the classic poles of psychotherapy—neuroses and personality disorders—remain basic to my analytic perceptions. But the natal chart and transits provide me with other structures for assessment that make many psychological categories appear absurdly simplistic.

This is not to say that the general diagnoses of psychology are necessarily wrong or have no value. Where illness is clearly involved, psychological diagnosis can be immensely helpful. Also, astrological patterns are sometimes so complex that we are forced to mentally simplify them to avoid being overwhelmed by all the levels and possibilities.

This issue involves more than critical judgments between the systems of astrology and psychology. Included are the talent, intelligence, and experience of individual practitioners. There are wonderful and terrible counselors in astrology as well as psychology. Good astrologers realize that clients deserve much more from them than textbook delineations; good psychologists do not limit themselves to the classical diagnoses of their clinical backgrounds. A violinist without technique or heart will not play better simply by owning a Stradivarius, but a virtuoso can make even a pawnshop fiddle sing sweetly.

I try to share my information and insight with my clients in a straightforward manner that avoids the stigma of categories (whether psychological or astrological) and helps me to establish a more intimate relationship with them. I don't wish to be seen as either a doctor or a cosmic authority, and while there is no way to prevent some people from placing me on that shaky pedestal, I do everything I can to convey to my clients that we are equals in the exploration of Life's mysteries, specifically their personal mysteries.

However, the absence of medical diagnosis does not prevent astrologers from rampant stereotyping. Astrology was popularized in large part by reducing the system to its lowest level, that of Sun sign categories. Too many astrologers characterize their clients as if they were the configurations that fill their charts.

The confusion between astrological tools and human beings is difficult to avoid. Charts are so personalized, so reflective of the people whom they describe, that it is very easy to slip into believing that the chart is the person. In a medical X-ray, what are we seeing? The consciousness of the person? No, only the structure of the body. It is the same with astrological charts. We are looking at a diagram that reveals the structure of the person's psychological/spiritual vehicle. *Charts are not the same as people.* Those astrologers who believe they are identical are promoting an essentially mechanical world view. They propagandize for spiritual materialism, the belief that consciousness itself is nothing more than a formula, that life is "written in the stars."

Very few astrologers would consciously admit to that orientation. I feel certain that most would vehemently deny it. But their denials, along with their ideals, are often undercut by the actual process of their day-in-and-day-out work with clients, which may be rife with the very inferences they find so offensive. Humanistic posturing is all too common; well-grounded integrity is another thing entirely.

Yes, But Is It Good or Bad?

Beyond this general tendency to confuse the vehicle with the driver, astrology suffers from an even worse offense. Traditional astrological interpretations, both the kind found in textbooks and those delivered daily by thousands of practicing astrologers, too often tend to reflect a polarized orientation into either "positive" or "negative" symbolic factors.

The idea that astrology reveals the "good" and "bad" of a person's personality or circumstances is deeply planted in the public mind. Even when we use softer terminology, such as "strengths and weaknesses" or "talents and liabilities," it still comes down to good and bad. This notion is held not only by much of the public but by many astrologers who should know better, and it remains one of the most vexing of all the silly attitudes about our system.

It is an insidious, almost irresistible approach to interpretation that has fostered a new double standard: In theory we support relativity, but in practice we still focus on positive configurations versus negative ones. Far too many students learn that trines and sextiles are "good," while squares and oppositions are "bad." Such a near-sighted mindset represents one link to traditional therapy that I hope we can eventually sever.

I suppose it's inevitable that human beings tend to evaluate their experiences in these terms, given the way Christianity has been reduced to absurdity after 2,000 years of religious politics, given the dialectical nature of thought processes in Western culture, and given the lure of instant solutions, the "quick fix" mentality we suffer from in contemporary America.

Perhaps it is the superficial understanding of metaphysics that pervades this society, a culture that continues to cling tenaciously to propaganda holding that the "emperor" of science can alleviate all the ills of mankind with the "new clothes" of technology. Or it could be the vaguely fearful authority people sometimes associate with intuitive professionals, especially Hollywood-style "psychics."

I don't know. Whatever the reasons, I do seem to have to deal with the issue of good versus bad more than, say, a plumber does. If my toilet leaks, a plumber may tell me, "Look, Mac, your toilet needs a new wax ring." I might say, "Is that good or bad?" The criteria for good versus bad in this situation is simple and straightforward: How much will it cost?

Some people seem to believe that having a session with an astrologer is similar to a visit from a plumber. They seem to believe that life is like a toilet—there's one right or "good" way for it to be put together, and any deviation from that must mean that their life has gone wrong. And they want to know how wrong it's gone, how much it will "cost" to fix.

I might say to a client, "You are on the Earth to learn about personal power and how to use it well." Or, "Your emotional intention is to transcend the inhibitions of exclusivity and jealousy in personal love." Or, "You're moving through a ten-month period where your basic life-purpose needs to be shifted away from passive mental images of your past toward assertive physical productivity." Usually, I offer this kind of information in response to something the client has said about a real-life situation. Such comments are usually offered as an aid to understanding and strategy. But more times than I can count, the person sits there dumbstruck for a second, as if hit by lightning, then looks me straight in the eye and says, *"Yes, but is that good or bad?"*

Do people really believe I'm making moral judgments about their lives? Or that I would even want to? Do they actually believe that life is so formulaic? I am not a plumber, and my clients lives are not leaky toilets. Plumbing is mechanical; human lives are not. They are mysterious, sublime, and full of exquisite paradoxes that demand not repair but integration.

For all the multi-leveled abstraction of its symbols, astrology is ultimately pragmatic. Charts say *this* is the quality you need to create and experience in a certain area of your life, and *that* is the quality you need to create and experience in this other area of your life. If there's a conflict between the two qualities, then it's up to you to use the conflict as fuel for your growth while you gradually learn to embrace both sides.

It is neither "good" nor "bad" to have Venus in Capricorn, Mars opposite Uranus, or Mercury in the 12th House. How we understand and live these patterns may be helpful or harmful in light of a particular situation, but that has little to do with astrology per se, and a lot to do with us.

So let me lay this issue to rest, once and for all. Everyone I know, including myself, struggles with the issue of positive and negative meaning, of good versus bad. As foolish as it is, we are constantly judging ourselves to be good or bad people because we want something or don't have something or need something else. It's been that way since we crawled out of the slime a million years ago, and it's likely to continue, regardless of whatever I say about it here. I'm going to keep doing astrological counseling sessions, and more often than I like, people are still going to respond to my information with the question "Is that good or bad?"

But please understand: *The tools of astrology—charts, cycles, and the like—do not contain moral judgments about the individuals whose lives they describe in symbolic terms.* Goodness or badness, like beauty, is in the eye of the beholder.

Power and Prestige

One of the most significant differences between astrology and psychology surrounds the way the two institutions have developed in our society.

Largely because it grew out of medical practice, psychology has carefully carved out a niche for itself, in spite of much skepticism by the general public. Psychology created hierarchical structures or acceptance into its club, including standards and practices, educational requirements, and certification procedures. In addition, psychology courted public favor by presenting a very formal image of authority. In remaining linked with the medical establishment, it achieved the dubious benefit of insurance coverage for its services. Finally, it associated itself with the great American "religion" of Science.

Psychology has posed as the handmaiden of Science, although in actual counseling practice it uses as much hoodoo-voodoo as any other discipline. We simply don't know much yet about the inner workings of the psyche. The surface has been barely scratched, many of the conceptual frameworks are arbitrary, and *all* forms of counseling remain much like the blind men and the elephant—each can identify a certain part or texture, but none encompasses the whole.

Where psychotherapy has really shone brightly is in its smashing success *as an institution*. It may not have lived up to its billing as an infallible tool to reduce human suffering, but psychology is a powerful institution in the culture. The same cannot be said of astrology.

For those of us attuned to participation in the larger culture, there is a definite ostracism associated with being an astrologer. In choosing to pursue the study and practice of astrology, we tread a path that is largely mocked. Despite increasingly widespread private interest in astrology, our culture is not merely cautious but downright condescending in its adamant refusal to even consider that there may be value here. Many of us have clients who occupy positions of influence—CEO's, politicians, doctors, lawyers, etc.—but even though these individuals consult astrologers, the institutions of which they are a part continue to scorn astrology. Where anything esoteric is concerned, our society reacts with childish fear.

Decades ago, the American Medical Association decided that chiropractic represented a threat to the power and influence of traditional allopathic medicine. Adopting an official policy of non-recognition, they began an unofficial effort to undermine chiropractors and subvert their success. To some extent, there was a real philosophical debate over methods and practices, but basically the issue came down to power, influence, and money. The AMA represented the "haves"; they sought to keep chiropractors the "have-nots." Finding themselves in a David and Goliath situation, chiropractors fought back by creating professional organizations and lobbying groups. Recently, the courts upheld that there was in fact a conspiracy against chiropractic by the AMA, but the battle still goes on.

By its nature, chiropractic tends to be somewhat more esoteric than Western medical traditions. It relies not on technology and the concept of bodies as machines but instead on the more holistic idea that healing is a function of body, mind, and spirit. As a result, chiropractic attracts a larger percentage of individuals interested in the metaphysical implications of health and disease. However, because of the power struggle waged between the institutions of chiropractic and traditional Western medicine, many chiropractors have been forced to practice in the shadows.

While there is no such clear-cut battle surrounding astrology, we labor against similar cultural biases. Our struggle may be less well defined, but it is just as real. Like chiropractors, astrologers tend to be seen as radicals or fuzzy-minded flakes. But there is a difference between chiropractors and astrologers. From a statistical point of view, the temperaments of those interested in formal medical training tend to be more grounded in linearity than those of astrological students and practitioners.

By and large, astrologers are an idiosyncratic lot who tend to eschew professional organization and regulation. From my perspective at least, the odds of our creating a strong central lobby are very slim. Astrology will probably never attain the influential status psychology has achieved as an institution. Discussion surrounding "standards and practices" will undoubtedly continue among certain groups of astrologers, but part of what draws people to this field in the first place is the renegade status of our discipline.

Working with Clients

Beyond cultural acceptance as an institution, there is another level where the distinctions between psychology and astrology stand out in bold relief. Psychology has been particularly successful *as a business*. Once again, the same cannot be said of astrology. The issue here revolves around the nature of services, the packaging and marketing of those services, and the frequency of purchase by customers.

Psychologists realized early on that what they had to sell was the promise of greater fulfillment through personality change. They packaged their services so that the process of interaction was in the foreground, while their tools remained almost mystically shrouded in the background. And they marketed on the basis of repeat business through continuing work in ongoing sessions.

Astrologers have consistently succumbed to the illusion that we sell mere information. We package our services as if the tools were the product. And we market those services on a hit-or-miss, one-shot basis.

The result is obvious: Thousands of consulting psychologists have overflowing practices that earn them a good living. Most astrologers in this country would starve if they depended solely on the income from sessions with clients. And it's a mystery to me why astrologers don't wise up.

It is not unusual for psychotherapists to see their clients three, sometimes even five, days a week. One session per week is a general minimum. Most astrologers consider themselves lucky if their clients come back at all. And for repeat business, once a year is not uncommon. Even those precious few astrologers who maintain a regular clientele do not see the bulk of their clients more than once a month.

When a psychologist enters into a relationship with

a new client, the emphasis is placed on the client's life, not on the psychologist's tools. People expect that they will need to talk to a psychotherapist, to explain their situation and their feelings about it. The product—fulfilling change—is a result of the interaction, and people know going in that those results will take time to reach—often a year of sessions, and sometimes more.

Astrology is almost universally marketed as if the tools and techniques are an end in themselves. Both astrologers and their clients tend to focus on charts rather than on the clients' lives. This is a ludicrous mistake. The product of astrology is not chart interpretations! It is awareness, effectiveness, and harmony with oneself and the universe. Focusing on charts as our product is not only an unsophisticated approach to the use of astrological tools, limiting the help astrology can provide, but, more to the point, it is a virtual dead end for generating return business, thus keeping the astrologer dependent on an endless stream of new clients to make even a modest living.

But wait, you say. Haven't astrologers addressed that problem by creating a whole package of different interpretations: natal reading, progressed reading, relationship reading, career reading, relocation reading, etc.? My answer is no, absolutely not.

We need to stop marketing ourselves as if we sell "products." Astrology will never support successful careers for any but the most brilliant (and fortunate) among us until we begin teaching our students and the public at large that the product of astrology is life-enhancement and that working with an astrologer is an ongoing process, not a one-time purchase.

It is boringly common for prospective new clients to call me on the phone and say, "I've already had my natal chart done. All I want from you is progressions." They offer this request as if one 90-minute session with any astrologer for a "natal reading" is sufficient for them to completely understand all the implications of their birth chart! As if the process of self-understanding involved little more than mechanical chart interpretation from some textbook. They think of it like a piece of furniture— buy it once and it's "done."Another common statement from prospective clients is "I'm calling you because I'm interested in learning about my chart."Again, this is offered as if the chart were the end product, complete unto itself.

Why do so many people have such ridiculous misconceptions? Because *astrologers*—some who are well-meaning and some who are flat-out idiots—have *promoted* these misconceptions.

High Expectations

While people may seek out astrologers for many of the same reasons they might engage a therapist, their expectations of astrologers tend to be much higher. In my practice, it is no surprise for a new client to start a first session by saying, "Well, what did you find in my chart?" or "Tell me what you know about me." These questions come from someone I have never laid eyes on before! Very few people have such outrageous expectations of traditional therapy.

Picture an initial psychotherapy session. Can you imagine a client expecting the therapist to know in advance not only what his personality is like, what his precise circumstances are (as well as when they began, when they will end, what they mean, and why they're happening), but also exactly what his problems are and how to solve them? No way!

M. Scott Peck, psychiatrist and author of main-stream books on psychotherapy, mentions in his book *The*

Road Less Traveled a client with whom he conducted 150 sessions before he even had a diagnosis of her problem. Three times a week for a full year this client spent an hour with him (and God knows how much money), and in all that time he didn't have a clue about what was going on with her, much less how to help her! If I were so brazen as to suggest to my clients that we have even one session—much less 150—without my offering professional insights, opinions, or conclusions, they probably wouldn't come. People expect astrologers to know a great deal about them, and they expect us to know it immediately.

In truth, one of the distinctions between astrological counseling and traditional therapy is that our system is much more revealing as an information base than most traditional approaches to counseling. We do, in fact, often know more, and we usually know it more quickly. This factor is one of many reasons I became an astrologer.

When I began to make my living as a professional astrologer in 1973, one of my motivations was to provide an alternative to traditional therapy. I felt then that standard psychotherapy was, at best, a crapshoot, and at worst, a well-meaning scam where the costs in time and money far outweighed the benefits.

Some of that opinion was based on my own anger at the educational system. Undergraduate psychology had been less than enlightening. In fact, it had been downright deadening to my enthusiasm. My introduction in 1970 to astrology as a serious psychological system revved my interest as well as my hope. I gradually came to believe that I could offer as much in one two-hour session as many psychologists achieved in 20.

Over the years, my resentments have mellowed along with my bravado, and I have gradually come around to the idea of ongoing sessions having a value all their own. Real change—authentically conscious maturity—usually takes considerable time, effort, and commitment. What some call "change" is often little more than passage through automatic, relatively unconscious phases. We can lead the horse to where we think the water is, but whether the water is really there is as much an unknown as whether the horse will drink. The proof is often not in the pudding at all, especially when the pudding is intangible.

Low Expectations

Economic stupidity in astrology tends to promote a vicious cycle. The bulk of textbooks and classes offer only rudimentary training in astrological technique and analysis, much of which contains questionable wisdom. Students are often cut adrift without ever being exposed to the wide range of non-astrological, human skills necessary to convert interpretive technique into effective counsel. After achieving what passes for sophistication in astrology, most "professionals" have difficulty attracting a working clientele, so in desperation many turn to the lowest common denominator. They hire themselves out to write Sun sign columns and booklets (the kind found on grocery store check-out racks). They write textbooks filled with shorthand, cookbook-style interpretations, which starts the treadmill all over again for a new generation of unlucky students.

A few achieve relative success by creating mail-order businesses that specialize in computer-generated interpretations. Such enterprises may generate sales in volume, but however comprehensive they may be they further the unfortunate belief that information is our product. On the whole, these services take food out of the mouths of working astrologers by fostering the mistaken impression that if people can get a supposedly "bona fide" interpretation from a computer for only $19.95, then why pay anywhere from $40 to $100 per hour to talk to a real astrologer? It's all the same, isn't it? Information is information, whether it comes from a computer or a person, right? Wrong. Insight is not the same as information. The kind of mature life-enhancement that astrology can offer does not emerge from pre-packaged natal interpretations or shrink-wrapped daily transit guides.

Some astrologers argue that there are benefits to mass marketing, that even superficial products result in increased awareness about astrology in the public mind. I would counter that such a result is a benefit only if you don't mind rigid misconceptions about what astrology is, what it offers, and how it works. The law of supply and demand applies here. We condition the public to want only kindergarten levels of astrological sophistication, resulting in a virtual tidal wave of lowered expectations in the marketplace. Even the best astrologers must be very strong swimmers to persevere against this current, and most students will drown in the undertow without ever realizing that real artistry is possible.

Feed people a steady diet of junk food, and how many will appreciate the subtle delicacy of gourmet cuisine? A few will; most won't.

The force of my opinions concerning the practice and marketing of astrology will, no doubt, offend some members of the astrological community. My arguments will be criticized as stuffy elitism, so let me be clear. As in every other field of human endeavor, those interested will reflect a multitude of attitudes, beliefs, and talents. A wide range of approaches are required to serve a diversity of needs in the marketplace, and many levels of sophistication can and should coexist in services and products.

What disturbs me are the relative proportions. Too much of what is offered comes from the bottom of the scale. What passes for excellence in astrology is frequently little more than sophistry. From the initial creation of Sun signs in the 1920s as our first mass-marketing device, far too many astrologers have demonstrated a disregard for serious development and public consideration of our system that is shortsighted, cavalier, and largely self-defeating. A certain percentage of astrologers are blind to this issue, preferring a rose-colored, naively occult vision of the world. Others complain bitterly, but continue to support the status quo by pandering to the public hunger for garbage. Most astrologers are guilty of contributing in one way or another to the problem.

The great tragedy of 20th-century astrology is that we have done this to ourselves.

Why Use Psychology?

In Minnesota, where I live, it is illegal to practice psychological therapy without Board Certification. But in reality, that means only that you cannot call yourself a therapist without running afoul of the authorities. As long as your work is performed under a different name—astrologer, psychic, consultant, personal counselor, etc.—you can practice therapy with relative impunity. (It is worth noting that laws vary widely from state to state, both in their letter and their spirit. Most states have laws against everything; often, those laws go unenforced. If you wish to use astrology as a basis for psychotherapy, you would be wise to check out the formal laws governing such practice in your particular area of residence, as well as the characteristic enforcement of those laws.)

So if the institution of psychology has gone to such extreme measures as legal prohibition to prevent outsiders from practicing therapy, if it is still so careful to publicly avoid any hint of association with astrology, then why don't we just walk away and forget it? As astrologers, why should we even try to increase our sensitivity and skills in the area of psychological counseling? Why? *Because astrology alone is not enough.* It never was, and it never will be. Life is bigger than astrology, so to use our astrological tools and perspectives in a way that really connects to our clients' lives, we need to recognize and account for the many non-astrological factors that influence those lives.

The kind of astrology currently used by the majority of astrologers and students focuses on the reality of individual life. Although many astrological writers direct their thoughts toward the use of astrology to reveal evolutionary trends in the larger collective, the bread-and-butter, day-to-day practice of astrology is almost always directed toward particular individuals. Natal charts certainly contain information that goes far beyond the uniquely personal, but those levels of meaning are relevant only insofar as they relate back to the individual life being analyzed.

Especially for particularly fervent students and professionals, astrology is regarded as a kind of "Holy Grail," a mysterious but all-encompassing system. They believe it to be capable of revealing everything about a given individual, if only the chart could be explored in sufficient depth, using the right techniques. This reflects a brand of fanaticism that is sad to see.

For instance, I notice certain repetitive patterns in the individuals and couples who make up my clientele. Often these patterns surround the emotional perspectives clients have on their situations, and more to the point, their expectations of what our work together will provide. Some patterns have nothing to do with astrology; others are the direct result of uninformed opinions concerning what astrology is, how it works, and what it can reveal.

A client telephones to set up an appointment. For me, that's a straightforward secretarial procedure. All I need to know is how quickly the person wants to see me. Is it an emergency? A routine check-in? A special occasion?

For some clients, however, calling to set up an appointment is not nearly so cut-and-dried. Although many have entirely positive motivations for sessions, some clients are laboring under any of a number of different anxieties or insecurities, and they want to address these in the phone conversation before they schedule a session. Naturally, every conversation is different because each person's situation is unique to his/her life-drama. But there are recognizable patterns.

Wake Me When It's Over

The telephone rings. I answer.

Bill: "Hello?"

Client: "Hi, Bill, this is Jane Doe [or John Smith]. I saw you back in December."

Bill: "Oh yes, I remember. What can I do for you?"

Client: "Well, I was thinking of coming in to see you for another session."

Bill: "Fine. When would you like to come?"

Client: [sidestepping my question] "Uh, well see, I've been going through some financial difficulty [or relationship problems, family issues, general confusion, etc.], and I was wondering if the chart might have anything to say about it."

Bill: "Jane, charts contain a great deal of information about every level of your life. I'm not exactly sure what you're asking."

Client: "Well, I'm real tired of this, and I was sort of hoping that my chart could tell me when it's going to end, you know, when things are going to get better?"

At this stage of the conversation, it's obvious that

we're firmly stuck in what I call the Wake-Me-When-It's-Over Syndrome. This person is undergoing an unpleasant experience that she doesn't understand. She's tried to cope with it as best she knows how, but she's gradually worn down. Nothing has worked, and now, after a long on-again, off-again period of stress and struggle, she's finally calling me out of desperation.

Jane knows enough about astrology to understand that there are many natural cycles in each person's life. However, she probably doesn't have an astrologer's awareness of the symbolic and multi-leveled nature of these cycles, perhaps believing instead that each cycle is about some very specific part of her life, perhaps even a concrete event.

She's no longer really interested in the dynamics of the situation, although she worries about it constantly. The idea that there might be meaning or purpose to what she's going through has long since vanished. And the possibility that she could conceivably learn or even benefit from her experience by understanding or acting differently is not on her mind. All Jane wants now is to survive whatever it is that's giving her fits, to outlast it. To that end, she's looking for a cosmic authority (like astrology, or more technically, an astrologer) to tell her that whatever has her by the tail will come to an end.

Jane's also probably divided inside herself about having a session with me. On the one hand, she wants to see me, because she hopes I will have "good news": "Oh sure, what you're describing is right in the chart. It started on such-and-such a date and it will end on such-and-such a date, so if you can just hang on for another couple days [or weeks, or months], this awfulness will be over, and everything will return to normal." [Translation: These "bad" factors in your chart will fade out, and you'll be all right.]

However, on the other hand, she's anxious about having a session for fear I may say: "Your chart says this is permanent. It's fated to be. You're going to have to put up with it from now on." [Translation: It's your karma, and you can cry if you want to. . . .]

Her expectations, both hopeful and anxious, are very understandable. First of all, she's human, which means she's subject to limits of understanding, strength, objectivity, etc. The puzzle of individual human life often is more than the best of us can gracefully handle. In addition, her beliefs about astrology have probably been formed largely by pop culture propaganda. She may even have been to one or more "professional" astrologers who reinforced these images and expectations because of their own superficial understanding or unexamined beliefs about astrology.

The Relativity of Astrology

Our symbolic system is not a single, unified body of knowledge. There are as many different "astrologies" as there are people practicing it. Each individual adapts the system to fit his/her particular evolutionary path. Certainly, the ongoing study of astrology can alter a person's paradigms of understanding, and every working astrologer has had the experience of clients being dramatically affected by some tidbit of astrological insight. But at any given moment, most of us compress "pure" astrology into something more selectively limited, something that fits our current levels of comprehension, maturity, and consciousness—all of which is unavoidable, of course, but it is, nonetheless, important to remember.

In addition, charts don't "say" anything. They hold their secrets silently. It is only when a human being interprets a chart that it reveals its mysteries.

Certainly there are conventions within astrology,

basic meanings upon which most astrologers can agree. Being a competent astrologer presumes a thorough understanding of these conventional interpretations since they represent the background of experience and wisdom amassed by our astrological predecessors, both living and dead. But such meanings can be learned through rote memory without delving further into the assumptions behind the interpretations.

If we digested the contents of every textbook or treatise ever written on the subject of astrological interpretation, we might suffer a kind of cortical brownout because each author's interpretations are produced in part by the metaphysical value systems s/he is using. Assumptions, attitudes, and expectations are critical to the art of astrological delineation because they represent the value systems that shape the raw symbology into an interpretive fabric that has real, practical implications.

Through the Looking Glass

We don't look at charts "directly." Instead, we look at them through the lenses of various value systems. Change lenses and the meanings derived from the chart shift in much the same way that a child's kaleidoscope will form new patterns as we rotate the cardboard tube. We have to decide what lenses we're going to use in working with this symbolic system. Even if we don't actually choose, it's still important to let our clients know what our basic presumptions are likely to be.

The astrology inside my head and heart—the astrology I practice with my clients—is not about knowing how long we have to "put up with" something. Nor is it really about the passive experience of "things getting better." Yes, I can understand that there are astrologers who use the system in that manner, especially given the high percentage of people who want them to use it that way, but I believe that's not even close to its real or best use.

Sure, I too have had that seemingly universal human feeling—When is This Crap Gonna End??? I have no trouble admitting that I'm a Bozo in good standing. But if that's how I use astrology, especially with my clients, then I'm not giving them the best of who I am. If that's how I look at charts when they ask me for help, I'm not using the best of what this symbolic system has to offer.

In my opinion, life is not about getting past things, suffering through them blindly until they pass away. Life is to be experienced, not avoided, and in the willingness to experience, experiment, and create lies the possibility, however intangible, of real learning—the kind of learning that brings growth and realization, not the kind that is essentially an endless repetition and magnification of unconscious or previously imprinted patterns.

Whose Life Is It, Anyway?

Viewed from one metaphysical perspective, we create our own lives. In this view, we are responsible for everything that happens in our world, either literally or figuratively. At this level, we can choose to change our behavior or our feeling patterns. We can recognize our part in the events and experiences of our living, and we are free to change at any time. Even when we do not recognize how we influence our environments, we can still work within the spiritual paradox of Acceptance versus Change, patiently observing ourselves and the world around us until the realization of causes, effects, and correlations become apparent, helping us to awaken into truer responsibility.

Interpreted from the opposite perspective, life happens to us, and we are mainly responding to what occurs. In this view, we are individuals living in a world we did not create, a world with its own perverse logic. We have to adapt to that world, adjusting our lives as required by circumstances often well beyond our limited control. But even then, we have a responsibility to ourselves to understand as much as we can so as to consciously respond rather than unconsciously react. We still have to observe ourselves and the environments around us, if only to maximize the effectiveness of our responses.

These two viewpoints appear to be paradoxical, which is to say "mutually exclusive." But the experience of countless sages over millennia suggest that they are not. Each way coexists with its opposite. Even further, each contains within it the seed of reflective inference that makes the other not only possible but necessary. Philosophically, one perspective could not exist without the other.

Astrology, with its symbolic techniques of natal charts, transit cycles, composites, etc., reveals meanings from either of these extreme perspectives equally well. As such, it is a discipline particularly well-suited to the investigation of life's ironies, especially when applied to individual experience.

Meanwhile, Back at the Ranch . . .

I should not leave the impression that all my clients see me because of "problems" involving negativity or other suffering. Many of the people with whom I work are motivated by the positive search for enhanced self-awareness and increased fulfillment. But once I have established a working relationship with a client, further sessions naturally tend to occur during times of heightened stress or personal challenge.

When Jane Doe (or John Smith) calls me for help with a problem, I already know that what she thinks she wants from me is not what she's likely to get. My job is not merely to give her information. On the contrary, it is to help her change any habitual mental or emotional patterns that may block her ability to act effectively. I try to help my clients gain access to more of their natural grace, freedom, and intelligence by shifting their metaphysical perspectives back toward consciously creative responsibility (read: the ability to respond).

How will I do that? I'll use the basic information from her natal chart, transits, and any other astrological tools that seem relevant to help her remember her life-purpose, her mission, and the mountains that stand in her way. I will assist her as well as I can in disconnecting from invisible hysteria or the subtle negativity of emotionally reactive states. The very same natal configurations or transit patterns that correlate more or less with her current predicament will offer other options for understanding and self-expression that may help her remember *who she is* and why she's here.

Could You Give an Example?

OK, let's say that my client Jane Doe has Mars at 10° Cancer in the 2nd House of her natal chart in trine to the Sun at 7° Pisces/10th House. Then presume that Saturn and Neptune are simultaneously opposing Mars in transit, as they were in 1989.

There are infinite scenarios we could conceive out of this limited set of factors using basic, "conventional" interpretations. In an event-oriented interpretive framework, we might discover that the financial difficulties she spoke of involve unexpected challenges concerning an external source of income. A loan she needs may be denied for no obvious reason; a death in the family could result in a legacy or will locked in probate battles; property settlements in a divorce or other partnership dissolution could be contested; a critical real estate closing might be delayed or she could be in danger of mortgage foreclosure on her home; she may have "apparently" won a contest involving money or prizes that she comes to count on, only to discover a catch in the fine print; an important team project she's leading in her work could be threatened by infighting, management changes, office politics, competition from another company, etc.

All those scenarios are based on the crudest, old-line symbolism of the significant factors: Mars in Cancer in the 2nd is interpreted as a battle over personal finances and the desire for security through money. The two simultaneous transits are oppositions in the 8th House, inferring blockage. Saturn is used here only in its most negative meaning—that of frustration, delay, or denial—and Neptune is interpreted as adding elements of illusion, fantasy, or subterfuge, clouding the issue and making the blockage impossible to understand logically.

The interpretations are utterly devoid of any humanistic or psychospiritual content. They are anachronistic, and could hardly be considered sophisticated. But they are conventional, and they do reflect much of the pessimistic thinking that swirls around astrology, both on the part of some of its practitioners and many of those who naively seek it out for advice.

Viewed from a more positive framework, we could suggest that her desire for self-worth (Mars in the 2nd) has now come to a culmination, a period of fulfillment or realization (transit oppositions) where she needs to integrate the idea of polarity, to understand the connection between the value that is hers alone (2nd) and the value that comes through relatedness (8th). The fulfillment is "forced" because of the involvement with Saturn, and Neptune's presence may correspond to her experience of circumstances as mysterious or beyond her control.

To fulfill personal desires now requires her to take fuller responsibility in her relationships with others. These reality demands interweave with fantasy, and the imagery from either her fondest dreams or her worst nightmares may bleed into situations. She could dissolve old attitudes involving anger over money or struggles surrounding selfishness, or she may drown in those same attitudes as they expand and spill over into her world. This time in her life allows literal manifestation of conflicts that had previously been relatively private to promote transcendence of any twisted attitudes that may have kept her from experiencing personal fulfillment and collective responsibility together.

Whatever lens we use, there are an endless number of possible scripts. In my own work, rather than try to figure them out in advance, I simply wait for my clients to explain their situations to me. What is actually occurring in their lives usually turns out to be more astrologically far-reaching than anything I could think up on my own. The interpenetrating weave of circumstances and their extension into actual life is often downright fantastic in light of the astrological factors involved. In fact, one of the things that has kept me from burnout over 16 years as an astrological counselor is the amazement I feel in hearing peoples' stories. Time and again, the circumstances are "tailored" to the chart in a way no Hollywood screenwriter could dream up. Truth is indeed stranger than fiction.

I must also state that no single approach is always infallibly correct or helpful. My preference with clients is to use the humanistic approach whenever possible because I believe in astrology's potential as a *raja yoga* (or royal path). Similarly, I lean away from the kind of old-line textbook interpretations I used as illustrations some paragraphs above.

But I cannot deny that those crude and negative orientations do often show up in real life. During the 7,000 sessions I've done with people, I have heard every conceivable kind of horror story, from the ridiculous to the sublime. So my point is not to suggest that these old-style, fire-and-brimstone interpretations cannot or do not occur in actual fact. They can and they do, in spite of positivist philosophies.

Astrology can be downright scary in its often uncanny ability to "predict" what will go wrong and when it will happen. And even when prediction is not the issue (since most serious astrologers eschew the fortune-telling mode), astrology is better than any system I have ever seen in confirming through symbolic correlation what has gone wrong in a given individual's life, when it happened, and why it occurred.

However, that's not the point. If all I do with my client Jane Doe is listen to her story and tell her that, yes, it's right there in her chart, and that the cycles will be over in November, I am doing her a disservice. That may be exactly what she wants to hear, and it may comfort her to know that these "awful" transits will come to an end, but it leaves out the whole question of how she might better work with reality now. Such simplistic advice presumes that the symbols in her chart have only one level of meaning—those indicated by the negative circumstances over which she's currently obsessing.

In telling her that the transits will end, am I relieving her? Or am I merely putting a Band-Aid over the wound while I inadvertently give it more importance than it deserves? Actually, I'm reinforcing her belief in life as a series of unavoidable "wounds" that are inevitable and must be suffered. I'm also suggesting that her difficulty is solely the product of the phase of circumstances, issues, and choices symbolically revealed by her current pattern of transits, which may or not be true. I've seen many emotional patterns far outlive the transits under which they began. The transits stop, but the person continues to rev on the patterns with which they correlated. Also, real circumstances have their own natural momentum, and there can be little certainty that the end of the symbolic associations with which they correspond will also represent an end to real-life repercussions.

For example, an individual may undergo a particularly challenging set of astrological factors surrounding finances. Questionable decisions, bad luck, or numerous uncontrollable factors may combine to produce bankruptcy. If, as is often the case, there are transit cycles that correspond to the initial period of difficulty, the cycles will probably end far before the effects of the bankruptcy. A Saturn/Sun or Neptune/Moon transit cannot possibly endure more than a year or two at most. However, the bad credit rating will remain for 10 years, continuing to affect the individual's life despite the fact that the transits have long since ended.

Certain outer planet transits to Venus correspond to a period of upheaval in personal relationships that may sometimes result in eventual loss, heartbreak, or grief. Again, the transits will end, but often the emotional depression lives on, affecting the person's ability to handle future transits.

Merely understanding astrology is not enough. Mastering the technical side of interpretation is insufficient. Astrologers need to understand more than that. We have to understand what being human means. And that requires us to shift our view of the chart to fit the person we're trying to help.

A Different Path

Consider the previous example with my client "Jane Doe" who has Saturn and Neptune in transit opposition to Mars. I may discuss with Jane the implications of her circumstances at any of various levels: mental, emotional, psychological, familial, socio-cultural, mythic, sexual, spiritual, etc. Each level can be addressed by looking at the chart through the lenses of different value systems. My job is to help Jane ease out of her fearful fixation into a more creative and fulfilling sense of herself and life around her. I will pick the lenses that seem most suited to that task.

We could discuss the nature and purpose of desire itself (Mars) and the way those desire patterns are linked with survival emotions that were imprinted in her infancy or early childhood. We can move the conversation back to her childhood if that seems feasible, helping her to remember incidents that echo what is happening now.

Having established that there may be a frightened child still living within her, I might then discuss the idea of "parenting one's inner child," an issue of special importance for her because of her 10th House Pisces Sun. I could suggest to her that the experience of responsible parenthood is crucial for her in terms of life-purpose (Sun in 10th) but that she might become confused about it, sometimes losing herself in fantasies of external authority (Sun in Pisces).

We could consider her relationship with her father or other significant authority figures. I might then suggest that she has unconsciously grown dependent on other people or positive external circumstances to take care of her inner child's need for security, and that when life didn't cooperate, her personality succumbed to the resulting fear tantrum. I could even suggest to her metaphysically that the very reason these negative circumstances are occurring might be as a way for her higher self to put her back in touch with the importance of assuming the role of responsible parent to her inner child.

None of these ideas are objectively true or false. For instance, I don't really know whether or not she has a "higher self," and the idea of its intervening in her life is an unprovable assumption. But offered to the right person at the right time, and conveyed in the right spirit, such ideas can sometimes have the effect of awakening that person out of a habitual state of expectation.

Furthermore, these ideas aren't just random. I'm not making them up out of thin air. Everything I've said so far, and a thousand other ways of looking at and discussing her life, are there for the finding in the symbolism of her particular astrological patterns.

The point is that it's all in her chart. What I'm saying isn't chosen haphazardly, nor is it the product of an arbitrary psychological system. To an observer, our interaction might look like more traditional counseling, but the content is still solidly based in astrological technique.

Perhaps a "family systems" approach won't work with Jane. She might not be emotionally secure enough to discuss her family. She could have a psychological blind spot with regard to one parent or the other. Also, the metaphysical suggestion of a "higher self" might backfire. Her religious background or beliefs might be offended by such blatant metaphysics. Or she might take the mythic poetry of my metaphor too literally, becoming convinced that her higher self will run her life for her.

There are many reasons a particular approach might not work with a given client. But that's no problem. I'm not limited to only these lenses as ways of reaching her. The chart provides information and direction no matter what approach I take. I just have to be sensitive enough to Jane to know when one approach isn't suitable, and intelligent enough to switch gears.

For example, I could discuss the general symbolism of the Saturn/Neptune conjunction, explaining that it's a repetitive cycle recurring about every 36 years with definite implications for humanity as a whole. I could talk about how cultural institutions periodically reach a point of stagnation and that this conjunction of outer planets correlates with a dissolving of old structures to make way for new visions of how we can create collective life. I would explain that certain individuals are "selected" to be representatives for this mass change by virtue of their natal charts containing certain sensitive points activated in transit by Saturn and Neptune. We could then discuss how her circumstances fit into this larger perspective.

There is no guarantee, of course, that my client will "get it." God doesn't sell that kind of insurance. No, that's up to her and me. She has to be receptive and creative with her intelligence. I have to be skillful and sensitive as an astrological counselor. She has to be patient with her problems, taking responsibility in accepting certain aspects of her life, as well as changing her circumstances and self-expression as she can. I have to remember that life is bigger than astrology.

But time and again, going back to the basics of the chart works. At least the feedback I get from clients and the visible, long-term changes in their lives suggest that something positive is occurring. More than that I couldn't measure anyway, since my work is not about rats in cages nor statistical norms of definable behaviors. Instead, it is about real people and the subtle experience of moving toward fulfillment.

The Bottom Line

I believe the astrological community would benefit from the recognition that our clients' needs are not best served by an approach that ignores the value of counseling. Astrological insights are helpful only when they can be heard. In other words, the actual, technical process of astrological interpretation is far and away the easiest part of our work with people. By and large, interpretation is a snap. Accessing information is easy. The real challenge lies in reaching people.

I want to interact with each client in a way that works for that particular individual at a certain time in his/her life with respect to the unique chemistry of our relationship. It is pure joy when I work with clients who are in synch with themselves, with me, and with my information. The sessions take off and fly in the shared exhilaration. But that doesn't happen every day.

Clients usually consult me when they are grappling with an issue, a challenging set of circumstances, or a new experience for which they have no previous understanding. When they are working through Wake-Me-When-It's-Over, Is-It-Good-or-Bad, or any other typically human blind spot, my first responsibility is to help them out of the hole. Sometimes information from their chart or transits is very helpful to that process. Sometimes it is not. Other times an explanation of the astrological frameworks behind the information may be more effective. Or it may not be. Often, what works best has nothing to do with astrology.

There are many paths. Not all of them lead home with every person in every situation, but some will. All the various astrological tools and techniques at our disposal can certainly help us determine which lenses might be of benefit, but common sense is important, too, as is good intuition.

Every person has an "inner grid," an emotional, mental, and spiritual framework for interpreting reality. My job is not merely to shovel information into that pre-existing grid, especially when the grid itself is so often the problem. My job is to alter the grid.

The revelations of astrology can assist us in clarifying the presumptions, expectations, and unconscious attitudes of the grids under which our clients may be laboring. It can also aid us in finding new directions to offer them in their journeys, and more importantly, more effective ways of looking at the journey itself. But one thing is clear: ***Astrology alone is never enough.***

Without the development and use of other skills, we will remain handcuffed, despite our knowledge of astrology. Without communication skills, our wisdom will be mute or misunderstood. Without cultural awareness, we will miss powerful, mythic factors that go far beyond individual experience. Without the active involvement of our minds to look inside someone, we will overlook the patterns of his/her inner thoughts. Without the receptive opening of our hearts to gently embrace one's reality, we will never finally gain trust. We need to listen to our clients, and feel them, and see who they are.

Then the symbols come to life, and astrology becomes the wondrous tool it should be.

Gray Keen

Keen was a teenage professional musician and music teacher. Following two years of course study in law and criminology, he worked in law enforcement but returned to the print media where he had begun a part-time career at age 15. His media career spanned 25 years as newspaper editor, publisher, radio producer, television news director and broadcaster. He has taught classes in journalism and astrology.

At age 11, Keen discovered astrology in a volume by Lord Francis Bacon. For ten years, he has practiced full-time in the Bay Area, serving business, professional counselors, as well as a wide range of clientele, including residents of many foreign countries. Although his practice is traditional, he studied Hindu astrology with professor P. K. Singh of India and is an initiate in Kriya Yoga.

Keen has written articles for *Geocosmic News* and *Today's Astrology* and contributed to the first volume of this series, *Spiritual, Metaphysical and New Trends in Modern Astrology*.

Married, he is the father of eight children.

PLATO SAT ON A ROCK

While currently adopted astrological doctrines and dictums might not vary quite as extensively as the cultures and languages on this planet, it should be readily apparent that they are too diverse to treat with singularity. So to propose a consulting regimen to such a broad spectrum is a little like trying to put a size eight shoe on New Jersey.

Still, there are fundamental values that no sincere, self-respecting astrologer can ignore. These qualities are very rarely seen in print, so cautionary reminders *out of sight* are *out of mind*.

Most intelligent and conscientious professionals are mindful of rules of the road, but there are astrologers who might never have had an opportunity to experience the words. Because these precepts are such an integral part of one's professional worth—and comfortability too often eclipses one's receptivity to "new" information—this might be the time to acquaint yourself with some patterns from experience. Even some professionals might benefit.

A prime requisite for the consultant should be a grounding in *technical skill competency* and *a humanitarian orientation*. But perhaps more important is the *ethical accountability* involved in providing a *valid client recipe that works*.

Although an "Oath of Ethics" is a primary part of

the membership application of some astrological organizations, the astrological community lacks its own "police force" to provide supervision or regulation of the opportunists and parvenues. One has only to visit his/her local library and scan the Yellow Page listings of various cities under the category "Astrologers" to discover not only the frequent *absence* of a legitimate representative of the profession, but quite often an activity other than astrology!

Whether this condition should be blamed on Motherhood or Pisceans is probably unimportant. What is important: *Astrology is a major life force that should be administered by responsible presenters whose primary motivation is more than a simple glamorous attraction to astrology.* While it is usually true that those who love astrology and people do it best, it can hardly be denied that astrology comes first, the astrologer, second.

Often, Plato was said to sit on a rock and, with his followers at his feet, deliver his discourses . . . which reflects the obvious tenet that any discussion is preferably based on a *philosophical union between the parties involved.*

It is a known occurrence that, at times, a client seeks an astrologer's audience simply to experience the presence of one who has a high profile by virtue of authored books, income, or television exposure. Even though the astrologer can enjoy the stroking, such posturing can lure one into "sitting on his/her rock" and talking *over* the client. I call this the *Plato Syndrome.*

As an adjunct to the foregoing sense of inflated ego—although sometimes quite innocently—an astrologer's *environment* can intimidate the client from the outset. As a student, were you ever called to the principal's office because of some behavioral infraction? Upon your arrival, you found this serious-looking person sitting behind a desk, and beside or in front of the desk there was an empty chair reserved for you. Of course, this is the archaic psychological technique of establishing "who is in charge." It is also intended to intimidate.

While many astrologers assume this to be proper professional protocol, it seems to be unnecessarily ego-centric and could hardly be expected to place all clients in a relaxed, open-minded mood. Besides, the client *knows* who is in charge and *presumes* your lofty posture, or most likely would not be present entrusting intimacies to you.

A proper environment could range from a casual office, den, living room, or even a dining table setting. Many professionals disapprove of too casual a setting, such as a park bench or a café booth. Two unacceptable locales would include your car or your bedroom. These scenarios are not only totally beyond the realm of profes-sionalism, but such a choice might place you in someone's memoirs, or land you in *small claims* court! For the same reasons, it is strictly inadvisable to make house calls.

Then there is the matter of appearance. I have heard from quite reliable sources that there are still astrologers who appear in a colorful flowing muumuu—sometimes adorned by a large medallion dangling on a long chain from the neck and, perhaps, topped with a red bandana headdress. Of course, most of these types are women.

This I call the *Messiah Complex*. But whether it's the Plato Syndrome or this complex, such aloofness would tend to shoot astrology in the foot! With mastery of the art/science, there would seem to be less need to impress clients with one's worthy personage than to indoctrinate them in the principles and wisdom of the cosmic science! This writer has never seen instructions anywhere that an AFTRA (American Federation of Television and Radio Artists) union card is required to perform a consultation.

The unseasoned consultant can sometimes be un-mindful that clients can also be not just uneasy but appre-hensive, skeptical, diffident—or worse—deceptive, antagonistic, argumentative, and neurotic or psychotic. So we must be cognizant of the client's perspective, which seems to reduce to two qualities: the *environment* you provide for the consultation and the matter of your *appearance*—which would also include your *demeanor*.

Still, although all people are different yet the same, there is likely to be disparities between the client and the consultant. One notable mismatch reported to me involved a client who visited a "spiritual astrologer." The client was startled when hastened into an immediate prayer session followed by a guitar-accompanied unison sing! Another signal incident involved a business executive who said his visit to a highly recommended astrologer involved her reading him a "printed report," followed by a discourse on some Neptunian land of Utopian ideals. This might have been peaceful and inspiring, the client said, but he booked the visit hoping to obtain answers to some current vexing business problems.

Disgruntled clients insist upon relating their unpleasant encounters when they arrive to give astrology another try. Additional "reports" that cling to memory:

A 29-year-old woman wanted to know if she could safely circumvent an astrologer's warning (given when 17) that she would never marry! The client said that she had turned down several excellent marriage proposals because she was afraid to countermand the astrologer's warning . . .

A client reported she was charged $500 per hour by a high-profile consultant, and only one thing told to her during the hour ever materialized . . .

Another astrologer rejected a client's request for assistance because, she was told, she (the client) possessed too much karma . . .

A client sent to me by referral was extremely upset by his visits to several "well-known" astrologers—actually in fear of his life—because the last astrologer he visited told him he was likely to commit suicide at the end of the following month!

More than one attractive female client has referred to "having difficulty" fending off some consultant's advances.

What has bothered this writer most, for years I guess, is the generic word *astrologer*. This label incorporates "spiritual," "Jungian," "esoteric," "Theosophy," "Uranian," "Tarot astrology," "psychic astrology," "Christian astrology," and myriad other homogeneous forms of practice. The client's confusion is well justified and might be likened to a patient sitting in a doctor's office with a severely lacerated arm before discovering that s/he had walked into an allergist's office. Although all physicians call themselves "doctor," their specialty is well posted. In the case of astrologers, it appears that all astrologers are not astrologers, and all treatments and prescriptions do not always reflect some *conventionality*.

Is it not grossly apparent, therefore, that not only *specialization* but *abilities* are unknown factors at risk for the client until *after* the consultation? Thus, our earlier premise bears repeating: A consultation should be based on a philosophical union between the parties involved. An attempt to achieve this in preliminary discussion with the client would be the *responsible* approach to eliminating this complication. Unfortunately, in some instances it appears that the ringing of the cash register is louder in the "advisor's" ears than the urge for ethical conduct.

There are many competent, diligent, hard-working, conscientious astrologers—some with high profile, others not—who save this institution of astrology every day by the services they dispense. It is by the hands and minds of this collective that what we would hope to be the best representative image of the profession remains alive. . . .

But there are too few.

Our quandary seems to be reflected in what the public never sees, for to them astrology is represented by the highly visible "astrology" columns in the periodicals. The people have no idea that beyond that veil *practiced* astrology has as many flavors as an ice cream store. So, if you're a budding consultant, why not endure this little questionnaire to which no answers will be provided.

1. What are your perceptions of what astrology is, and does it agree with any widely recognized authority?

2. Have you developed a concept of astrology by compiling several diverse techniques?

3. Do these techniques conform to the universal standard of erecting a client's birth chart, bringing it up to time by progressing it, and augmenting it with a solar return for the year or imposing current transits upon it?

4. Do you utilize established, published "cook books" for developing an interpretation of the charts, construct interpretations based on traditional key words, or do you develop these from your own "instincts"?

5. Did you find astrology so complicated or involved that you gave up and took a shortcut by shoring up what you'd learned with other persuasions, such as divination or palmistry or tarot? Or did you simply extend your creations into Uranian or Neptunian concepts because you felt they left windows open for invention?

Astrology can represent too imposing a challenge to some students, and, of course, there is the "I Got It Syndrome," which is a kind of occupational disease that overtakes some persons upon their virginal exposure to an astrology book. This latter condition is typically followed by soliciting a family member as one's "practice client." It is the next step—the premature ejaculation into the public arena—that can create problems . . . not just for the client but for the astrologer as well.

Psychologist/astrologer Noel Tyl has been quoted as attributing an octillion (look it up) variables to the tradition of astrology—which reflects the expansiveness of the territory. Thus, it can be fairly stated that boundaries of dedication or intellect are the likely defaults preventing some students from patiently carrying on their studies until full comprehension sets in, which, it can be said, is perhaps the equivalent to scaling the east wall of Mount Everest. But like the pot of gold at the end of the rainbow, those who persevere ultimately will find rewards—psychological, philosophical, and spiritual rewards.

When a consummate astrologer departs from this plane, s/he leaves as a *student*, for this profession does not come in a nice, neatly wrapped, compact package. It's a little like an investigative reporter's assignment that never ends. The foundation of astrology is indeed based on empirical evidence—*just as all science*—requiring a lifetime recipe of modification to compensate for learned refinements and social alterations. So budding astrologers might well be advised to think of themselves as being "from Missouri"—until their returns are in. For it is those moments of discovery—those confirmations of astrological philosophies that bloom brightly from client relationships—that make the trip worth the price. And, there's a prize at the bottom of the Cracker Jack box: self-esteem.

Where else can you buy veracity and reputation?

Remember that virtually all astrologers are self-taught, or taught by someone who was self-taught by someone else who was self-taught. But before all that, we have a human being who comes to the endeavor with stars in his/her eyes. We can dispense with a secondary education requirement because this can too often produce a mono-intellectual who might come with counterproductive conflicts. More importantly, who was your family, how were you raised, and what do you bring from that environment? If you were steeped in religious dogma, you might arrive with an intellectual corset—although it is not fatal nor an impossible shackle to break out of any more than the singular focus of some secondary curriculums.

A child who grows up amidst the richness of "Dutch Uncles"—a family of philosophers who derived their wisdom by surmounting hardships—brings an appropriate background to the activity. If the experiences left a positive taste in the family mouth, then the result is called a caring, humanitarian attitude. Empathy and compassion earned the old-fashioned way. The person who has been dealt what is commonly referred to as a "hard life" is often well fitted to assist others . . . and lest we forget, astrology is a "helping profession," when practiced with its value system logically applied.

My grandfather and I were sitting on his front porch one lazy August afternoon. As he rocked his chair, swatting at a fly, I broached the subject of a new girl friend I was beginning to regard seriously.

"Son, forget about marriage until you've got a good job and some money in the bank. Nothing pours cold water on a romance more than bill collectors knocking on your front door."

I was 13 at the time, and although grandfather never experienced frustrations with bill collectors, this was simple common-sense advice. Plato or grandfather didn't invent it, but neither did Freud or Jung. Call it simple "Dutch Uncle" common sense.

So if you had a close family member who gave you good, sound advice from life experience or knowledge—or better still, if you lived it yourself—then you are privileged because it is the legitimate purpose of astrology to accomplish the same thing. But, in astrology the common sense is derived from a chart from which, by empirical discovery through time, appropriate procedures have been developed.

What has life experience got to do with reading a chart? A simplistic person who has spent a sheltered or cloistered life will be prone to interpret a chart in a naive way, while a person who has a broader life experience is usually more eclectic and views a chart from a wider perspective, attuning to a wider range of humanity and a more complex application of astrological procedures.

While no credible astrologer would disagree that certain qualities should be inherent with the practicing professional, you can bet your dime-store whistle that astrologers would likely *not* agree on what these qualities are. So, I accept the challenge to propose some qualities which, it is hoped, are acceptable to all who believe that the higher the professional's principles, the higher the public regard for astrology will be.

The astrologer should:

1. Be rudimentally grounded in traditional astrological concepts, and if a divergent philosophy or personal concept evolves, its premise should stay within the boundaries of scientific and/or rational humanistic credibility.

2. Possess an ethical, moral, and professional personal philosophy.

3. Have a deep sense of compassion and responsibility that is not overwhelmed by ego.

4. Acknowledge that a Pollyanna or dilettante mentality has no place in the realm of astrology, and that one should, above all, not allow the "all-knowing," "all-seeing" delusion to divorce the self from the real world . . .

from which the client arrives. Thus, the astrologer's character should reflect a person who is well-read, worldly and
sophisticated in a traditional, practical way.

5. Acquaint the client with the workings of astrology rather than allow him/her to become immaturely dependent since we assume that the client's welfare is para-
mount and not secondary to the astrologer's. You should
impart the knowledge that you do not think you are God,
nor a magician, but simply a skilled craftsman and techni-
cian steeped in an ageless formula devised to aid man in
negotiating the paths of life.

6. Be able to communicate regarding a spiritual
level. There is something beyond the mechanistic equa-
tions of astrology, a spiritual quality. Admittedly, there
are clients who will be unreceptive to this subject or with
whom it will be inappropriate to discuss, or this may be an
area not within the parameters of the consultant's lexicon.
But given certain intellectual qualities possessed by both
astrologer and client—or perhaps a verbalized indication
that this involves a root concern of the client's—it would
seem proper to address the issue of the existence of the
"Creator" to enable the client to understand that there is a
larger force at work than you and the client. This does not
include offering of organized religious dogma or preach-
ments, but suggests an allusion to a general spiritual concept—a grounding principle that can help to galvanize the
client against an anarchistic philosophy. At least, ideas of
humility and conscionability might be apt areas to peruse
in the person's chart.

But What About Your Clients?

So you have a comfortable feeling about your own
credibility, your environment, your appearance, and
you're waiting for your client to arrive. The client workup is conveniently at your side. Since you have never seen

this person, but have eliminated some preliminaries by phone and what you have learned from the chart, you are curious about what s/he will be like in personal conversation.

Let's categorize some typical clients:

1. There's the *perennial seeker*. This person has visited a number of fortunetellers, psychics, tarot readers, or even other astrologers, and continues to do so on a revolving basis. S/he is in search of something that is unattainable, but doesn't know what that "something" is. Whether you accept the task of helping find that "something" is strictly optional. It could be something as simple as being locked in a retrograde Saturn return.

2. The *unrealist* is someone who has quite thoroughly deluded him/herself throughout life. S/he treats foibles and shortcomings with a convoluted perspective that rationalizes reality into unreality as well as unreality into reality. This person can occasionally be either neurotic or psychotic, and if it is blatantly obvious that this client should have a net thrown over him/her, you might diplomatically make a referral to your "associate," who just happens to be a psychoanalyst or psychiatrist. (If the counselor also utilizes astrology, the transition should be easier.) But if this client simply took the wrong fork in the road, then astrology is tailor-made for "self-discovery."

3. The *skeptic* or *challenger* has little, if any, concept of traditional astrology and how it works. This client has, perhaps, a fundamental religionist or material science background or comes from an environment of disbelieving, unsophisticated associates. This is an uphill climb for the consultant, only resolved by time. The astrologer can present a credible piece of work and hope that its effectiveness is sufficient to provide some acclimation . . . and future acceptance.

4. The *dependent*. This is a person who gets out of bed each morning and constructs his/her daily itinerary based on your astrological projections. This client is likely to call you for the proper time to brush his/her hair! The elimination of such dependency and more training is necessary. The client should be made aware that s/he needs to manage his/her own life through more generalized astrological dictums—structured from an understanding of *who s/he really is* as an individual. Obviously, this client usurps the science of astrology and the astrologer as a substitute for his/her distinct, responsible identity.

5. The *misinformed*. This might be considered an addendum to Number 4, but with a twist. While this person's confusion may derive from experience with inept consultants, rejection and disillusionment can be diminished by teaching that astrology has a specific structure ... that astrology's primary purpose is to awaken one's awareness of self, beyond which the client can learn to shadow-dance with the auspicious and inauspicious indicators in his/her progressed chart. Sometimes, this client's "deficiency" is due to limited intellect or spirituality.

6. The *normal* client might be considered someone who has a general working knowledge of astrology's parameters but needs your fine-tuned professional expertise to solidify his/her perceptions. Often, this client can almost do it alone and can be the easiest and most pleasant working relationship you experience.

7. The *curious* client also exists. The most common quote issued by this client will sound like: "I've never been to an astrologer before. I was curious to see what it was like. . . ." (Nothing to do on a rainy afternoon?)

So, let's assume that optimum conditions prevail . . . that you learned how to interpret a chart with a good

teacher to guide you step by step, who intercepted erroneous or inexperienced judgments. . . . You have examined
the chart and developed any focus that preliminary discussion with the client might have indicated, such as romance, employment, finances, or possibly relocation.

But before you see the client, a precautionary note.
It's the lack of knowledge and misconception by the public that causes a large number of people to assume that the
astrologer dispenses the same quotients as a psychic,
palmist, phrenologist, fortuneteller, or crystal-ball reader.
In general, it should be recognized that many persons—if
not most—lump astrologers with all of the foregoing so-
called "advisors" as "those who know special things."

If you do your part to indoctrinate those you serve
in the actual mechanics of astrology (that, for example,
you do not have E.T.'s phone number), then you will do
much to enable the profession to be recognized for what
astrologers *really do*. Also, try not to "sit too high on your
rock." That's reserved for guys like Plato.

*There's a human being knocking at your door. Hear it?
Give it your best shot.*

P. S. One last thing. Be mindful of the ageless legacy
of doctors, lawyers, counselors, and consultants called
"client confidentiality." If you wish to be identified as a
legitimate professional, then moral responsibility dictates
that information divulged during the client/astrologer
exchange remains secure with you.

Ginger Chalford, PMAFA, Ph.D.

Ginger Chalford is a psychological counselor and healer, writer, speaker, astrologer, and seminar trainer. She has been a "Renaissance metaphysician" since 1967, amassing spiritual and occult knowledge from many varied mystical paths. She has a doctorate from Walden University in Educational and Social Change with a major in Synergistic Psychology. A certified practitioner of the MariEl System of Healing, Neuro Linguistic Programming, and Circles of Life Integrations (Educational Kinesiology), she has worked with Lazaris of Concept: Synergy for over 11 years.

A member of NCGR and AFA, Dr. Chalford has two books published by AFA titled *The Inner Personalities of the Chart*, a synthesis of transactional analysis and astrology, and *Pluto, Planet of Magic and Power*, a study in transformation and empowerment. Her third book, *Emotional Mastery*, is nearly complete.

She has developed the "Imagix" and "Love Heals" seminars for personal development. Happily married, she and her husband Francois live in Miami's Coconut Grove area and raise rare tropical fruit trees.

HEALING WOUNDED SPIRITS

An Astrological Counseling Guide to Releasing Life Issues

Few astrologers train as counselors before they find that with chart interpretation comes a vocation as a counselor. Some astrologers find counseling easy and natural to do. Others are uncomfortable with the authority, responsibility, and facilitation demands of counseling and prefer to refer their clients to psychological specialists.

However, even those who are not interested in building therapy skills can find themselves with a sobbing client "in crisis." How do you calm the client and guide him towards a successful session's closure? In these circumstances, step-by-step guidance can come in handy. This chapter addresses this guidance for not only psychological crises but general counseling situations as well.

About "Wounded Spirits"

We all know that people come to an astrological consultation for more reasons than just "entertainment." They are often looking for life direction and support, and they expect the astrologer to provide this. Many clients who seek emotional or psychological help through astrology are those who find the traditional psychotherapeutic route intimidating, too lengthy, or too expensive. They are often *wounded spirits*, traumatized, anxious, and/or emotionally ready to change. Hoping for an inner healing of themselves, they need that extra "something" from the consultant right on the spot.

While it is often easy to refer people to financial planners or medical specialists, the emotional intimacy that counselor and client can experience in a session gives an extraordinary opportunity for the astrologer to help the client start healing immediately. Sometimes this intimacy isn't available with psychological professionals who need time to undo the intimidation in their relationship.

Wounded spirits are people who have been tragically disappointed by other people, results from dedicated and passionate work, or their lives in general. All wounded spirits have tried hard to accomplish something—a happy relationship, a successful business, a healing of a serious illness, or a spiritual dream. They have struggled to make a better life for themselves and for their loved ones. Although they have glimpsed a Vision of what they could fulfill, it has been dashed—along with the spiritual joy and delight it could have brought.

When the future they counted on seemed lost, they became dismayed and hurt. Something stood in the way of their hopes. Trying harder to make it "work," they failed even more. Helpless and frustrated, they wondered if their Vision was an illusion. Were they just fooling themselves? Will it ever be safe to dream again? Sadly, some wounded spirits become cynical, building a shell around their pain.

But many people recover from these challenges to their hopes and dreams to try again. Some succeed. Others eventually tire, become discouraged, and withdraw into the part of their lives that works best. For example, broken-hearted people may become workaholics, claiming "I don't even want relationships anymore. They're too much trouble." Others, financially disabled, create deeper bonds with their families and loved ones for emotional support and security.

Although it is great to have some successful area of life, people are not fulfilled until they enjoy *all* parts of their lives. Most of us are wounded spirits in one area or another. Whether or not you as a counselor are one of the walking wounded, your job is to give people hope and to guide them in some way towards their dreams.

Wounded spirits can come into a session asking "Will I ever have a good relationship? Will I ever be successful?" Doubting themselves, they want a guarantee from the astrologer that the next business venture or relationship will pan out before they commit themselves to it. An inexperienced astrologer may give these people a definite yes or no, trying to be helpful, but we all know that nothing, bad or good, can be guaranteed. Life is risk-filled by its very nature. The consultant must provide an environment of safety so that wounded spirits can take a step back from their problem. That way they can focus on ways to heal and rebuild direction.

How to Help Wounded Spirits (and all clients)

As an astrologer, you have a responsibility to help clients discover their life themes and issues so they can move with purpose and direction towards their highest good. Even without crises, direction must be given on how to clarify, handle, and heal life issues. This, in essence, is *processing* and is what successful psychologists do.

Life themes are personal focuses of this incarnation which direct the person to his greatest self-discovery and spiritual freedom. They often show up as urges or spiritual needs. *Issues* are life themes that have not been learned about or handled successfully. In the process, the individual is wounded and issues turn into painful limitations, blockages, or negative scripts. *Unresolved issues trigger difficult symptomatic, repetitive life situations.* The issues and their situation patterns are what many therapists and clients call "old tapes." Below are steps I've found useful in healing these old negative issues while also handling client crises.

Step One: Prepare Yourself for the Counseling Session

Before the client walks in, check your mood, your energy. Do what is necessary to raise your consciousness so that you are feeling optimistic and looking forward to meeting your client. This may not be the day you are faced with a client crisis, but you want to give all your clients the gift of your highest energy.

Some people use a meditation in which they bring white light all around and into their body, feel it dazzle and sparkle, and sense all body cells beginning to dance as they drink in the light. Those of a serious disposition find that laughing works fine to engender the right state.

Naturally optimistic counselors have an easier time here, but still they may need to ground and protect their energy field from being drained. If you feel that you want this, it can be easily accomplished by imagining a ball of mirrors surrounding your body. The mirrors face outward, reflecting negativity but *absorbing* positivity. Sometimes just visualizing this little picture in your mind, especially before meeting with a potentially difficult client, can keep your energy up for the rest of the day!

Step Two: Be a Professional—Act Knowledgably

To comfort all clients, and particularly wounded spirits, the astrologer must communicate three certain messages. First, the astrologer is *enthusiastically working for the best interests of the client*, not the astrologer. This I call a *Positive Intent*. Second, the astrologer cares for the client while remaining *detached from his own trips*. After all, the client doesn't need to hear stories about the astrologer's life. Third, the astrologer *takes charge of directing the session towards understanding/insight, emotional healing, and closure.* These messages give clients confidence that they can "be" themselves while gaining needed insight to heal their life issues.

Start by putting your client at ease. Tell him to make himself at home. Provide water or juice if you like. Reassure your client that he is free to speak his mind and that you will make no judgment on anything said. Project confidence that the session will turn out well.

Breathe easily. Demonstrate that you're interested in your client by giving him your rapt attention. For some people, this means more than anything you can say. Respond to him as if what he is saying and feeling is valuable and significant. However, don't let your client ramble aimlessly. If you do, he will go home to listen to the session's audiotape only to hear his own voice.

Throughout the session(s), keep your energy, vitality and aliveness up. Be enthusiastic about interpreting the chart, as if your client were a V.I.P. or a celebrity. I once did a reading under pressure when I was tired and very uninspired. I lost that client, and all of her potential referrals. If you can't feel "up," then look at the possibility that you've overbooked yourself or that you really don't want to do astrology.

Empower your clients. Respect what they already know. Avoid criticizing their beliefs and attitudes. If you find them stuck with a limiting belief, such as "I can't" or "They will always do this or that to me," gently suggest that it may be helpful for them to foster a more useful or more successful belief in their lives.

Tell clients what you see in the chart, not only what you think they want to hear, but don't be tactless. Any truth you see can be told nicely, even if the information is difficult or unpleasant to say. Also, don't imply that your way is written in stone. Say, "The way I see it is _____." Information you give about "negatives" can become educative with helpful suggestions or available options presented.

When you do see possible negative outcomes, give positive potentials as well. For example, a Saturn transit could indicate a loss or separation. But it could also suggest a business venture or the building of a new perspective on life. Usually, people are already aware of the negative possibilities of a situation. They don't want to deny or ignore difficulties but to find preventive measures that can balance or correct the situation.

Don't persuade your clients to take any specific course of action. This is tempting to do when they vacillate, waver, or otherwise appear confused. Remember, if they follow your advice and it turns out poorly for them, you may get blamed, even if they didn't follow your directions correctly! Gently insist that they alone must make their choices. Offer at least two options for consideration. Then they realize their power of choice.

Most importantly, never tell clients "There's nothing you can do." Remind them that *they can influence, emotionally if not physically, the final outcome of their challenging situations.* Wounded spirits may need to be presented with images of feeling good about themselves, even if their situations don't appear to be successful.

Step Three: Set a Tone; Hold Your Positivity throughout the Session

When you hold your positivity, you:

1. Show that the future is bright. Build hope, motivation and purpose. Some people go through very difficult periods and need cheer. Others already enthusiastic feel supported and nourished by your optimism.

2. Bring up any low energy of clients to your higher, more vital level. Refuse to empathize or identify with low states, or they'll stay there. They'll come up if you stay up. Inspiration, understandings, and healings can occur with this upshift. Not only do clients accept your optimism, but they start to pick up your attitudes and outlooks as well. Their negative energy transmutes into positive energy without much effort on your part. Best of all, clients don't feel pushed into feeling good. If they don't come up to your "high" immediately, just stay there. It takes time for some clients to join you. A few may never get it consciously, but there is an impression you have made on them that will assist them anyway.

3. Keep yourself from being drained by the negative emotional states of clients. You can maintain this positivity easily by sensing a protective light around you as you work. After all, you've got to keep yourself clear and productive, and other clients may follow this one. It wouldn't be kind to be debilitated for them. Also, you don't want to lie awake at night mulling over other people's problems.

Remember, what you say has impact on your clients. They respond emotionally. Some clients bring truckloads of problems to a session to sort out; others carry only one. At any point, a client may break down crying, go into depression, or have a fit of anger and hostility. It's not aimed at you, so don't take it personally.

Whether or not a crisis is occurring, notice and avoid sharing a client's negative moods. For example, if he is suffering, don't say "Yes, I know. I went through that one too. It was awful." By the time you've remembered your own difficult experiences, you're feeling down, too! A better approach: "Yes, I know that is difficult. How are you managing? What are you planning to do now? What options are you considering?" You take charge of the energy this way. You also gain information from your client that can take you out of some crises, back into the charts, and into resuming the session.

Care for your clients. When they look upset, pause and ask them, "What's going on?," not "What's wrong?" Don't reinforce their negative states of mind by letting them moan with self-pity and helplessness. It's not fair to them or you. When clients fall apart during a session, it indicates that they are moved by an emotion connected to their major Core Issue and that they have touched a wound. This issue is important enough to defer the rest of the reading to its processing.

When a "crisis" occurs, be prepared to start a healing process or to recognize if a client has taken you into territory about which you know too little to be of help. If you feel more comfortable not processing, then don't try to be an authority. With humility, you can say, "I don't know about that. However, I have suggestions. If these aren't appropriate, let me refer you to someone who knows more about this subject." On the other hand, if you are willing to work with your client, you need to know what to do next.

Healing is the process of transmuting negative energy or limitations into positive energy or freedoms. Your intention is to empower your client to be free to choose what he wants in life and to act on it. A great benefit for you is that you can be healed as well through the insight gained on *your* current issues! After all, clients tend to show up with your issues!

Step Four: Identify the Traumatic Pattern

Let's use an example. Crying, your client may complain intensely, "My husband doesn't talk to me anymore. All he wants to do is read and watch TV. I'm tired, too, but I'm willing to be there for him. Why doesn't he want to be there for me?"

Her complaint reveals a difficult situation. Ask her to detail this picture. Does this type of situation happen often? Has it happened earlier (in prior relationships, in the childhood family)? Get a sense of any common denominators between this situation and others that have occurred before.

Recurring difficult events of a similar dynamic form a pattern. Usually the client has little control over patterns which are not resolved or healed. Each situation within the pattern consistently produces the same negative emotions. With repeating occurrences, the client will come to *expect* the same painful outcomes. People can go through the same sequence of destructive actions and feelings in relationship after relationship, job after job. When the pattern is destructive, it can also be called an *addiction*.

Negative patterns, big or small, will continue to occur until the underlying painful emotional sequence is released and healed by the client. Then the pattern is broken and it's possible to replace it with new, freer, more loving situations.

Continuing with our example client, ask "When this pattern situation happens, what emotions do you feel?" If she replies with a judgment, such as "It's stupid," gently remind her that you are looking for a *feeling*, not an opinion. You can suggest emotions to her if she is unable to think of any (which is common). Say, "Do you feel frustrated? angry? scared? hurt? anxious? helpless? (any others you may think of)?" Most clients will agree to one or more difficult emotions. Generally, these are the emotions that triggered the crisis or problem.

Detail what the emotions are about. For example, this client may be angry because her husband won't tell her why he's quiet, or maybe it's because she feels put down by his behavior. Don't say authoritatively, "You are angry that _____." If you think you know the important details, state them in question form. Ask "Are you angry that _____?," and let your client nod agreement or make a statement of his feelings. Any acknowledgments he makes allows the client to take responsibility for his feelings. This first step in taking charge of feelings helps calm any crisis.

However, emotional denials are common. If anger has been forbidden since childhood, your client may not feel comfortable with your knowledge that he is right-eous, angry, and filled with rage. In that case, repeat a reassuring statement such as "Anger (or this negative feeling) is normal when you experience a situation like this." If the client still does not acknowledge his feeling or interrupts with another subject, go on to other feelings until you find one your client will accept as a focus of discussion. Trying to push clients into recognizing some-thing can backfire as they start seeing you as a parent figure and react against you.

If you find clients emotionally frozen or "para-lyzed," encourage them with this important message: *Emotions are good and natural, and it is safe to recognize them, express them, and release them, particularly here in this session. There is nothing wrong, weak, or bad about you when you feel because difficult emotions are simply messages that the ways in which you're trying to handle your life aren't working. When you acknowledge and express unpleasant feelings, you can heal your life, no matter what anyone else does. YOU have the power to make a difference.* Something *can* be done about unruly emotions—a comforting thought for a frustrated or miserable client.

Most frequently, this message unfreezes him and he feels it's safe to feel whatever emotion occurs. If he looks more at ease, ask for clarification: "What specifically do other people do that triggers your feelings?" Have him explain the behavior of others involved in the situation. If your client says he is only angry with himself or tries to otherwise judge and blame himself, acknowledge that. Say "I hear you. And who else are you angry at? Who else is acting inappropriately?" You can look for other people, society, even God. Then ask for the self-evaluation. It can be rather harsh and judgmental, or defensively righteous. Ask "And what do these feelings make you feel about *you*?" But don't let the client ramble on about the emotions or the situation.

If your client hears your comforting message and is still too uncomfortable to acknowledge and share his feelings with you, you may need to pause while he regains composure. Then, continue into some other area of your consultation. A client who won't identify his emotions with the situation is not willing to heal at this time. The best you can do is to keep him out of self-pity. Hand over tissues or anything else required and suggest that he needs to work slowly, evoking the emotion gently over time. If you feel confident that you can assist your client emotionally, see him again at a later time when you can take him through visualizations and emotional release processes without having time restraints. Otherwise, continue the session and refer him to a therapist at the end of it.

Step Five: Identify the Underlying "Core Themes/Issues" at Stake in the Problem Situation or Pattern

By now, your client is ready to discover how the difficult situations he experiences threatens his life's purpose or orientation. A *Core Life Issue* needs to be identified here, and it's easy to do when you have the symbolic language of astrology with which to work. Since each sign, planet, aspect, and house has its Theme/Issue, every chart has at least 40 active issues. Keep it simple. Look for the Core Issues first. Core Issues are found in the Sun, Moon, and Ascendant Signs. A significant planet conjoining these three will add its supportive Theme/Issues as well through the sign it rules. Houses specific to the situation's players or subject (such as children in the 5th House) will add more, too.

The *Ascendant* represents the **Projected Self-Image**, that is, what the person wants others to see in him. Simultaneously, an individual can have an inner, hidden, negative self-image, often erroneously thought of as the "true" self. The *Sun sign* represents the **Essence** of what makes the self happy, valued, and fulfilled. To realize one's true identity and personal worth is a major goal of one's lifetime.

The *Moon sign* represents **That Which Motivates** a person. Everyone is motivated one of two ways—either by the "carrot" (positive feelings of value and self-esteem) or by the "stick" (to avoid negative feelings of pressure, punishment, or pain forced on the individual by society, family, or religion). For example, overwork can bring excitement and power (carrot). It can also avoid the pain of failing to meet family financial needs (stick). When issues stop a client cold, the stick is usually the motivator.

In the following pages I've given Core Theme/Issues for each sign with some of their obvious identifying symptoms. Predictably, you only have to look in the houses and signs respective to the Issue to clarify and reinforce your depth of understanding. Relationships will add 7th House issues. Parental issues add the 4th and 10th Houses. Societal issues (social and peer group themes) will be found in the 5th, 6th, 11th, and 12th Houses. Communication skills and cultural exchange are found in the 3rd/9th House polarities, and children are in the 5th.

ARIES—Theme/Issue: Selfhood's survival and creative pleasure. **Planets:** Mars and Pluto. **House:** 1st. **Value:** Power of originality and inspiration/upliftment. **Most difficult states:** Denial, responsibility, guilt.

Symptomatic Patterns: Me versus them (or my way versus their way); doing versus thinking, impetuously thinking "too late"; everything is a confrontation, no negotiation; must be there first, be the most original—or not at all; doesn't listen to or hear feedback; runs from intimacy; angry and impatient/blames others' lack of support; selfish, thinks only of own desires.

Keys: Develop negotiation skills, giving/receiving of impact and acceptance.

TAURUS—Theme/Issue: Trust, both of self and of others. **Planet:** Venus. **House:** 2nd. **Value:** Honesty, integrity, practical know-how with resources. **Most difficult states:** Vulnerability, risk of hurt, failure.

Symptomatic Patterns: Refusal to be pressured (stubbornness); deep sadness and hurts (over disappointments and expectations); tangible outcomes needed, intangibles may be dismissed; won't admit needs, appears aloof from neediness; fear of being visible, known, and controlled; involved with resource control (such as money) for financial security.

Keys: Develop intuition, positive expectations, prioritizing skills, and ability to come to own conclusions.

GEMINI—Theme/Issue: Personal space and freedom to change. **Planet:** Mercury. **House:** 3rd. **Value:** "Street smarts," practical savvy for ingenious survival. **Most difficult states:** Responsible commitment, waiting, confinement.

Symptomatic Patterns: Emotional shallowness, uncaring attitudes; curious—has to know everything, but not at great depth; fear of "enmeshment," relationship approach-avoidance; has elite/trendy social circle, drops names, can be snobbish; witty humor covers up feelings, especially old hurts; suspicious; fearful of containment or loss of identity.

Keys: Develop ability to change belief systems, intimacy, balancing emotions with the intellect and physical activity.

CANCER—Theme/Issue: Security/survival in love, money and values. **Planet:** Moon. **House:** 4th. **Value:** Recognizing essence and truth, being vitally necessary. **Most difficult states:** Angry guilt, dependency, failure.

Symptomatic Patterns: Underdog's protector, defends rights; motivated by needs, urgent requests, pressure of expectations; plays parent-child roles, dependence-independence anxieties; bonding through favor-giving and getting, i.e., "indebtedness"; heavy emotional family issues, guilt and shame; avoids confrontations by "good behavior" or running away; stuffs emotions, can have eating disturbances or weight problems.

Keys: Develop ability to release expectation pressure and anger safely, self-acceptance, egalitarian relationships.

LEO—Theme/Issue: Impact—making a difference, being heard/seen. **Planet:** Sun. **House:** 5th. **Value:** Attracts love, ability to move and inspire others. **Most difficult states:** Humiliation, being ignored, intimacy.

Symptomatic Patterns: Self-image, shyness, visibility concerns; remembers relationship hurts deeply; takes things personally; needs to be attended to, wants to be special and enjoy "perks"; plays social roles for outer validation, political savvy; can be high fashion or outrageous in dress and behavior; feels one emotion, shows another ("grin and bear it" school); doesn't listen to feedback for fear of criticism and rejection.

Keys: Develop intimacy, self-awareness, uniqueness, positive ego, self "realness" through honest expression.

VIRGO—Theme/Issue: Search for perfection and truth. **Planet:** Mercury, particularly in Earth signs. **House:** 6th. **Value:** Putting in hard effort no matter the price, doing things excellently. **Most difficult states:** Self-pity, feeling unappreciated, rage.

Symptomatic Patterns: Martyr (self-denial), overgiver, workaholic; low self-esteem, self-criticism; analysis and rationalization of everything; feels the need to earn deservability, doesn't receive easily; worry, looks at negatives much more than positives; high expectations of others as well as self; perfectionism and impatience with error and/or self-image.

Keys: Develop self-esteem, self-love, freedom to make mistakes, self-respect.

LIBRA—Theme/Issue: Selfhood's acceptance and sharing. **Planet:** Venus, particularly in Air signs. **House:** 7th. **Value:** Ability to suggest solutions; good companion/friend. **Most difficult states:** Confusion, fear of abandonment.

Symptomatic Patterns: Negotiation results in too much compromise; overconcerned with others' behavior, enmeshment/dependency; has refined manners, pleasant, but sometimes too passive and indecisive; anxious about being bold, aggressive—overestimates impact; fear of committing a social *faux pas*, becoming embarrassed; fear of losing options, getting "pinned down"—needs way out; upset about unfairness; fears that preferences hurt others.

Keys: Develop ability to prioritize, self-trust, self-confidence.

SCORPIO—Theme/Issue: Personal empowerment by knowing the bottom line. **Planets:** Pluto and Mars. **House:** 8th. **Value:** Problem-solving ability, personal knowledge, magnetism. **Most difficult states:** Helplessness, paranoia, exposure.

Symptomatic Patterns: Silent self-judgment and criticism; refusal to forgive, holds harbored anger, grudges, jealousy; strong, superior powerful person (image) others can lean on; expects total dedication of everyone or won't do anything at all; fears loss, can have very negative future expectations; suspicious of another's negative intent and possible sabotage.

Keys: Develop ability to express anger safely and forgive easily and the manifestation of know-how/techniques.

SAGITTARIUS—**Theme/Issue:** Personal freedom of movement/learning. **Planet:** Jupiter. **House:** 9th. **Value:** Teacher of great ideas, inspirational, knowledgeable. **Most difficult states:** Waiting, being "stuck," not knowing.

Symptomatic Patterns: Mentally arrogant, "know-it-all"; fears the physical restriction of routines; emotional escapist (runs away from intense situations); gets the overview but misses the details; fears loss of options, identity and opportunity; thoughtless, tactless, self-centered and busy; high-principled and enthusiastic, but poor follow-through.

Keys: Develop gratitude, intimacy, responsiveness to others, adventuresome lifestyle.

CAPRICORN—**Theme/Issue:** Safety, controlling its secure availability. **Planet:** Saturn. **House:** 10th. **Value:** Energy, youthfulness in age, a "get it done" person. **Most difficult states:** Guilt, worry, fear of loss of control.

Symptomatic Patterns: Overly responsible, burdened by others' needs; impatient, interrupts/rushes others, tense, won't let things "be"; parental in relationships and businesses, uses "shoulds"; frets about survival, when put on the spot is defensive; shows tremendous self-control and discipline—the "boss"; uses humor about awful situations to distract from inner misery; guilt and pain from lack of family togetherness/unification.

Keys: Develop self-worth awareness, sensitivity to others, ease, caring for self.

AQUARIUS—Theme/Issue: Individuality and freedom of expression. **Planets:** Uranus and Saturn. **House:** 11th. **Value:** Is a noble "genius maverick" and a good friend. **Most difficult states:** Feeling "pegged," misunderstood, denial.

Symptomatic Patterns: "Spacing out," out of touch with body/emotions; expects mental respect, but may not always give it to others; rebellious, outrageous in self-estimation, but appears normal; easy, tolerant, friendly demeanor—unflappable, laughs off heavy issues; giver of inspiration, not action, i.e., high thinker, slow doer; poorly defined personal needs but clearer with social idealism.

Keys: Develop intimacy, ability to act on ideals, self-respect.

PISCES—Theme/Issue: Search for the ideal and for truth, visionary. **Planets:** Neptune, Jupiter. **House:** 12th. **Value:** Charming, caring companion; creative brainstormer, expresses self ingeniously. **Most difficult states:** Loneliness, rejection, hurt.

Symptomatic Patterns: Fantasizes, mind wanders, indecisive; easily influenced, distracted; puts teachers on pedestals; intuitive, a sense of "knowing"—confused when it's not there; impatient for change; hopes ideals are achievable goals; disappointment/disillusionment problems, gives up needlessly; dedicated to service to the point of self-denial/martyrhood; says yes much too easily, then backs out when it's time to act.

Keys: Develop self-love, application of spiritual know-how to mundane life, responsibility for focus.

With the Themes/Issues handy, search for the Core Issue(s) in the Theme or Value listings given above. Discover which Issues apply to the pattern. In our example's situation/pattern, our client's husband (and possibly other people) somehow "robs" her of her sense of value, diminishes her, or threatens her with the loss of her Theme. Since she is involved in a difficult personal relationship, start with her Rising sign (Libra), then the Sun (Scorpio) and Moon (Leo) Sign. If she had a career pattern, you would start with the Sun. For family/parent issues, begin with the Moon.

Decide on a question out of her Theme/Issues that will evoke feelings. For her Rising sign, you might ask, "Does this relationship make you feel like he isn't accepting who you are or (go to the Value) that you can't suggest solutions because he won't hear them? No? How about this (you go to the Sun sign)—do you feel powerless and don't know what's really going on?" You can read down the symptoms list for fears and insecurities if you don't get a yes on the Core Theme/Issue and ask, for example, "Do you suspect he has negative intentions towards you? Are you afraid of losing him?" Don't antagonize a client by going for the areas he may be sensitive to. In this case, "Do you harbor grudges against him? Are you jealous?" would be inappropriate as it may take time for her to see the other side to the situation, i.e., his.

If these questions haven't prompted an affirmative signal yet, I'd go to her Moon sign and ask, "Do you feel that you need to be heard, that you can't make a difference here? Are you feeling (as per the Value) unattractive, unlovable?" Generally, one or more of these questions will register emotionally with our client. Her head will nod yes or she'll confirm your joint discovery with details, just as she did with the earlier "list" of emotions.

Step Six: Find the *Reason* Behind the Negative Pattern

If you choose to work with your clients in later counseling sessions, or if you have the time available in the crisis session, you can continue the counselor's process. You and your client are ready to understand the "message" or "reason for being" of the negative pattern. Start by looking for what the client learned, both positively and negatively, from previous incidences of the difficult pattern or situation. Review two or three examples.

Our example client may have learned to not trust people, that she could survive a lot of pain, or that men are too mysterious to ever be part of a happy relationship. The learnings will come in the form of beliefs or generalizations about herself, people, a group (such as men), relationships, etc. Keep her Core Issues in mind until she deduces her inner message or remembers it emotionally. When the client finds it, knows it, and says it, there is an "aha"—a shift or release occurs, giving a sense of accomplishment and peacefulness.

Look next at the source and potential future impact of that learning. From which parent, sibling, or childhood situations was this pattern originally learned and adopted? How? Go into the future. What will be the client's future in a year, three years, seven years, if the negative pattern is never released or changed?

A client sometimes goes into self-pity when staring down the long, hard road he has taken. Gently suggest that the negative pattern was once a necessary or positive choice for survival. He did it for positive reasons and goals he wanted or needed to achieve at that time. When the client understands this, he ceases to blame himself, realizing the option to *rechoose*. The pattern *can* be changed. A light of hope and victory is turned on! It's another "aha" moment, nearly indescribable. Much of the healing happens right here.

Step Seven: Forgive

By now, you've identified the emotional tangle underlying your client's Core Issues and are ready to release it, along with the pattern. If you are uncomfortable with your own emotions or emotional expression, don't take your client further. Send him to someone who is comfortable with feelings and won't risk "losing it." Alternatives are to prepare audio cassettes or pamphlets on handling emotions or to refer clients to the many fine tapes on emotional release by Lazaris. You'll find them in lavender audio-cassette packages at your local metaphysical bookstores.

Emotional release work is *the* most important personal growth processing anyone can do. After all, love and happiness are found in healthy emotions, not disturbed ones. Most of those who do spiritual work or are interested in growing tend to express very evolved mental and spiritual selves. However, the emotional self is often left far behind like an abandoned child. When emotional self is healed, it grows up too. Negative life patterns and issues heal—and so do your clients' spirits!

Choose one of the example situations you and your client discussed earlier, or another one. Say, "Imagine that you are in the picture—in the situation." You will see that he is "there" by slight changes in skin color or breathing pace. Continue with "Now, in your imagination, step out of the picture so that you are watching yourself in it." This disassociation creates two selves—one is the younger self who is being wounded, and the other is the current self who can grasp the overview, providing a higher resonance for the suffering self to change (transmute) into.

Ask your client to visualize the situation unfolding, seeing his younger self caught up in it while simultaneously remaining detached. Suggest gently that this younger self wasn't acting foolishly on purpose but was doing what he *needed* to do in order to feel the best possible under the circumstances. However, few resources beyond the old habitual behavior patterns were available, so the younger self did what anyone would do in the same circumstance—what had been done before.

From this sympathetic viewpoint, the client can start to care for and forgive the younger self for having done only what he knew to do at the time. It also helps for the client to thank the younger self for handling all that pain in order to grow. At this time, the client can come to a deeper understanding of what was "learned." More emotions will emerge as another level of healing happens.

Once self-forgiven, the client can turn his attention to forgiving the other people involved in those difficult scenarios. But first, all negative feelings must be expressed. Rage, anger, and expressions of hurt, grief, sadness over the loss of the Vision apply.

A useful technique is to have your client place each person, one at a time, in a bubble of light to tell him anything and everything negative the client feels or felt. This can be done out loud or mentally. If your client cries, draw him back to expressing negative emotions, such as anger, until they are expressed fully. Generally, within five minutes or so, he will begin to appear peaceful and slightly tired. Suggest that your client forgive each person, release the dreams (the reasons for being with the person), and let them be. Tears are appropriate here.

If you use other healing techniques, such as MariEl healing, Light Touch, Rebirthing, etc., include them, for they can help this process wonderfully. When you are psychically sensitive, you will feel a major energy shift happening in the room as emotions are cleared. This shift also means that the Issue and situational pattern are also healing.

Step Eight: Replace the Old Negative Pattern with a New Positive One

Ask your client what he would like to change about the old pattern and to what. Focus on the *emotional outcome* as a client's new goal, not the physical circumstances. You can ask a question, such as "What would be the outcome you'd prefer, and once accomplished, what would it FEEL like?" Some clients don't want to think and will say, "I'll feel good." Don't accept "good" as an answer. Get specific details on one's feelings.

Sometimes it takes a while to narrow the feeling down to feeling worthwhile and valuable, but this self-esteem is important. In our sample situation, the client may say that she would feel valuable and loved, two very important basics. Next, detail a "Success Scenario Using Your Client's Imagination." This is a script or plot outline of how the difficult patterns-situations can resolve pleasantly and feasibly. Even though she may not initially believe solutions can be found, she can start to imagine herself feeling better inside and responding differently to other people in those traumatic situations. Include the concepts given in the "Keys" portion of the Issue listing by sign to help build the new pattern. This encourages her to access positive feelings within herself and build confidence in her bounce-back ability.

If you don't have session time left to replace the space left by the negative pattern with something uplifting, give your client homework. Ask him to write out a NEW positive pattern for himself with the same depth and intricacy of detail that he discovered in the old, negative pattern. Make sure he includes new beliefs, attitudes, thoughts and feelings, and goals.

You can also ask him to talk this technique out with you if you have time. Help him visualize how the new pattern replaces the old pattern in similar future circumstances by using one or more of the sample situations you worked with earlier. Have your client *see and feel the difference* as he triumphs in his imagination. If different negative emotions from those processed earlier should show up in the imagined new pattern, process those secondary patterns as well.

Imagine and brainstorm ways of handling all the possible new situations to alleviate any uncomfortable emotions. Encourage your client to make a definite commitment to watch for his old pattern. Every time it shows up, he will remember to choose the new pattern. This strengthens the client's confidence in himself and anchors the new pattern in the subconscious mind. Now he is empowered to begin building his Themes, not Issues.

When it is time for you to close, close. Some beginning astrologers will stay with a client in "crisis" for several hours, dropping their other obligations and sacrificing themselves to the client's needs. Despite its saintly appearance, this doesn't help the client. But it does give both of you more time to wallow around in messy psychological or lifestyle details. This also drains you, the astrologer, and discourages you in your work. Know what time span works best for you, and when you reach the end of that period, interrupt the session. Say, "I believe our time is unfortunately coming to a close. Do you wish to pursue this further with me, or would you rather I refer you to a specialist?"

Close with any other options that you feel are necessary to mention in this session. State a summary or overview. It gives your client a feeling of emotional closure and satisfaction that something was done. Often the most satisfying part of a session for my clients is this summary part where they realize how good they feel or how much clearer their options have become.

Once a session is over and your client has left, make sure you have some way of clearing your energy field of his pain. There are wonderful meditations on tape that can help you do this. A simple process I use is "washing" my energy field (aura) with light and rebuilding my mirrored protection. When I imagine this, my intention regenerates me. It's easy to absorb your clients' emotional debris and be totally unaware of it when you don't clean your energy field regularly. If you hold other peoples' "stuff," your empathy can draw emotional and even physical health problems to you.

A client who fears that he can't release emotional pain on his own when it comes up may need to come back for more processing, at least in times of crisis. Even though you may be past the current crisis, long-term healing (releasing and building) is often necessary for entrenched, painful, long-held issues. Theme empowerment is not had in a day, but by self-loving growth over time. If your client can do no more with you, or you have hesitations about assuming responsibility for his long-term development process, refer him to specialists in related, supportive methods.

Helpful Related Methods

I recommend three supportive methods that heal emotional wounds quickly and enable the client to get back into his life with a minimum of fuss and work. The first is a great method called *Neuro Linguistic Programming*, or *NLP*, which repatterns excellently. An NLP Practitioner may be found in the Yellow Pages under "Psychologists" or through the metaphysical community in ads and by word of mouth.

A second technique that I mentioned earlier, called *MariEl healing*, is very powerful. One session alone often heals not only the emotions and their patterns but also health disturbances which are physical corollaries of the Issue. Network in your local metaphysical community to find a practitioner.

Since negative patterns start in childhood, I use a third technique frequently, which I call *"Inner Child Self" therapy*. In it, therapist and client return through visualizations to the client's childhood and/or adolescence. There the client forms a relationship with his younger self, giving it everything it needs so badly—the Themes (healed Issues), the safety, and the unconditional love. When the younger self has everything it needs and desires, an emotional peace descends upon the adult self. Since there are few therapists who advertise their child work, you'll have to find this technique in workshops and in books (fortunately, there are several now becoming available).

When you wish to counsel professionally as well as be an astrological "reader," you will want to release and heal your own Issues as well as your clients'. Take yourself through the process of this chapter. If you can feel the shift of healing taking place within your psyche, you won't feel ill at ease when a client breaks down in your presence. You'll be able to guide anyone, and be a *healer of wounded spirits*.

Donald L. Weston, Ph.D.

Donald Weston received his Doctorate Degree in Clinical Psychology from Boston University in 1958. He has held teaching appointments with Harvard and Johns Hopkins Medical Schools. Becoming involved in astrology in 1967 when the Director of the Laboratory in the mental hospital where he was working used astrology, he introduced it into his practice after 13 years of study.

Dr. Weston has a private practice as a psychologist/astrologer in Portland, Oregon. He uses astrology to focus issues for therapy and works with clients who are not interested in or comfortable with astrology.

He has lectured at Astrological Conferences on the West Coast and for the Calgary and Edmonton, Alberta, Canada Astrological Associations. His teaching style is reflected in his Leo Sun, Gemini Ascendant and Sagittarius Moon. His main focus is interpretation of psychological issues in the natal chart. He feels asteroids have psychological significance in chart exploration and believes that employing astrology in clinical psychology brings the whole person into focus.

ASTROLOGY AND

THERAPY/COUNSELING

As a Clinical Psychologist using astrological tools, I am asked by astrologers, "How did you get involved in astrology?" Mental health workers ask, "Does astrology work? How do you use it in your practice?" This article seeks to answer these questions and discuss the role of the asteroids in psychologically based astrology.

How a Psychoanalytically Trained Psychologist Becomes an Astrologer

My Doctoral Degree in Clinical Psychology resulted from study at Boston University, a school respected for its psychoanalytically based training. My work experiences began in the Department of Psychiatry at the University of Colorado, the University of Rochester and the University of Maryland Medical Schools. I also held research or teaching appointments with Harvard and Johns Hopkins Medical Schools.

I became Chief Psychologist of the 400-bed mental hospital serving the Portland, Oregon metropolitan area. Equipped with intelligence tests, Rorschach's inkblots, Thematic Apperception Test pictures and other tools of the psychologist's craft, I led a staff of psychologists in providing psychodiagnostic and therapy services.

The laboratory director was involved in astrology and would ask physicians for birth dates of patients. She would report back, "I think you gave me six schizophrenics and six alcoholics," and she was right. Here was a woman using the horoscope to know what we psychologists were determining by psychodiagnostic techniques.

I began reading about astrology and did "cook book" work on interpretation of Sun signs, planets in signs, planets in houses and aspects, i.e., the angular relationship of planets in the horoscope circle. I studied with Diana Stone, a Portland astrologer interested in psychological interpretation of the horoscope. Thirteen years after beginning astrological study, including an "Intensive" with Zip Dobyns, Ph.D., and having read horoscopes of all my friends who would tolerate it, I felt ready to present myself as a psychologist using the tools of astrology.

As a psychologist/astrologer in private practice, I see people who are not interested in therapy but want a horoscope interpretation to understand their psychological patterns. There are clients who want to use astrology to focus on early life experiences and resulting emotional issues for therapy. On the other hand, there are probably some clients who would run out of the office if they knew astrology was done there. Their lack of awareness occurs in spite of certificates of astrological training displayed on the wall next to diplomas, Certification as a Diplomate of the American Board of Professional Psychology, State License and other "necessary" evidence of competence.

Does Astrology Work?

Carl Jung stated: "As a psychiatrist, I am chiefly interested in the particular light the horoscope sheds on certain complications in the character. . . . I must say that I very often found that the astrological data elucidated certain points which I otherwise would have been unable to understand."

In writing about synchronicity, Jung explained the

mechanism of astrology. *Synchronicity* is evidenced when two events occur in parallel but without causality. Each part of a synchronous occurrence reflects the other, but there is no causal interaction. When you look in the mirror in the morning, you are reflected in the mirror. You do not cause the mirror to look the way it does, and it does not cause you to look the way you do. You and the mirror are synchronously related.

The natal horoscope is literally a map of the position of the planets in the heavens at the time of a person's birth in relation to the point on Earth where s/he was born. The astronomical pattern, i.e., the position of the planets, is synchronously related to early life experience, personality patterns and other aspects of human experience. Because the Earth wobbles on its axis, a specific horoscope is repeated once every 260,000 years, a Biblical Age. This demonstrates the uniqueness of the horoscopic pattern and each individual.

Astrology is a symbol system where the planets, signs and houses signify persons, actions, objects or functions. Because of this system, its units can represent different facets of life, giving astrology many applications.

There is *natal astrology*—to study the individual. There are *progressions*—to study the chart of current experience or advance the natal chart to future periods. *Synastry* provides the key to understand relationships by examining the interaction of two persons' natal horoscopes. *Medical astrology* explains how to understand physiological processes, health and illness. There is *political, economic* and *mundane astrology* that focuses on events in the economic, social and natural world, i.e., earthquakes, plane crashes, etc. *Horary* and *electional astrology* techniques answer questions and establish a time when astrological patterns support initiation of specific actions. *Astro-meteorological astrology* researches the relationship of astrological and weather patterns. This variety of applications is possible because astrology is a *symbol system*.

Astrology is one approach, or model, for understanding the Universal Truth with a capital *T*. There are differing scientific, religious and philosophical models, all of which have their view, and probably some element of this Truth inherent in them. Much greater understanding of Truth could be gained through collaboration by proponents of the different models, rather than negation of the other's understanding.

Astrology provides information about personality structure. Basic to this astrological/psychological approach is the knowledge that our experience of life is shaped by our beliefs about the universe in which we live. Stated another way, our understanding creates our reality. With this view, astrology—like psychology—becomes a way of *understanding* behavior and experience, not an excuse for it.

Psychologically based astrology communicates that the stars do not cause anything to happen in people's lives. *The map of the horoscope shows different ways of being in the world, of moving through life, the available choices.* Because it shows choice, it is—like well-conducted therapy—*empowering*.

The horoscope reflects *challenges* in life, but it never depicts challenges without indicating how these can be approached and resolved. Too often, astrologers focus on "problems" in a horoscope without showing ways for positive resolution.

A student once quoted an astrologer who told her she would die a violent death in the kitchen. Mars was in Scorpio in her 4th House. When asked how this helped her, she laughed and said, "I'm sometimes very afraid to go in the kitchen." Is there any positive information in this kind of interpretation?

Psychologically based astrology shows areas where *learning* may be focused during a lifetime. In the sense that something is to be learned through life's experiences, this can be called *karma*. In the astrological framework, karma as endless retribution or reward does not make sense. If people want to apply the idea of learning in this lifetime to a series of lifetimes, this is within astrology's conceptual framework.

Clients may have already resolved challenges of the natal chart through life experiences and/or therapy. Yet, exploration often shows that basic personality issues continue their influence. Early emotional patterns form the foundation of adult functioning in the world and tend to persist unless there is a high level of awareness about these patterns and the experiences which activate them.

Psychologically based astrology recognizes that significant messages of a horoscope are repeated. It is as if the Universe wants us to grasp the information reflected in the horoscope and, assuming we may not readily understand, repeats major themes in a variety of ways.

Elements and Qualities

Among the sources of information are: (1) the *pattern of the ten planets* (actually eight planets and two luminaries) in the 360° of the horoscope. This gives a backdrop of how a person functions. (2) the *distribution of the planets in the traditional elements* (Fire, Earth, Air and Water), which indicates how the individual approaches new people, problems and situations. Those with a preponderance of Fire use an instinctual and impulsive approach, Earth people are aware of practicality and the outcome of their actions, Air folks refer to what they know or can learn about a situation, and Water individuals tune in to their emotions and intuition. (3) the *planetary distribution in the qualities* (Cardinal, Fixed, and Mutable), showing how a person takes action in the world. They may (a) be comfortable with conflict and tend to confront and solve problems (Cardinal), (b) take firm stands in the hope of avoiding conflict (Fixed) or (c) assume excessive responsibility and self-blame for problematic life situations (Mutable). (4) the *psychological challenges associated with each of the Sun signs* (5) the *planets in their signs and houses* and (6) the relationship of the planets to each other, the *aspects*, which provide more detail. Significant themes of the horoscope are evidenced in several of these sources.

Planets and Signs

The *planet* is the *verb* in an astrological sentence, e.g., Pluto digs beneath the surface to transform and change, Uranus throws things up in the air for excitement. The placement of the planets in the horoscope is determined by the position of the planets in the heavens at the time of birth. Psychologically, the planets symbolically reflect people, events and processes in a person's life experience.

The *sign* is the *modifier* of the astrological sentence, giving more information about whatever is represented by the planets. The signs are determined by the position of the luminary or planet against the backdrop of the zodiac of the constellations, i.e., Aries, Taurus, etc., as seen from the Earth in its annual path around the Sun.

Astrology's detractors state that the shift in the relationship of the Earth and planets to the constellations, called *precession*, makes astrology invalid. This shift over eons resulted from the Earth's wobble as it rotates on its axis. In practice, contemporary astrology uses the *names* of the constellations, but not their current location. The Tropical zodiac is determined each year as the Sun passes from the Southern Hemisphere to the Northern Hemisphere at the Spring Equinox. This point in the zodiac is 0° Aries, and the other astrological signs are measured in 30°

units from this point. Sidereal astrology relates the location of the planets to the constellations, not to the position of the Earth in relation to the Sun.

The portion of the zodiac in which the Sun is seen at the time of birth, the Sun sign, shows a great deal about how an individual will *express* him/herself in the world. It also reflects early experiences of parental figures and prominent psychological issues. The sign occupied by any planet shows the manner in which the things symbolized by that planet will be expressed. The sign is like a *filter* altering the hue of light passing through, expressing it in that sign's unique way, e.g., actions of Mars in Aries will be assertive or aggressive; the action of Mars in Pisces may be indecisive and indirect.

Houses

Astrological houses reflect *areas of life* in which people, events or actions symbolized by the planets will be most experienced or expressed. In all house systems, the houses reflect areas of life experience, e.g., early life, relationship with the physical world, day-to-day aspects of work, intimate relationships, values and beliefs, etc.

There are a number of ways to divide the zodiac into houses. There are "time-based" house systems, like Placidus and Koch, which use the time it takes the Sun to travel a segment of the ecliptic, the Earth's apparent path around the Sun. There are "space-based" house systems, like Campanus and Regiomontanus, which involve projecting the North and South horizon points of the place of birth onto one of the Great Circles.

The Earth's daily rotation on its axis determines the degree of the zodiac sign on the eastern horizon at the moment of birth, the Ascendant. The Ascendant reflects the *inner personality*, the personality that the individual may have brought into this life from past-life experience.

Some astrologers suggest the Ascendant indicates the Sun sign of the immediate past-life experience and that people grow, in this lifetime, toward their present Sun sign. When the Sun sign personality is under stress, a person utilizes the characteristics of the Ascendant sign in his/her coping behaviors.

More detail about the personality can be gained by interpretation of the East Point and the Anti-Vertex. The *East Point* is the location of the Ascendant if a person were born at the *Equator*, i.e., 0° latitude. The *Anti-Vertex* is the location of the Ascendant if the person were born at the *Co-latitude* of birth (90° – the latitude of birth = the Co-latitude). If these *minor Ascendants* are in the Ascendant sign, there is no need for interpretation. If they are different, it is helpful to indicate to the client, "You generally function in the way described by the Ascendant sign, but the chart suggests that sometimes you also function in these ways," describing the signs of the East Point and/or Anti-Vertex.

Aspects
The number of degrees separating two planets in the horoscope circle define *aspects*. When two planets are conjunct, 0° separation, they synergize. Their working together can be very positive or it can be difficult, depending on the nature of the planets. The *easy aspects*, the sextile (60°) and trine (120°), show ready positive integration of those things symbolized by the planets. These aspects are often not appreciated and do not lead to change. The *hard aspects*, the square (90°) and opposition (180°), indicate that more energy must be expended to harmonize the learning concerning things symbolized by these planets. Because of the tension involved, squares and oppositions promote growth and change. The quincunx (150°) illuminates features in the life where re-examination, reorganization and restructuring are necessary.

The aspects show how the nature of early life experiences, as reflected by the planets, is expressed, as indicated by the signs, in specific areas of life, delineated by the houses.

Applications of Astrology in Counseling and Therapy

The most important application of astrology in therapy is *understanding psychological patterns*. Using astrology diagnostically allows early discussion of psychological issues and life experiences, making clear areas needing therapeutic intervention. There are significant reasons why this use of astrology is possible: (1) The horoscope allows the client to *shift attention from him/herself* to discussion of the meaning of astrological patterns. This encourages earlier identification and discussion of potentially painful emotional material. (2) As a symbol system, astrology provides a *conceptual framework* for the therapist and client to use in their communication.

In using astrology diagnostically, it is impossible to indicate details. There is "positive" and "negative" expression of all planets and signs. In looking at a chart, you do not have knowledge of specifics in a person's life. Therefore, it is helpful to say something like, "There is a pattern here which suggests that your father may have been very limiting and restricting in your life, may not have allowed you to be spontaneous, creative and childlike. This pattern may also reflect a father who was so involved in teaching you how to be 'safe' in life that you felt very restricted. How did you experience this pattern?" or "How have you lived this out in your life?" Horoscope interpretation provides a structure similar to a projective technique which allows discussion of early experiences and their consequence in adult life.

Many people seek out an astrologer/psychologist because they are interested in greater psychological understanding. In my practice, a horoscope consultation of one and one-half to two hours is conducted with these people. This interpretation focuses psychological patterns of the chart and current astrological/psychological patterns, is taped for the client's future use, and sometimes leads to therapy.

There are clients who, knowing the psychologist is an astrologer, seek a horoscope reading as the way of initiating therapy. With these clients, the first session is a two-hour horoscope reading, which is taped so the material is available for the client's review. The information from this interpretation is used in the client's therapy.

Clients who are not aware that the therapist is an astrologer may ask about the birth-time question on the client information form. If they indicate interest in using astrology in their therapeutic work, parts of the next several sessions will focus on astrological patterns and the client's psychological experience.

In the initial interview, the therapist makes sure the client discusses experience in four areas of life: (1) work, (2) friendship/support system and intimate relationships, (3) recreation, play and personal growth, and (4) sense of meaning in life or spiritual understanding. Pleasure through the first three of these may be recognized as Freud's prescription for the "psychologically mature person." Freud, having only one planet in the "transpersonal" or spiritual part of his chart, did not focus on the meaning of life. The 8th House emphasis in Freud's chart reflects his involvement in uncovering and understanding unconscious content.

In the second session, there may be discussion about the pattern of the chart, the elements and the qualities. In the third session, the psychological issues of the Sun sign as they relate to material being presented by the client are taken into consideration. With these clients, astrological discussion parallels and facilitates disclosure of psychological themes.

This is not a situation where the therapist/astrologer defines for the client his/her psychological issues. This would violate the client's readiness to deal with emotional issues in determining the pace and direction of psychological work.

The client who is not interested in using astrological data or is uncomfortable about astrology can be informed that the therapist will be doing a horoscope for his/her understanding. The therapist's acknowledgment that astrology is important for his/her understanding of the client often leads to a request for chart interpretation.

Discussion of psychological issues is facilitated by the displacement allowed in focusing on the horoscope's patterns rather than directly on the client's experience. For example, during a horoscope consultation it is possible to say to a client, "There is a pattern here suggesting the possibility that you experienced much negation, violence or possibly abuse in your early childhood. Does that make any sense to you?" This is a much more gentle and open approach than "Were you abused as a child?"

If the client says no, this may reflect that abuse did not occur, or it may reflect his/her inability to be aware of these experiences at this point in therapy. These experiences may have been so painful and difficult that they have been repressed from consciousness. During therapy, these early experiences may be expressed somatically in dreams or conscious memory so they become part of the therapeutic material.

Talking about the horoscope rather than questioning an individual's experience often allows material which would not come into therapy until the sixth to eighth session to be identified and discussed earlier in treatment. Therapists anticipate that a period of time is required to establish trust in the therapist and the therapeutic process before more painful issues are presented. Astrology's focus on understanding the horoscope presents the possibility of earlier work with these issues.

In astrologically based counseling, the astrologer must avoid the oracle role, not feeling that s/he must prove the validity of astrology by being right about the client's life or psychological experiences. This is truly a mutual exploration to illuminate the individual's life experiences and psychological patterns arising from these experiences.

In counseling or therapy, astrology provides a conceptual framework for discussing a client's experience. In beginning a horoscope session, the therapist presents an understanding of the horoscope. This includes the fact that the planets do not cause anything to happen to a person and that astrological understanding allows greater choice, greater power.

With the client whose chart has been previously discussed, it is possible for the therapist to say, "That sounds like the Mars/Jupiter pattern where you feel that you move into relationships with such energy that you frighten others away." An important point here is not expecting the client to learn astrological jargon—unless the client is a student of astrology who wants to learn the source of all astrological/psychological statements. Using planetary names gives a reference point so the client can begin asking questions in astrological terms, i.e., "Is that my Saturn stuff again?"

The client may begin using astrological concepts to discuss feelings and events of life. It may be much easier to talk about "my Mars energy" than to talk about "my anger." While some therapists would say that clients must ultimately "own their anger as part of themselves," it can be effective to discuss feelings at the level of displacement provided by astrology. The client is aware that s/he is talking about his/her own emotional process, not someone else's. Through astrological patterns, clients can develop understanding of sources of their emotions and alternative ways of constructively expressing these feelings.

The horoscope reflects *problems* or *challenges* in one's life. Many astrologers prefer the term "challenges" because a client does not need to leave a horoscope reading with additional identified problems than at the onset.

In working psychologically with the horoscope, it is imperative to recognize that for every challenge in the horoscope the chart reflects potential solutions. In reading the chart, the astrologer must continually ask, "Have I suggested ways of working with this pattern?" If ways of responding to challenges have not been incorporated in the consultation, the client leaves the session without a sense of options, not feeling empowered.

Which options are best for the client is his/her decision and in his/her control. The therapist or astrologer who tells a client what s/he "should do" is falling into the pattern of a dependency-creating parent. The therapist or astrologer who tells someone what s/he should do is also unfair because the therapist does not have to personally experience the consequences of the client's action.

One therapist used runes with a woman who had been hospitalized as the result of a beating by her husband. Although the woman was exploring a shelter for battered women, the therapist interpreted the runes as reflecting that she should "return home and face your problems." She went home and was rehospitalized in much more serious condition because of a subsequent beating.

Astrology can be used to help a client understand present psychological issues by examining the *progression of the natal chart*. People do not experience psychological issues, unless the potential is indicated in the natal horoscope. Clients who have been in therapy for some time will frequently talk about an issue in their lives and ask, "I wonder how this is reflected in my horoscope," or they may ask about transits. *Transits* are the current positions of the planets in the zodiac. It is often helpful to use progressions and transits to relate current psychological emphasis to natal psychological issues.

Secondary progressions give a psychological pattern for the year of the life. For example, the position of the Moon shows areas of the life in which change will be emphasized and experienced. Planets changing signs or houses or in early or late degrees of a sign indicate the beginning of new ways or the ending of old ways of living out whatever is symbolized by the planet, the area of life being reflected by the house of the natal chart, e.g., Jupiter, the planet reflecting how a person relates, moving from Scorpio, where relationships tend to include anxiety about rejection, into fiery confident Sagittarius will show a much more outgoing, extroverted nature.

The *Solar Return*, a horoscope for the time when the Sun returns to its natal position each year, gives more specific information about psychological patterns for the year. The Solar Return Moon's location in the natal chart shows where there will be impetus for change. The relationship of the Solar Return to the natal chart indicates whether the emphasis of the life for that year will be on personal growth, issues of relationship, or matters of profession and life's meaning.

The sign on the Ascendant of the Solar Return shows how the energy of the natal horoscope will be expressed during the Solar Return year. The issues of the Ascendant sign will be emphasized in the life. The Midheaven is the point of the chart which relates to the "profession" with which one identifies. Its location in the Solar

Return will give information about the vocational life during the year.

Because the horoscope circle has 360° and the year has 365 days, it is possible to use the Solar Return as a timing device with one degree of the horoscope crossing the Midheaven each day. Some astrologers use the planetary conjunction with the Ascendant and Midheaven of the chart for prediction of patterns in the Solar Return.

Psychologically, it is possible to suggest what issues will be emphasized at certain periods of the year. These issues are often sequential, so the client is given a road map for the work ahead.

Patterns of transiting planets also reflect current psychological influences in life. The fast-moving planets reflect brief and momentary impact in life. The slower-moving planets may reflect issues which are in the foreground for several months. The "generational" or slow-moving planets reflect issues which are prominent for longer periods of life and feel less personally imperative.

In using transits for psychological understanding, it is easy for a client and the astrologer to slip into the view that "the planets are doing it." With our basic view that psychological understanding creates our experience of the world, it is important to use the transits as a way of identifying psychological issues and increasing awareness of themes involved in current life experiences. The prevailing potential issues shown by transits must always relate to psychological issues reflected in the natal chart.

Therapy and astrology are processes of empowering the client through understanding how past experience influences current decisions and actions. This understanding of astrology allows early discussion of life experiences and psychological issues arising from them. It also gives the client a conceptual framework for his/her therapeutic work.

Asteroids and Psychological Understanding

The asteroids offer a more detailed look at psychological issues. Discovery of the asteroids and their integration into astrology is another example of synchronicity.

The first of the asteroids, discovered in 1880, was named for *Ceres*, the protector Goddess of Sicily. The first four asteroids were named for women and reflect the roles of *mother, daughter, wife* and *sister*. As a result of increasing interest in the relationship of depth psychology and astrology, astrologers began placing these asteroids in the horoscope in the early 1960s. Synchronously, this coincided with the beginning of the women's movement. These asteroids reflected the feminine aspects of both men and women at a time when the culture was beginning to recognize that men can express feminine energies and women can express masculine energies.

Some astrologers have avoided using the asteroids, stating that they obtain all the information they need from "the basic chart." Because of the small size of the asteroids, with Ceres the largest at 500 miles in diameter, some astrologers feel the asteroids cannot be significant. One prominent and highly respected astrologer suggests the asteroids be called "transiting gravel."

Resistance to using the asteroids is very understandable. Astrology with ten planets, twelve signs and twelve houses is complex. Adding asteroids seems like complicating an already overwhelming task. Yet, many astrologers feel they are not "getting all there is" in reading the basic horoscope.

At the time of this writing, there are over 4,200 asteroids with defined orbits, and 11 to 12 asteroids could be located on each of the 360° of the natal chart. No wonder the task seems overwhelming. It is not important to place all of the asteroids in any particular horoscope. Another synchronicity shows the way to work with this problem.

Asteroids are named by the discovering astronomer. Astrologers place these newly found asteroids in their horoscopes and find that the names given by the astronomer, who generally does not "believe" in astrology, fit the issues reflected by the asteroid in the horoscope.

Dr. Zipporah Dobyns, who has done extensive work with the psychological and mundane application of the asteroids, illustrates that astrologers *can select* their asteroids, depending on the nature of the questions or issues they are studying. For example, ***Atlantis***, having to do with positive use or abuse of power, has been prominent in the chart of every nuclear event from the initial chain reaction at the University of Chicago laboratory in 1942 to the Chernobyl nuclear accident.

In using the asteroids for psychologically based astrology, it is necessary to become familiar with only those asteroids relevant to your areas of interest. For example, the asteroids Washington, Moscow or Iran probably would not be useful in a horoscope seeking psychological understanding. However, they are very significant in mundane astrology.

Psychologically, if we are interested in how a person relates, we look first at the natal chart and then at three asteroids of relationship—***Eros***, ***Amor*** and ***Sappho***. *Eros* reflects the excitement of new-found romance. Strains of "Falling in Love with Love" sound when Eros is prominent in the chart. Depending on the sign placement of this asteroid, it is easy or difficult for the individual to fall into and out of love relationships. While attraction to a new love object may be easy, Eros is not known for staying around long enough to work through the issues which come as part of any significant growth-producing relationship.

Amor reflects the *spiritual* side of relationship, the love of parent for child, which is devoid of sexual energy, the love of Saint for humanity as exemplified by Mother Teresa, or Parsifal's search for the Holy Grail. Depending on sign placement, Amour will reflect the importance of a partner's spirituality and the nature of the spiritual tie with a partner.

Sappho mirrors the *sensual* side of relationship. Although Sappho was sexual with the women with whom she worked in writing music and poetry for the heterosexual bridal chamber, her asteroid shows how an individual expresses sensuality—not just genital sexuality. Sappho is often prominent in the horoscope of lesbians as they become aware of their sexuality and enter or end a relationship. For all people, Sappho shows ease or discomfort in expressing the sensual side of the self. Comparison of the Sappho positions of two people shows the ease or difficulty of blending their sensual expression.

There are asteroids which represent areas of life in which people want to strive or excel, e.g., **Hildalgo** and **Icarus**. Synchronously, of all the asteroids *Hildalgo* moves highest above the plane of the ecliptic—the plane defined by the movement of the Earth around the Sun in its annual path. What better way to show flying high and striving for high goals.

The asteroid *Icarus*, named after the mythological man who did not pay attention to his father's advice to not fly too close to the Sun when they were attempting to escape the labyrinth of the Minotaur, reflects "trying to fly too high and not paying attention to advice." This is best illustrated by transiting Icarus conjunct Richard Nixon's natal Sun at the time he was implicated in the Watergate Scandal. When Rosemary Wood was exposed for erasing Watergate tapes, transiting Icarus was conjunct her natal Sun and in a stressful aspect to Nixon's natal Sun.

Lilith, not the dark moon Lilith, is an asteroid which illustrates an area of life where there is something of unconscious meaning which needs to be explored at some time in the life. When it is conjunct the Moon, this relates to mother; if conjunct Saturn, the father; if conjunct Jupiter, relationship patterns must be examined, etc.

In beginning with the asteroids, choose a limited number which have interest to you and your clients. The asteroids of relationship mentioned give a breadth in readings and allow understanding of how the asteroids are expressed in a chart. These suggestions may ease the way in working with asteroids: (1) Read astrological patterns before entering the asteroids. (2) Use a different color for asteroids than for planets in the horoscope. (3) Narrow asteroid orbs to 1°. (4) Read only major aspects, perhaps beginning with conjunctions and oppositions.

Employing the asteroids in the horoscope is much like turning up the power of a microscope. It is true that the basic horoscope with the planets, signs and houses reflects the potential for the client's psychological issues. The asteroids give more detail about personality structure and how it is expressed.

Psychologically based astrology has a great deal to offer the mental health worker, counselor and astrologer. For those working in understanding human feelings, behavior and experience, astrology provides a valuable tool. We have discussed the specificity which can be gained through astrology and how this can be integrated in therapy, counseling and astrological practice. Examples of the operation of synchronicity and its role in increasing understanding of human behavior have underscored how astrology *empowers*.

Susan Dearborn Jackson

Susan Dearborn Jackson has been in private practice as an astrologer for 10 years and has studied astrology since 1975. For five of those years, she was the on-staff astrologer with the Eugene Center for the Healing Arts in Eugene, Oregon. During that time, she consulted regularly with the center's counselors and therapists.

Her astrological practice focuses on counseling, to which she brings a comprehensive background in Reichian analysis, Bioenergetics, Gestalt, Tibetan Buddhist Psychology and Jungian Analytic Psychology. In addition to counseling, Susan has led workshops and lectured in the Pacific Northwest, including a presentation at the 1988 Welcome to Planet Earth Conference. Her astrological book reviews have appeared in *New Realities* and *Welcome to Planet Earth*.

Currently, Susan is enrolled in a two-and-one-half-year program in Jungian Studies to enhance her understanding of mythology and symbolism and its role in her work.

READING THE BODY, READING THE CHART

dedicated to my first mentor, Judy Tobias Franzen

Astrology is, in my estimation, the best diagnostic tool available for psychotherapy and counseling. It not only describes personality types and psychological issues but also reveals a client's history and background. Likewise, astrology clearly describes predictable cycles and transitions in human development.

Many different schools of psychological and philosophical thought have been correlated to astrology. Transactional analysis can find parent, child and adult through the placement of Saturn, the Moon and the Sun in a horoscope. Jungian analytic psychology can identify the shadow by looking at natal Pluto and Saturn. The Kaballah and Tarot have been cross-referenced to astrological signs and planets. Id, ego and superego find their way into astrological interpretation as well.

There is yet another therapeutic frame of reference available to astrologers for diagnostic and counseling purposes. This is the work of Wilhelm Reich in the first half of the 20th century. Originally a student of Freud's, Reich discovered a vital body energy that he termed "orgone." Orgone energy is identified as the life force and is similiar to the Kundalini fire of Eastern philosophy. Reich's studies led him to postulate that as children we find ways to protect ourselves which aren't appropriate later in life. However, the childhood defenses and protections create energetic blocks in the physical body in the form of chronic muscular tension. The orgone in the body then "freezes" in particular patterns of held tension. Thus, the emotional issues and defenses in an individual can be seen on an energetic, physical level.

Alexander Lowen expanded on Reich's theory through his development of Bioenergetics. This therapeutic approach works directly with the body to release old emotional blocks. Both men suggested five basic defenses which hold emotional stress as tension in the body. Each defense manifests as a specific body structure and corresponds to a particular stage of childhood development.

Again, each of the five defenses or character (body) structures can be correlated to astrological indicators in the birth chart. Using the Reichian typologies allows the astrologer to identify the client's emotional issues and may provide information invaluable to the individual's healing process.

No one falls clearly into just one of the five character types or body structures. Each of us is made up of a composite of defenses and issues, much like the Earth is composed of a variety of different types of rock and sediments. Yet, at the core of our being there is a propensity toward a certain way of protecting ourselves, which was originally developed in childhood. Often in Bioenergetic therapy, the client's body will change as different emotional issues are uncovered. Thus, the physical body holds the answers that lead to psychological healing.

A word of caution: The names given to these five types are labels only and tend to overgeneralization. Like all labels, they serve the function of allowing identification of a client's background and psychological issues. And, like all labels, they can also create barriers and separations from the real, live client in front of us. Also, the Reichian terminology is derived from classical psychology and can conjure up uncomfortable associations. For clarity, I have chosen to present Reich's and Lowen's original terminology. It is best to keep in mind, however, that these labels are for the benefit of the counseling astrologer only and, in most cases, should not be shared with the client.

In presenting an overview of each character structure, I will discuss its formation at a particular age or stage of development, the childhood environment and behavioral manifestations. The issues or core conflicts indicative of each structure will be described. The astrological correlations and how these issues show up in a chart will be discussed, followed by an example chart and a brief case history. All charts utilize Placidus houses, and birth data is withheld for confidentiality. The final section of this chapter will examine appropriate therapeutic approaches and techniques for each structure.

The Schizoid Structure

The *schizoid* structure is formed very early, either in utero or shortly after birth. If, for any reason, the mother is unable to bond with the child, whether due to illness, depression or her own fears, the child will be unequipped to develop a strong sense of self. This *lack of emotional bondedness* leads to *total adaptability* on the part of the child.

There is a tremendous fear of annihilation in this structure. The message the child receives is that without mother s/he won't survive. Thus, the child learns to *split off from his/her body and emotions* as his/her primary defense mechanism. The schizoid structure is often, then, ungrounded, has little sense of ego and is disconnected from the body.

The positive feature of the schizoid is a *highly*

developed imagination and strong fantasy life. Not limited to its five physical senses or to his/her body, the child has no sense of personal limits or boundaries. This openness leads to a strong desire to achieve other states of consciousness and an ability to tune in to different states of awareness. This is the child who can see auras, hear voices and get lost in daydreams and fantasies. Because s/he is ungrounded, s/he does not develop the capacity to realistically interpret his/her perceptions.

As an adult, the body itself will often be *tall and skinny, looking hard and fragmented*. There is generally little or no energy in the body extremities, manifesting as cold hands, a blank face and disconnection of the feet. There may be a marked split at the neck so that the head seems unconnected to the rest of the body. This may indicate an attitude of trying to keep the head above water. In other words, the schizoid will dissociate from his/her emotions. Energetically, the first chakra or energy center—the seat of the survival instinct—will function in a diminished capacity. The schizoid is often seen as "Mr. Mellow," the superspiritual type who is ungrounded and spaced-out.

The schizoid structure lives in a *world of extremes*. Behavior and attitudes assume black and white, either/or proportions. This theme extends to the emotional realm as well. Generally, the schizoid will avoid feeling—"If I feel, I'll die." Terrified of close relationships, the schizoid will literally retreat from a relationship rather than feel. Being touched or slowing down brings up emotions that the schizoid tries to evade. Conversely, this structure may be overwhelmed or flooded with feelings.

This body type can *vacillate between a sense of specialness and a feeling of "nothingness."* S/he may believe that s/he is actually a king or queen in disguise. S/he may feel singled out for a divine destiny, and because s/he has an incredible sensitivity to other states of reality, the line between illusion and illumination may become quite thin!

Lack of boundaries characterize the schizoid structure. S/he literally doesn't know where s/he ends and
someone else begins. A sense of helplessness, self-doubt
and confusion may also be present. <u>There is always terror at
the core of the schizoid.</u>

Astrological Indicators

Astrologically, the schizoid will be indicated by an
emphasis on *Pisces, Neptune or the 12th House.* Psychically
sensitive and emotionally empathetic, the schizoid knows
how to break down boundaries, whether through music,
prayer and meditation, dreamwork, or drugs and alcohol.
The symbolism of the ocean and its waves, associated
with Neptune and Pisces, is appropriate to the schizoid
structure. Unclear boundaries, the inability to set limits
and feeling overwhelmed are all issues related to the
Piscean theme. Spiritual awareness, creative inspiration
and a rich inner life are also strongly connected to this
astrological motif and the schizoid structure.

There is often a *preponderance of Air and Water* in the
birth chart. Underlying this is a dissociation or splitting
off of the thinking function, represented by Air, from the
Watery, feeling function. The Moon, symbolic of our
emotional nature, may be in an Air sign or house. The
schizoid cannot let him/herself feel or the terror will
threaten to engulf him/her. Often, the Air/Water combination creates confusion just as fog and clouds are formed
from Air and Water.

Mars may be placed in Pisces or in the 12th House,
further indicating an underdeveloped sense of ego.
Similiarly, Mars may be conjunct Neptune in the natal
chart. Based on my clinical experience, Mars also may be
found in Aries or in the 1st House. Rather than indicating
independence or assertiveness as traditionally interpreted, the issue is the need to form a solid self-image. The

schizoid has no clear self-identity and, like a chameleon, can adapt to the environment.

Schizoid Case History

When Rachel's parents were married, they each already had children from previous marriages. The first time Rachel's mother discovered she was pregnant, her new husband was surprised, but indulgent. However, when she became pregnant with Rachel a short ten months after the birth of their first daughter, Rachel's father felt trapped and betrayed by his wife. The morning Rachel was born, her father went out and got drunk.

Because Rachel has spent 15 years in therapy and is a highly skilled therapist, she has been able to recall her experience in utero. It felt like a hostile environment, full of terror and chaos. Rachel's mother was an alcoholic and had a history of semi-psychotic episodes. All the turmoil and confusion that the mother felt was communicated to the unborn child.

The craziness didn't end at Rachel's birth. Her father was emotionally absent, and Rachel's mother claimed the child as her own. There were no boundaries between them. In the symbiotic enmeshment, the mother began to sexually abuse the young baby. Most of the abuse occurred during drinking binges and continued until Rachel's grandmother came to live with the family when Rachel was three years old.

Rachel's experience of her childhood was that there was no one around to protect her from her mother. She describes her mother as "a study in extremes." One moment she was loving and generous, the next moment she was calculating and perverse. Clearly, Rachel's mother had a split in her own psyche.

The turning point in Rachel's life was the birth of her daughter. Prior to this time, she had lived on the edge, continuing the pattern of her childhood. With the birth of her child, Rachel, at 24, had a focus around which to center and structure her life. She was determined to play out the role of mother, and she did. She remembers feeling spaced-out, depressed and always anxious.

Rachel began therapy in her mid-twenties. She became aware that she felt like she had been walking around in a black cloud all her life. Odd memories surfaced and nightmares haunted her sleep. Rachel credits her husband and her daughter with providing support and caring in this phase of her healing.

Presently in her early forties, Rachel uses her sensitivity and awareness in her counseling practice. She has developed her intuitive abilities to a fine art. Laughingly, she describes herself as "having antennae with a capital *A*"! On occasion, Rachel still experiences attacks of terror and feels like she is enveloped in a war-torn environment. Now when new insights burst upon her, she is able to integrate the information more quickly. Rachel makes her sensitivity *work for her* rather than being overwhelmed by it.

Rachel's birth chart is atypical of the schizoid structure. In spite of this fact, I chose to work with her case history because she has both the awareness of her emotional dynamics and the ability to clearly communicate her experiences. Usually, there is a greater emphasis on Air and Water in the horoscope, indicating the splitting off of feelings. Rachel's chart contains several planets in Fire signs, which, again, is unusual for the schizoid structure. I feel that the emphasis on Fire has been a major factor in her ability to heal the old emotional wounds as well as evidence of her highly developed intuition.

Her horoscope contains a 12th House Aquarius Sun and a Pisces Ascendant. Along with many other astrologers, I connect the 12th House to the prenatal experience. The emphasis on Pisces and the 12th House describes

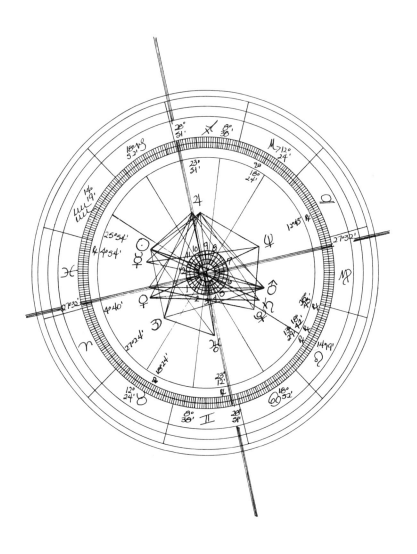

Rachel's Chart
Schizoid Structure

Rachel's hypersensitivity, her experience of enmeshment with her mother, and the alcoholic, dysfunctional environment in which she grew up. Lack of boundaries and an underdeveloped sense of ego are also themes associated with Pisces rising and a 12th House Sun.

The chart ruler, Neptune, falls in the 7th House of relationships, which further emphasizes unclear boundaries and unhealthy symbiosis in relationships. Rachel recalls her first few years of marriage as very enmeshed with her husband. Neptune also opposes Venus, natural ruler of relationships, reflecting again the loss of self in the experience of relatedness.

Two of the feminine indicators in a chart, the Moon and Venus, are located in the 1st House in Aries. This suggests that Rachel's mom did, in fact, claim the child as her own and didn't see herself as separate from Rachel. Here, the emphasis on Aries and the 1st House is associated with the schizoid structure. Rachel had to discover who she was—her own self-identity separate from her mother's self-image.

Several planets in the chart are retrograde, including Mars, the planet of self-image, and Mercury, planet of the mind and its capacity to create maps of reality. The retrograde motion implies her inward focus and rich fantasy life. Indeed, these factors suggest that the path of healing and repair leads to the inner world of the psyche.

The Oral Structure

The formation of the *oral* structure occurs in the first two years of life. At this stage of development when the child is reaching out to have his/her basic needs met, s/he experiences *deprivation*. This most commonly happens when either the mother is unable to respond to the child's needs or there is a lack of contact from a nurturing, supportive caregiver. At the core of the oral structure, there is *fear of abandonment*.

The child responds to the sense of abandonment by denying his/her needs. The message is "Don't reach, or you will be rejected." The child feels that s/he has lost the right to need when the nurturance of the mother has been withdrawn. *The oral learns not to make any demands*. "I don't need anyone" is the core statement of the oral body type who believes that being dependent means being weak.

Thus, any sign of neediness will be masked by an *outer display of strength and independence*. The oral is often very nurturing towards others and likes to feel needed while maintaining an illusion of boundless vitality. Yet, under stress, this structure falls apart and collapses. Such individuals are unable to sustain any energy in their bodies and are subject to *intense mood swings*. Depression and rage are common. Both feelings are related to the experience of fear and disappointment from having needs unmet and denied.

In relationship, the oral structure will look for a mother figure for nurturance or s/he will choose a partner who needs him/her. Either alternative allows the oral to *manipulate emotional contact* without having to experience one's own neediness. There is a tendency to cling to partners or to expect others to fill him/her up while diguising anxiety under a strong, independent exterior.

The physical structure of the oral may look much like the schizoid body type. While the schizoid body seems fragmented, the oral structure appears to be *either undernourished or overnourished*. Often, the *arms are under-developed* from fear of reaching out for nurturance and being rejected. The oral simply stopped reaching, and the arms reflect this. There may be a ring around the mouth, indicating that the sucking needs of the child were cut off too early. Likewise, there may be a ring around the neck from choking down needs. From my own experience working with clients, <u>I have often seen an energetic block</u> <u>at the fifth chakra, the energy center located at the throat,</u> <u>since the right to express or voice needs has been denied.</u>

The positive aspect of the oral structure is that this individual is *very loving, generous and affectionate*. The oral has a lot to give. This structure is very often *highly creative* as well.

Astrological Indicators

In a horoscope, the oral structure is indicated by an *emphasized 4th House, a prominent Moon or several planets in* *Cancer*. This theme represents the need for nurturance and the strong nourishing energy orals express towards others. It also symbolizes the significance that mother and emotional bonding play in the development of the oral structure.

Quite often, there will be a *Moon/Saturn* contact in the natal chart. The more stressful, challenging aspects, such as the conjunction (0°), the square (90°), the quincunx (150°) and the opposition (180°), will indicate emotional deprivation or difficulty in reaching out to get security needs met. Fear (Saturn) of abandonment (Moon) is an accurate interpretation for the oral structure.

There may be a preponderance of *Water* placements in the birth chart as well. The oral personality has a tremendous capacity to feel, indicative of an emphasis on Water signs. If the element Water is not accented, there may be several planets in the Watery houses—4th, 8th or 12th. Because the oral structure denies its neediness, there may be many unshed tears held in the body.

<u>The energy block at the fifth chakra may be</u> <u>indicated by a strong placement of</u> *Mercury or several* *planets in Gemini or in the 3rd House*. Coupled with the Cancer theme, this pattern symbolizes the necessity to express security needs.

Another astrological indicator of the oral structure I

have found in my work with clients is *Mars in Cancer*. This reveals how difficult it is for this body type to express its needs directly. It is also symbolic of the rage found in the oral that stems from feeling abandoned and having his/her needs denied.

Oral Case History

When Vince was born, the oldest of two children, his father assumed a major caregiving role. He fed Vince, changed his diapers and was very much present in the baby's life. His mother asserts that she had never seen a father who was as tender and nurturing as Vince's dad. Because his mother wasn't employed, Vince had virtually around-the-clock nurturance.

In August of 1961, when Vince was ten months old, all that changed. His mother took a full-time job and Vince was left in the care of a baby sitter. In October of that year, his father was recalled into military service because of the Berlin Crisis. Being the good Capricorn father that he is, Vince's dad felt it was important to fulfill his military obligation. Astrologically, Mars, the planet of war, was transiting Vince's 4th House cusp, and Jupiter and Saturn were squaring his Libra Sun, indicating his father's military recall.

The upshot was that Vince was "abandoned" by a primary nurturer at age one. Readers, please note that this was not a child left to cry alone for hours in his crib. Vince received solid nurturance from both parents. Yet, his experience was one of having the nurturance withdrawn at a crucial stage of development. For several months at a time, Vince didn't see his father, and when he did, he didn't recognize him. His father would come home as often as he could, but the pattern was established in Vince's unconscious. Together-separation-together, followed by another *separation*.

During the winter of 1961–62, Vince contracted

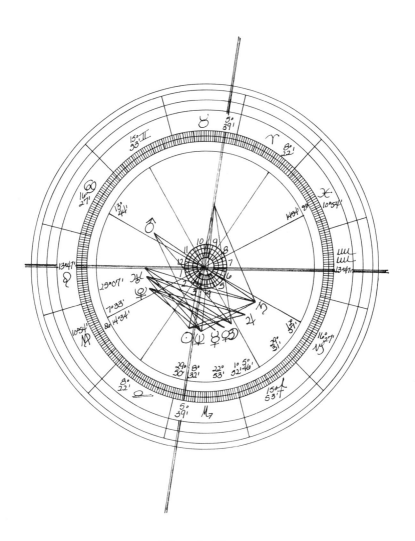

Vince's Chart
Oral Structure

pneumonia and was hospitalized. Pneumonia, which settles in the lungs, is an illness associated with grief and unshed tears. It is not too surprising that the small child was grief-stricken at the separation from his father.

Vince's physical body fits the description of the oral structure. While he is now a tall, slender man, as a child he was overweight, exhibiting the overnourished aspect of orality. Food filled that empty spot left by his experience of abandonment.

What is obvious to Vince as he looks at his early childhood is that the pattern of closeness-separation-closeness continues in his adult relationships. As we talked, what emerged was a sense of being either overly dependent on or totally separate from his lovers. His experience is also that if he expresses his neediness, his partner leaves, physically or emotionally. Control and manipulation have been part of the pattern as well. Most of his lovers were Cancers or had several planets in Cancer or in the 4th House. Some of them have also had a prominently placed Moon. Clearly, Vince has looked for a nurturing caregiver in his relationships.

Vince describes himself as having lots of vitality. He works himself into a frenzy, expending vast amounts of physical and emotional energy. The pattern continues as he either collapses or explodes in an emotional outburst when he can't maintain the frenetic pace. He then withdraws before resuming the cycle again.

Vince's chart reflects these characteristics. His 4th House, associated with the father, contains a stellium. He has a Moon/Venus conjunction, which indicates that he experienced his father as very nurturing. The Moon in Sagittarius also suggests the distance he felt when his dad left for military service.

The Sun is in the 3rd House, indicative of the energetic block at the throat chakra. Vince majored in music and voice while in college. He intuitively felt this was an important step in spite of the fact that singing was very difficult for him. It has been an important factor in overcoming his reluctance to verbally express his needs.

There are three planets in Water and four in the Watery 4th House. Vince is extremely sensitive and nurturing in his relationships with others. Furthermore, Mars in Cancer is the only planet above the horizon. When I asked him how it felt to reach out to meet his needs, Vince replied that his arms went limp when he had to say "I need." He admitted to feeling a lot of frustration and sadness at having experienced abusive and manipulative behavior with his partners when what he really wanted was closeness and nurturance.

The Masochistic Structure

The structure of the *masochistic* body type is formed between two and four years of age. Most of the emotional issues are created because the child experiences *too much pressure from the mother*. Often felt as suffocation, this pressure centers around toilet training and eating at this phase of development. Discipline often comes in the form of humiliation, nagging or guilt-tripping. Basically, the mother is more concerned with her own image and less with the child's well-being, pushing the youngster to be a reflection of what a good mother she is.

What develops is a sense of *anger and resentment that is held in* by the child. The inner pressure increases—and with it a resistance to pleasing the caregiver. An attitude of *inner rebellion and spitefulness* characterizes the masochistic structure. The core statement of the masochist is "Everything is too much." Along with this is an outlook of "I won't try" and "If I fail, it's because I didn't try." Thus, the masochistic maintains an *illusion of superiority*. Yet, there is a resistance to success.

Release is difficult for the masochistic structure. S/he may provoke fights in order to experience relief from the internal pressure of unexpressed feelings. Whining and complaining, yet remaining submissive, also characterize this body type. Because his/her *primary defense is to hold on and resign him/herself to stress*, it is often very difficult to break out of old patterns and experience inner freedom.

The physical body is generally *short and thick and looks compressed*. The masochistic body may look like a tomato being squeezed and about to pop. The body itself registers the tremendous external pressure that the child has experienced and now internalizes. There is *an appearance of suffering*; the shoulders may be rolled over or pulled in and seem to be burdened. Tension and tightness will show up in the jaws of the masochistic structure, giving the individual a "bulldog" appearance. In short, this person will appear *trapped in his/her body*.

The positive feature of the masochistic structure is *strength*. This body type has *endurability, patience and tremendous coping ability*. S/he also tends to be very *productive*. Given a naturally placid, sweet character, this is the salt-of-the-Earth type—the Earth Mother, always patient, slow-moving and tolerant.

Astrological Indicators

The masochistic structure may be indicated in the natal chart by a *preponderance of Earth planets (or Earth houses) and generally very little Fire*. The Earth element gives the masochist his/her slow but steady quality and is a major factor in the productivity and perseverance of this structure. If there is Fire in the chart, it is often unexpressed and can be the key to release in later therapy.

There is frequently an *emphasis on Taurus, a strongly placed Venus or several planets in the 2nd House*. This theme relates to tension in the jaws and the held-in resentments of the masochistic structure. Obviously, it contributes to the down-to-Earth, productive image.

Another astrological factor found in the chart is often a *prominent but difficult placement of Uranus,* reflecting the inner feeling of rebellion common to the masochistic body type. This structure longs to feel a sense of freedom and an urge to express his/her individuality; however, these longings are blocked by external pressure.

The presence of *planets in Libra or in the 7th House* is characteristic of the masochistic structure. Libra is one of the truly "nice guys" of the zodiac and has a hard time learning to say no and to set limits. The emphasis on this theme illustrates the bind that the masochistic structure feels about expression of anger and frustration.

Humiliation is a component of the masochist, and I have frequently seen *Pluto in challenging aspect to the Moon* in the birth charts of this body type. This aspect denotes the manipulation that the child experiences in childhood. The *Moon in Scorpio* may also suggest the masochistic structure.

Masochistic Case History

Melissa comes from a long line of strong women. Both her mother and grandmother are powerful figures, and Melissa displays enormous strength and energy as well. The history of these three women is fascinating, especially since it shaped much of Melissa's life.

From the time Melissa was born, the oldest of four children, her grandmother and her father played decisive roles in her upbringing. They both instructed and directed Melissa's mother in the proper care of the new baby. In fact, her mother was under constant scrutiny and pressure from other outside sources as well. Living in student housing when Melissa was two threw the young mother into a group of women whose sole concern was competing to be the best mother in the neighborhood. This pressure of the mother was passed on to the child. Her younger brother had been born only 14 months after Melissa, and at that point she felt she was expected to grow up and be a big kid.

The pivotal factor in Melissa's childhood, however, was her father's unpredictable, violent temper. Melissa was always terrified that he would explode, and she responded to the constant tension by making herself very small and keeping the lid on her own feelings. She also acutely felt the strain her mother was experiencing. She remembers sensing that her mother was barely keeping it all together with four small children under five years of age and a husband given to episodes of irrational rage and sudden violence. There was no room for Melissa to be scared, no room to express herself, and no room to need anything because her mother was already overwhelmed.

Melissa's father disappeared when she was eight, and the family moved to the West Coast to live with her maternal grandparents. Now Melissa had two mothering figures. Her image of this period is both women standing over her, telling her what to wear, what to eat and what to do.

It was at this time that she began to gain weight. Her three younger brothers and her grandfather teased and taunted her about her weight, adding to her sense of shame and humiliation about her body. Once again, Melissa experienced a sense of "too much" and retreated into herself. Once again, external strain caused her to try to diminish herself to avoid further anxiety.

Melissa's body reflects the years of pressure. She is short and ample, a miniature Venus de Willendorf. She looks like an Earth Mother whose lap is big enough to climb into and whose shoulders are broad enough to carry any burden.

Although she has been in counseling for years,

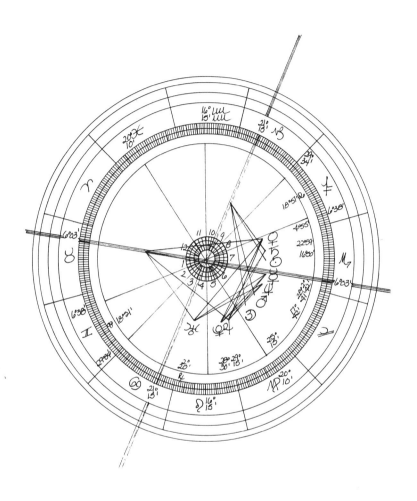

Melissa's Chart
Masochistic Structure

Melissa still experiences difficulty in expressing her resentments and anger. It is simply easier to hold it all inside. She is now beginning to realize how she has carried the burden of her mother and grandmother's unspoken resentments and unfinished business with each other.

Melissa's natal chart contains a Taurus Ascendant and Virgo Moon. The emphasis on Earth and Earth Houses (there is a stellium of planets in the 6th, Virgo's natural house) reflects her masochistic structure. Melissa does have four planets in Fire signs, which give her a feeling of aliveness. The Earth and Fire combination indicates her enormous productivity, so if she takes on one project, she is likely to take on several others as well. Needless to say, Melissa works well under pressure.

Her chart mirrors the frequent Taurus theme found in masochistic structures. Venus, the ruler of her Taurus Ascendant, is quincunx the Ascendant. Clearly, Melissa has had to make many adjustments and learn new ways to release resentments in her relationships.

Uranus T-squares her Mercury in Scorpio and Taurus Ascendant. This configuration reflects her feeling of rebellion and her urge to experience a sense of autonomy, free from the pressure she has dealt with all her life. The T-square is focused in her 4th House, indicating her father's sudden disappearance.

The emphasis on the 7th House, associated with Libra, is present with her Scorpio Sun and Saturn and Venus in Sagittarius here. The full 7th House is indicative of the tendency to be the "nice girl" and repress outward expressions of anger. Learning to say no to overwhelming pressure has been an ongoing challenge for Melissa. With Sun conjunct Saturn in Scorpio, Melissa is no stranger to adversity or challenge. She rises to the occasion like the eagle, symbol of Scorpio's strength and power.

The Psychopathic Structure

The *psychopathic* structure is formed between ages three and six. Generally, the child has been *controlled by the mother in a manipulative, perhaps seductive, manner*. The father may be physically or emotionally absent. The child, thus, has to be a "little man" and take care of the mother. The child may also be used as a wedge between the parents. Psychopathy is usually found in men, although the structure is not uncommon in women.

The issues of the psychopathic structure revolve around *power, control and one-upmanship*. Because the child has been used in a manipulative way, *s/he learns to perform in order to survive, also learning to displace or deny any feelings of fear, rage or powerlessness*. The illusion of the psychopathic body type is that "I can be independent if I stay in control." There is a lot of suppressed energy and denial in this structure. Underlying the denial is a sense of *helplessness and impotence*.

The psychopathic structure is *charming and seductive. Cleverness* is another key feature. Though often good with words, there is a lack of connection between words and feeling and words and actions. *Overinvestment in ego and in self-image* is another aspect of this body type.

In relationship, the psychopathic structure defends against any sense of dependency. This reflects his/her fear of being used or manipulated as s/he was in childhood. Sexually seductive, this body type displaces all feelings towards the head and the arms to maintain denial and control. There is a *disconnection from the feeling side of relating*. If needed by the partner, s/he has a sense of being powerful.

As an adult, psychopathy will be seen in a body with an *inflated chest, large shoulders and a highly charged head*. All of the energy in the body is displaced toward the upper half of the body. In fact, there is often a sense of a volcano getting ready to explode in the physical structure. The hips, waist and legs may be slender. There is a look of cunning and brightness to the eyes, which quickly changes to wariness and distrust if confronted.

It is important to bear in mind that while the rage of this structure can be destructive and explosive, the psychopathic body type has a lot to be enraged about. Underneath all the bravado, charm and denial is often a frightened child living a nightmare.

The truth is that the overdeveloped upper body hides a *huge heart*. This is the positive aspect of the psychopathic structure. S/he can be a strong humanitarian and defender of the underdog and is often *quite successful and highly productive*. There is a lot of love in this structure, buried underneath the pain.

Astrological Indicators

In the birth chart, the psychopathic structure is indicated by a *predominance of Fire and Water*. The combination of these two elements creates a pressure cooker which, like the volcano, can explode without sufficient safety valves. Fire and Water are also indicative of the potential for deep caring and compassion towards others, which are inherent in this structure.

There can also be an *emphasis on Scorpio, a prominent Pluto or several planets in the 8th House*. Having been manipulated as a child, an emphasis on this theme reveals issues connected to power, denial and control. The psychopathic structure is frequently found in children whose door to his/her private world had only one doorknob—on the outside. S/he had no control over who came in or out of that door. As an adult, s/he is very good at spotting others whose doorknob is fastened to the outside of the door.

Mars is another key planet in the psychopathic structure. The red planet will often be found in a Fire sign, indicative of too much ego and explosive tendencies. Mars may also appear on an angle in the natal chart or as a singleton. The prominent placement of Mars correlates to an overinvestment in self-image. Together, an emphasis on Pluto and Mars reveals the underlying rage of the psychopathic structure.

One further astrological indicator is an emphasis on the *5th, 8th* and *10th Houses*. All three houses are connected to issues of power. In particular, if Mars, Pluto or Scorpio falls in any of these houses and psychopathological behavior is present, it will be more than likely that there is a strong element of psychopathy in the individual.

Psychopathic Case History

Ted is currently married with two children and, after several years in therapy, has created a life for himself free from the horror of his childhood. He has a successful job with a large corporation and owns a home in the country where he is able to focus his enormous energy into home improvement.

The second of two children, Ted was his mother's favorite. By the time he was three years old, sexual difficulties had seriously threatened his parents' marriage. Ted's mother turned to her young son who did, in fact, become her "little man." While she was never overtly sexual with Ted, she was emotionally seductive towards the child.

Meanwhile, Ted's father was busy building his career and often was physically absent from the family. That he was also emotionally absent goes without saying. The sexual tension in the home was palpable, yet neither Ted's mother or father were able to face the issue. Instead, the two children, particularly Ted, served as buffers between the parents.

As a young adolescent, Ted was sexually molested by an older boy in the neighborhood. During much of

Ted's teenage years, he was accosted and propositioned by older men as he hitchhiked around the Midwest. Humiliation and shame grew within him.

Ted remembers feeling powerless and angry during his childhood and adolescence. Tension and jealousy between Ted and his father grew to such a fever pitch that physical fights broke out. Slamming doors and shouting matches were daily fare.

One of the people Ted felt most hostile towards was his older sister. While Ted had been an average student, his sister was bright, popular and active in school affairs. Finally, the subtle comparisons that Ted feels he experienced were too much for him. Embarrassed to admit it now, Ted recalls retaliating by sexually humiliating his sister in their late teen years. It was a classic case of regaining power and one-upmanship, according to Ted.

As an adult, Ted is charming and likeable. His relationships before his marriage centered around sexual conquest. He feels now that he has been able to work through a lot of old humiliation in his relationship with his wife. He is aware of his explosive tendencies and has found healthier outlets for his anger and aggression.

Looking at Ted's birth chart, one is struck by the stellium of planets in Scorpio in the 7th House. Clearly, Ted was one of those children who experienced invasion and manipulation growing up. Much of his energy is focused on relationships with the Sun, Mercury, Saturn, Venus and the Moon posited in the 7th House of relatedness. The ruler of the 4th House, the Moon, and the ruler of the 10th House, Saturn, fall in the 7th House, indicating Ted's experience of being the wedge between his parents in their marriage. Venus, the ruler of his Ascendant, is also in the 7th House and retrograde. Finally, the ruler of his 3rd House of siblings, Mercury, is in the 7th House, revealing his stormy relationship with his sister.

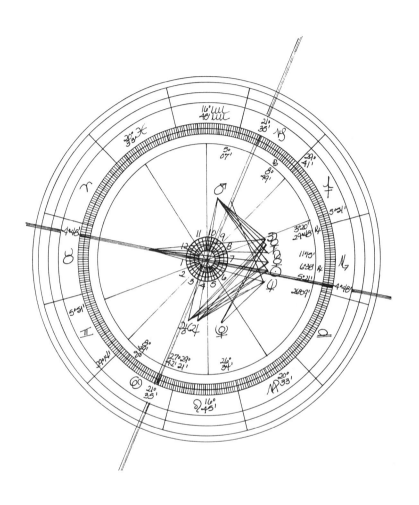

Ted's Chart
Psychopathic Structure

Other indicators of psychopathy found in this horoscope are the abundance of Fire and Water (the pressure cooker), Pluto in the 5th House, and Mars angular in the 10th. All three factors illustrate the rage and sense of impotency masked by the urge to be in control. While Mars is technically not the handle of a bucket formation in the chart, its placement as the only planet in the Eastern Hemisphere gives it a feeling of emphasis.

A final thought about Ted's chart is associated with the T-squares which again connect the 4th House of the father, the 10th House of the mother, and the 7th House of relationships. It has been my experience that T-squares indicate an individual who has gotten caught in the crossfire between the parents. Here, the energy is focused on the Sun and Mercury, which are square to Mars, Uranus and Jupiter. Competition, provocative behavior and argumentativeness are highlighted. Originally, Ted experienced all three between his parents (Mars in the 10th House opposing Uranus and Jupiter in the 4th House). Ingrained in his psyche, now these issues are Ted's to work out through discovering his own road maps and a sense of Self, free from the manipulation and control of his childhood.

The Rigid Structure

The structure of the *rigid* is formed between three-and-one-half and six years old. At this stage of development, the child reaches out to the opposite sex parent for approval and validation of his/her sexual identity. The parent's reaction is often one of fear and rejection, so the child represses him/herself sexually. The key to the rigid structure is *unaccepted sexuality*. Because s/he is seeking love and approval, the youngster will try to please the parent. Under the external pressure of parental "no's" and "should's," the child begins to stiffen.

The *stiffness and holding back* are two main components of the rigid. The child learns to conform. Programmed for success, *individuality and desire for change are repressed*. Thus, much of the structure develops around the issue of *avoiding pleasure*.

Pleasure is minimal because s/he has disconnected heart (love) from genitals (pleasure). This structure *does* receive love and nurturance during childhood. What they do not receive is support for their growing awareness of their sexuality and individuality.

As an adult, the rigid copes effectively in the world. These are the beautiful people—successful, ambitious, powerful and achievement-oriented. *Body image is important* and much attention is focused on attaining the perfect "10" body. The price the rigid pays, aside from plastic surgeon's fees and health club memberships, is the cutting off from human feeling and no sense of individuality. "Stiff with pride" accurately describes the rigid structure!

Physically, the rigid is *grounded and well-proportioned*. S/he carries a good energy charge in his/her body and, consequently, has an appearance of vibrancy. There is, however, a *tightness of the surface* of the body which creates muscular armoring. The function of the armor is to reduce anxiety. The rigid structure simply doesn't breathe deeply. Because so little air reaches the muscles, s/he is protected against deep feelings that might otherwise surface. The tight, energetic body of the rigid maintains the illusion of vitality. Scratch the surface and you'll find depression and lifelessness.

In relationship, the rigid structure is *controlling and manipulative*. These characteristics stem from the pain and rejection experienced in childhood. In order to avoid further betrayal connected to love and sexuality, the split between heart and genitals becomes more pronounced. The illusion of the rigid is that they are completely loving yet unappreciated by others. Unfortunately, they can remain stuck at the emotional age of seven or eight in adult relationships.

Astrological Indicators

Not surprisingly, the natal chart will usually contain a *preponderance of Fixed signs*. Change is difficult for the rigid structure. Maintaining the status quo ensures that the safe structures s/he has created in his/her life aren't threatened.

Often, there will be an *emphasis on Fire* in the horoscope as well as a good representation of the *Earth* element. The combination of Fire and Earth gives the rigid the ability to be successful and productive in the material world. The Fire will be repressed, but it accounts for the vitality associated with this structure and is also the source to tap later in therapy to bring out the playful child within.

The first Saturn square at age seven is when much of the rigid structure solidifies. The push against authority in order to separate and individuate is squelched. Thus, the rigid may never get beyond the structures of Saturn to achieve the individuality of Uranus.

There will be an emphasis on **both** *Leo, the 5th House or the Sun* **and** *Capricorn, the 10th House or Saturn*. This combination may be reflected in the chart in a variety of ways. Just as not all Pisces are schizoids, neither are all Leos and Capricorns rigids! The Sun may be placed in the 5th or 10th House, or Saturn may be conjunct the Sun. Several planets may fall in the 5th and 10th Houses, for example. Saturn may be angular or otherwise pronounced. However the rigid structure is reflected in the chart, the main theme is that *the individual is motivated by wanting recognition, approval or love*. The road to that acceptance is paved with performance and achievement.

Challenging aspects between Venus and Mars are

another indication of rigidity. Because so much of the psychology revolves around sexuality and pleasure, this is understandable. Relatedness, creativity and expression of sexuality make up the arena of the Venus/Mars contact. The rigid structure faces that arena probably much like the Christians faced the lions in the Roman Coliseum. In other words, s/he has a tiger by the tail!

Rigid Case History

Claire grew up in the All-American family. The second of two children, she was born 13 months after her older brother. With Claire's arrival, the family picture was complete.

And it was a picture of the perfect family: handsome father, pretty mother and two healthy, attractive kids. Both parents were educators and both found time to coach Little League and run Camp Fire outings. Outward appearance, the right manners and how you presented yourself were the governing concerns in Claire's growing-up years.

Claire recalls that she sought after and idolized her father. As a child, she remembers trying to be more like her mother in order to win her dad's affection. She respected him and never questioned his authority. Discipline came in the form of reasonable and logical explanations of right and wrong choices. When Claire moved outside the parameters of acceptable behavior, she keenly felt her dad's disappointment.

High expectations from both parents contributed to her fear of rejection if she failed. So Claire never failed. Wanting approval, she was the good girl, the dutiful daughter and the straight-A student. What Claire was really adept at was maintaining the illusion of being good. She learned early to use her charm and good looks to get what she wanted. As long as she kept up appearances and didn't rock the boat, life proceeded smoothly.

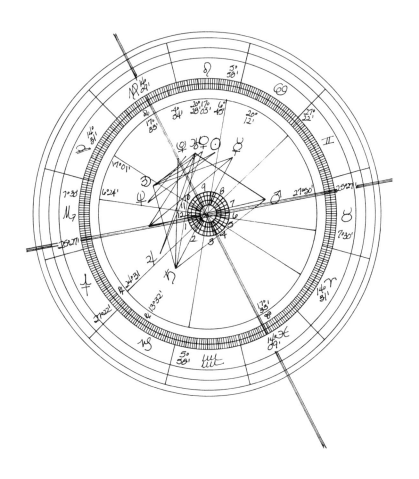

Claire's Chart
Rigid Structure

At 21, Claire married a young man from a different social class and background. Naturally, this was upsetting to her parents, but not nearly as unsettling as her decision to leave her husband two years later. Shortly after their divorce, Claire began to explore lesbian relationships.

Now at 29, she has been in a committed relationship with another woman for four years. She is currently pregnant with her first child. Pregnancy for Claire has been a transformative and sometimes difficult experience. Her body image has obviously changed, and this has not been comfortable for her. She has had to relinquish control and accept the changes her body has undergone.

When we talked about sexual identity, Claire was quite candid about her present feelings. For her, lesbianism is a conscious choice. In relation to her family, it allows her to relate to her dad as an equal, not as someone else's wife. All the distinctions she felt in her childhood between the skills boys were taught (like carpentry, mechanics and plumbing) and the skills girls were taught (like cooking, housekeeping and child-rearing) have had to be redefined by her father in his relationship to her. Claire's dad is forced to recognize her independence and competence. Being a lesbian has also given Claire the freedom to develop a sense of herself as a woman, separate from her mother's feminine values.

Claire's natal chart clearly reflects her rigid structure. She has a preponderance of planets in Fixed signs, including a Scorpio Ascendant. She is strong-willed, self-determined and driven. There is also a T-square to Uranus, planet of individuality, from her Ascendant and Mars in Taurus. The emphasis on Uranus indicates her ability to rebel against the mold dictated by her upbringing. Claire has four planets in Fire signs, which also contribute to her capacity to send her family patterns up in smoke. Combined with three planets in Earth signs, she is highly productive and achievement-oriented. In short, Claire is a go-getter, and her chart shows it.

The horoscope also contains an emphasis of Leo and Capricorn, indicative of the rigid structure. Claire admits to the ongoing struggle of trying to win approval and validation from others. This is not surprising with her Leo Sun and Saturn in Capricorn. As she said, "Everything about me has to be okay." Her Leo planets fall in the 9th House, and the theme of high expectations ran through her conversation about growing up in a family of educators. She was expected to go to college and she never questioned it. She was expected to be a winner, and she is very successful in her position as a university administrator, a fitting 9th House career.

While the Venus/Mars contact in Claire's chart is not exact, the pair are square by sign with Venus in Leo and Mars in Taurus. Claire's choice of an unconventional sexual lifestyle, fueled by the Venus/Mars aspect, is illustrative of the conjunction between Venus and Uranus. The maverick planet, Uranus, plays a key role in Claire's life. With all the changes she has been able to make, it is easy to imagine that Claire will move beyond the constraints of Saturn to the freedom of Uranus.

Practical Approaches to Counseling

So how do we, as counseling astrologers, use the diagnostic information available from character analysis? How can the material be integrated into our astrological practices?

It is important to keep in mind that Reich's and Lowen's theories were intended to be used with in-depth psychotherapy. The counseling astrologer, then, needs to know his/her own limitations in therapeutic situations. And knowing when and where to refer clients is as important as not going beyond our training or skill level.

Having a working knowledge of character analysis enables the astrologer to detect the dynamics inherent in each structure. With this awareness, you can remain detached from the defenses employed by each of the different structures and avoid the possibility of doing further harm to the client.

Schizoid Client

When you work with a schizoid client, be aware that the astrologer serves best as an adjunct to primary psychotherapy done with a skilled professional. However, a foundation can be laid with the schizoid structure that moves him/her onto more solid footing.

Educate this client. Teach him/her how to ground him/herself with both feet firmly planted on the floor. More than a few times I have jumped up from my chair in the middle of a session and demonstrated basic grounding techniques. Recommend exercising like walking, running, biking or swimming. Getting schizoid clients to work with their hands can be invaluable and grounding as well. Pottery, weaving, gardening and woodworking are a few possibilities.

Above all, don't do to your client what has already been done to him/her. In other words, don't confuse or be dishonest with your schizoid client. S/he will easily detect a mixed message or false feeling. Keep the session a little shorter than usual so s/he isn't overwhelmed or inundated with too much information. This is the client whose eyes glaze over after 45 or 50 minutes of interpretation.

Oral Client

The oral client needs to have a clear understanding of how you, the astrologer, work. Be specific about fee schedules and payment. Be definite about how long sessions last. The oral structure may complain about fees or want more of your time, and while it is important not to abandon the oral client, set fair, definite limits.

Suggesting nurturing activities may be beneficial. These may include massage, hot tubs and long, hot baths. Curling up with a comfortable quilt or blanket, rocking in a favorite old rocking chair, drinking herbal teas or sucking on oranges or even baby bottles are also possibilities. I often recommend that the oral client make a list of nurturing behaviors and keep it in a place where s/he can easily refer to it.

In the sessions, it is helpful to ask if the client is getting what s/he wants. "What do you need from me?" is an appropriate way to phrase the question.

Masochistic Client

It may feel frustrating working with the masochistic structure. Don't pressure or push the client. Remember, s/he is in a bind and you can't push or pull him/her out of it. And you don't want to get pulled into it either!

Instead, it is important just to sit with the masochistic client. S/he is frustrated and may provoke a disagreement or argument to experience a sense of release. Validate the pressure s/he feels and be ready to be very patient. Clear limits are crucial with the masochist. Assertiveness training and inner child work are valuable recommendations.

The client may respond to all of your suggestions with "Yes, but." Don't take it as a sign of your incompetence. It is at this point in a session that I begin to agree with the masochistic client that nothing seems to be working. What often happens is that then the client sees the usefulness of your suggestions and will move towards making changes.

Psychopathic Client

Generally, relationship issues prompt the psychopathic structure to make an appointment with a counselor or an astrologer. S/he walks into your office and starts asking you how you are! Gently deflect the questions. Don't let the client take care of you. This is how the psychopathic structure defends against losing control.

Avoid getting into power struggles. If need be, go to your own helplessness and give up your need to be right. The psychopathic client needs to have permission to be direct, not manipulative. Validate his/her needs. Assertiveness training is also helpful for this client. T'ai Chi with its meditative, inner focus is another useful suggestion.

Rigid Client

The rigid structure will try to please you, the astrologer, so it is important for him/her to understand that there are no expectations. Give the rigid client several different options, and then give him/her permission not to do any of them if s/he doesn't want to. Don't reject this client if s/he doesn't follow through on suggestions.

It is often helpful to recommend that s/he make a list of pleasurable activities that are enjoyable to him/her. Play therapy is useful. Non-competitive play is another possibility. Group work with the whimsical, spontaneous child can be suggested. I like to encourage rigid clients to work with their dreams or to do visualizations to reconnect with their inner life. Meditation may help with relaxation.

I also have an internal set of guidelines that I am aware of as I begin counseling with a client. The first rule of thumb I follow is I ask myself *if I like the person*. If I don't, I won't work with him/her. This is also good information for me in my own growth because it may point out aspects of my shadow self that need exploration. Secondly, I look at *my own intentions*. If there are places in my life that are ragged or unraveled, I can't expect fulfillment from the client. Next, I *let go of my need to be right*. Here I have to trust the client and his/her own particular style. My personal belief is that we each hold the answers to our healing within ourselves. I am just the guide to help discover those answers.

It is also important to remember that *there are always three people in the counseling situation* with you. These are the internalized child, the internalized parent and the adult that exist within the client. Just looking at the position of the Moon (internalized child), Saturn (internalized parent) and the Sun (adult) in the birth chart provides a key to the gestalt of the individual.

Another guideline is to *always be where the client is*. Respect who s/he is and what s/he values. To undermine his/her beliefs and attitudes ultimately does more harm than good. It takes a lot of courage to walk into a counselor's or astrologer's office, so respect is a primary consideration.

Listen to your client. One's words and language hold incredible clues to a person's internal make-up. The client's body language, whether relaxed, bored or defensive, is also valuable. I often mirror a client's body language if I sense that s/he is tense or uncomfortable. This simple technique immediately puts him/her at ease.

When I do agree to ongoing counseling, I am very specific in *setting guidelines* with the client. I use a contract that clearly states what my fee is, how long we intend to work together, what my cancellation policy is and how available I am outside the counseling session. I also ask him/her about his/her concerns and expectations. Working together on our mutual concerns builds trust between us.

It is important to have a skilled therapist for *supervision of your work* with clients. This is someone you can consult with regularly. Having the support of a supervisor guarantees the quality of your counseling, and if you get stuck or feel unsure of yourself, the guidance is there to get you back on track with your clients.

I believe that being in counseling yourself is important if you are going to counsel others. As counseling astrologers, we need to continue to grow in our personal as well as our professional lives. Otherwise, we can find only too often that our blind spots get in the way of effective, healing work with others.

Frequently, I begin working with a client through an examination or interpretation of the natal chart. This allows the two of us to identify the issues at hand and to pinpoint what is of concern to the client in the present. It gives the client the opportunity to check me out to see if there is a sense of rapport and an ability to create trust. The initial reading provides me with the necessary information about the client. For both of us, the time spent in an interpretative or educational setting determines whether we can work together effectively or if another form of counseling would be more appropriate for the client.

Astrology involves archetypes and symbols that lend themselves for use in dreamwork, visualization, imagery, Gestalt, journal-writing and art therapy. *Imagery* is a tool that allows clients to move away from the limitations of left-brain interpretation, giving them an opportunity to find related images meaningful to them. The use of planetary imagery supports the old adage that a picture is worth a thousand words. *Gestalt*, verbalizing the internal dialogue, is another useful technique. Giving voice to the planets or subpersonalities that seem to be in conflict with each other provides a creative third solution to be reached which allows all of our selves to be acknowledged. *Journal-writing* is a practical tool which offers the client a place to record and relate insights, dreams and other information gained in the counseling process.

Much has been written about the use of *dreamwork* in therapy. I usually ask my client to select one or two books from a recommended list of titles on dreams and to begin working with his/her dreams. Often, the images that appear in dreams correspond to planetary symbols and reflect current transits and progressions to his/her natal chart.

Art work is an innovative way to work with clients, and one that most clients enjoy. For those who feel intimidated by drawing, I encourage them to recapture the spirit of the six-year-old child who used to color and doodle for hours at the kitchen table. In combining two different approaches formulated by Richard Ideman and Tracy Marks, I've devised an exercise in art therapy. I create an image for each of three planets—the Sun, the Moon and Saturn—representing the adult, the internalized child and the internalized parent. Clients draw each image or a related image on a large sheet of paper. I ask them to label each of the three drawings. The final part of the exercise is to find a phrase or sentence that links all three images. The position of the drawings, the ease or difficulty experienced creating each picture, and the related thoughts and feelings that surfaced while drawing are all good material to work with in the sessions.

Finally, I draw heavily from *mythology* and *symbolism*. I encourage clients to read fairy tales and myths. I ask them which childhood books were their favorites. I tell stories from the ancient myths during sessions. What frequently emerges for the client is a connection to a particular myth that speaks to him/her. That one myth can provide hope as well as direction to the client who discovers that someone else has traveled the same path or explored the same territory that s/he now faces.

It is important for astrologers to embrace different techniques and methodologies to enhance their counseling abilities. Likewise, we must know the limitations of our craft and the extent of our skills. It is probably most valuable to recognize that our clients are our best teachers. Our clients are our source of inspiration.

Doris A. Hebel

Doris has been a full-time professional counseling astrologer in Chicago, IL since 1964. She also counsels clients in New York, Los Angeles, and many points in between.

In 1974 she founded the first Chicago chapter of the National Council for Geocosmic Research and served as Membership Secretary on its national board for five years. Currently, she is involved in establishing the first association for professional astrologers.

She is the author of *Contemporary Lectures* and *Celestial Psychology*, both published by Aurora Press.

BUSINESS COUNSELING

Language is your most valuable tool to efficiently present information in any consultation. Its value in counseling business people is heightened by your *familiarity with the specialized language*, even jargon, of the fields in which your clients operate.

Obviously, none of us could possibly learn all the terminology of every field. Even the often encyclopedic memories of astrologers would quail at that task! Some hints on where to start amassing your business vocabulary:

First, which fields does your own chart indicate you'd be most likely to work in were you not an astrologer? Put another way, what job or career did you follow before becoming an astrologer? Any or all of the areas you list are the first you should focus on for broadening your language skills. For instance, I worked in advertising and publishing before becoming a full-time astrological consultant. Not only do I still attract many clients from these fields but my earlier experience often helps greatly in counseling since I know at first hand some of the conditions encountered or the internal structure of such businesses.

Second, what other interests do you have? Many people find clients in the fields of their own hobbies. You may already have an extensive vocabulary in your personal interest fields. Mine have always been the expressive arts, and I find that many creatively oriented people from various fields make up the bulk of my clientele.

Third, subscribe to magazines and journals published for those in the fields that your chart or your earlier experience points toward. Much valuable information about specific business fields can be learned as you build your vocabulary.

Fourth, read the business sections in your daily newspaper, weekly magazines, and other easily available sources such as the *Wall Street Journal*. Read not so much to keep up on what's happening to specific companies, but to grasp trends in specific industries or fields. Building a general business and financial vocabulary becomes much easier when you understand some of what's going on. Remember, you aren't trying to turn yourself into a whiz of a financial or business consultant; you are acquiring language to enable you to communicate more effectively with your clients. Any specific industry "catch phrase" (if you thoroughly understand it) can condense your explanations to a client. Your apt use of slang, idiomatic phrases, proverbs and quotations also can assist in getting information through to the person you are counseling.

Finally, ask your clients for specific feedback; ask them to let you know how a particular business situation worked out, and match their reports to the forecasting techniques you've used for that period. You'll learn even more about how the planets, signs, houses and aspects function in such particular circumstances and/or in a general business trend.

Personal Style and Presentation

Always dress and behave in a professional business manner. Business people feel more comfortable consulting an astrologer who doesn't look like a holdover from the '60s or a New Wave punker! The only times you may dress more casually are when doing weekend or holiday consultations.

Your office also should project the most comfortable but businesslike atmosphere you can devise, even if you work in your home. In such a case, it's smart to have a separate and specific place for your consultations, much as other professionals do when consulting at home. In other words, don't interpret your client's chart while sitting around the kitchen table or on the couch in your living room. These areas should be for family or social use only. If you can't have a separate office at home, set up an office space in one corner of a public room in your house or apartment.

Presenting yourself in a businesslike way also has an immediate advantage for you—it will, with time, help you to focus your mind on the consultation at hand, rather than on whatever family or personal issues may be important to you, before your client arrives.

What to Leave Out

Most astrologers are used to dealing with the "big three"—love, money and health. In emphasizing business concerns, "love" becomes "satisfactions," and the others retain their usual importance, or even become of primary importance. Most business clients don't want to hear about anything spiritual or metaphysical, and they certainly don't want you to lecture them about ethics or inject your own moral beliefs and judgments.

Since many astrologers do believe that spiritual, psychological and ethical considerations should influence business circumstances, *watch for important transits and progressions through the client's 12th House* to bring up these nuances. At such a time, the client often senses an internal emptiness, mentions strong feelings of apathy, or complains that life doesn't seem to have as much zing to it as usual. This is the time when s/he is very open to a non-judgmental exploration of opportunities for personal growth and enrichment. Any transit of Saturn, Neptune or Pluto over personal points and planets can offer a similar opportunity for the astrologer to discuss personal growth.

Natal *Saturn* and *Neptune* in the client's chart also show where the client can, and perhaps should, make *contributions of time and energy to society*. A lawyer client of mine was distressed that he and his wife had chosen not to have children. Since he had Saturn in the 1st House and Neptune in the 5th, I suggested that if he did some volunteer work with kids or for children's organizations he would probably be able to deal with his distress more effectively. Since he also had Neptune opposite Mars, he chose to coach a Little League team and later donated some of his professional expertise to a charitable organization concerned with children's issues. He reported back about two months after starting coaching that he hardly ever felt upset about not having children anymore.

These kinds of suggestions to clients not only help them personally, it adds to the betterment of society. But don't make a crusade in telling every business client this kind of information. Wait until s/he tells you or hints at some lack in personal contentment.

Maintaining an objective point of view as you offer counseling on personal growth is imperative to avoid alienating the client. Make no value judgments, and suggest several possible alternatives the client can explore in effectively addressing any hidden personal needs.

Example: The client has transiting Saturn conjunct natal Mars in the 6th House. In addition to exploring the probable aggravation and frustration of getting the job done, dealing with coworkers, staff, working conditions or colleagues, and guarding the health, you may also suggest that the client give some thought to confronting an underlying pattern of negative Martian energy that can manifest as anger, hostility or excess competitiveness. You may think that the best or only truly effective way would be through, say, psychotherapy. This is where you would do best to remember to offer several alternatives in keeping with the planetary energy, such as learning (Saturn) a new exercise program or sport (Mars), rekindling an interest in athletics (Mars) from the past (Saturn), talking about problems with a valued mentor (Saturn), taking energy (Mars) vitamins and healthy foods to counteract the tamping-down effect of Saturn, getting body work like massage or rolfing to release long-held (Saturn) tensions in the muscles (Mars) and, of course, any other suggestions you can think of appropriate to the Saturn/Mars aspect in the 6th House. This gives the client leeway in choosing a remedy for the situation, and doesn't close the client's mind to the whole issue if s/he happens to be one of the many people who believe that going to a psychotherapist denotes craziness, shows weakness, or is somehow shameful.

While it is likely that a person with Venus in or ruling the 2nd, 6th, or 10th Houses may have work-associated romances and possible marriages, that's certainly not uppermost in the business client's mind. You do need to point out, however, that in speaking of satisfaction with work, colleagues, career or attaining recognition, we may also be speaking about opportunities for romance, or if the client is happily wed, temptations to be ignored. It is often helpful to tell your client that although a traditional

212 / Astrological Counseling

interpretation of this placement means a romance at work, nowadays it more often can point to *a need to love one's work* or *to seek work that can give real inner satisfaction* so as to avoid job- or career-hopping. Since women's liberation, many young female professionals abhor the idea of having a romance with someone they work with or for, so the older astrological interpretations don't necessarily apply in the same way as before.

More than anything else, choose words in describing sensitive issues that do not leave the client feeling you've made a negative value judgment about him/her!

House Interpretation

Not only is the *10th House* the highest in a chart, it is supreme when doing business consultations. We are all familiar with the 10th House representing the client's boss and/or the company for which the client works. But the astrologer also needs to *reinterpret the other houses in relation to the 10th House.*

When a client is self-employed, owns/runs a business, is a career-oriented person, is a professional in any field, or conducts him/herself as a professional, the 10th House and the other house meanings derived from it have even more impact and can reveal a great deal both in initial interpretation and forecasting.

10th House – The boss, the company, your career, profession, reputation, and standing in your field.

11th House – As the 2nd from the 10th House, this represents your *income from business, career or profession.* It's also the results of your 10th House activity, for when a significant transit or the progressed Moon goes through the 11th House, you often reap the results of what you did or the attitude you projected when that same planet was in your 10th House.

This is especially noticeable with transits of *Jupiter* and *Saturn*, the most clearly business-oriented planets.The results of hard work and intensive commitment to career or company come when either of these planets transit the 11th, rather than the 10th, House. Saturn especially, since it is noted for delay, will show its ability to reward one for a job well done as it passes through the 11th. Interestingly, having counseled quite a few people for the whole period that Saturn was in transit through the 9th, 10th and 11th Houses, I've noticed that the client doesn't want to make a change even if s/he is clearly "dead-ended" at a present position while Saturn is in the 9th House and much, if not all, of the 10th. S/he will wait until Saturn is late in the 10th House or deeply into the 11th House before switching jobs. How typical of Saturn!

In other cases, the benefits to the client come when either Jupiter or Saturn transits the 10th House, and they often continue in the form of income raises as the planets go through the 11th House. Or, perhaps some other form of recognition, improvement, or matters of value to the client come about in business life at these times. Frequently, there are promotions, even the attainment of upper-management positions (especially vice-presidencies) or the achievement of becoming the head or assistant head of a department, provided the client has "paid his/her dues" or is exceedingly well prepared, both Saturnian conditions. Jupiter can bring "luck" by elevating a worker before s/he can actually handle the job efficiently, though. When this occurs, the client needs to know not to "rest on his/her laurels" but work hard to develop the qualities that will enable him/her to retain this position after transiting Jupiter moves on.

Sometimes, of course, no particular improvement occurs when these planets transit through the 10th or 11th Houses. Occasionally, there are even firings! When one is fired under a Jupiter transit (yes, it does happen more than we might initially think!), the implication is that there is something better around the corner, or at least a new position won't be too difficult to find. True to Jupiter's expansive nature, sometimes several jobs must be attempted before finding the right match, and finding many positions usually presents no difficulty.

When a client is fired under a Saturn transit through either the 10th or 11th Houses, it's often a negative reward for a lack of commitment to the boss, company or position—at least in the eyes of the company! Clients will often admit to just "marking time" or not being challenged, yet not asking for any opportunities either, prior to being fired under this transit.

In cases where nothing of import comes about for the client under these transits or the progressed Moon through the 10th and 11th Houses, it points to the client as a "job-holder" or 6th House type, no matter how elevated his/her position might be! Even entrepreneurs whose companies don't show much change during such transits or progressions are likely to be 6th House types.

When a client is a 6th House type worker, the transits or progressions through the 10th and 11th Houses refer to what's going on either with the boss or with the company itself.

12th House – The most important thing the astrologer needs to do in interpreting the 12th House within the business context is to completely forget its unfortunate reputation in ordinary natal terms! The 12th is the 3rd House from the 10th, primarily representing the *daily climate of the company, the boss's attitude and communication abilities, and the internal structure of the company or organization.*

Many people with positive natal 12th House placements do extremely well working for corporations. Those clients with *Mars* or *Uranus*, and sometimes *Neptune* or *Pluto*, in the 12th may be better suited to free-lancing if they have the drive for it as they will often encounter major communication difficulties with bosses or dislike the way the company is run.

The term *institution*, commonly used in natal astrology to describe 12th House places, can be expanded in business astrology to describe those companies or organizations that, by virtue of their longevity or influence, are considered to be institutions by consensus among the general public or by the cognoscenti within a particular field or geographic area. Examples are Sears, Roebuck and Co., the *New York Times*, and Marshall Field's department store. Major companies or organizations in the client's view or geographic area also are likely to be appropriate 12th House denizens.

Many clients with natal 12th House Jupiter placements have become vice-presidents or attained other high advancement in their companies as early as their late thirties or early forties.

A client who owns his own real-estate development corporation has natal Saturn in Gemini in his 12th House. When transiting Saturn opposed, he won a bid to build roads in a neighboring state. In this case, the state was the 10th House (the boss), and the roads within that state probably couldn't be astrologically described more perfectly than by Saturn in Gemini in the 3rd House from the 10th!

A very large percentage of people work at jobs that are 12th House focused since their contribution to their companies or organizations is useful totally within the internal structure of the employer. These people rarely have empty 12th Houses. Those with many planets in the natal 12th House either have several different jobs within a company in the course of their employment there, try different duties at subsequent jobs, or continue to perform the same basic work but move from job to job, and not necessarily quickly.

When a client is employed by a company and also does free-lance work on the side, this additional work's potential is shown by the 12th House.

1st House – Since this is the 4th House from the 10th, it represents the *home of the company*. That can mean the "home office" if a client works for an organization that has branches, but it most frequently means where the company is locally. When aspects to the Ascendant or 1st House planets indicate a change or move, there also have to be appropriate 4th House aspects if the client is moving to a different home. When there are only 1st House change aspects, it's often the company that moves, with the client moving into a new office or space in the company or other changes at the office affecting the client. When a client moves his/her own business and works at home, the same rule usually applies. When the business is client-owned but not located in the client's home, a 1st House change aspect can still show some alteration in the status of the office.

2nd House – As this is the 5th House from the 10th, it represents any *investment* a company makes, and it also seems to show the company's *stock*. The most dramatic examples of this that I've encountered so far involved multimillion-dollar situations.

For some years I've been the astrological consultant for many upper-level management executives. In 1981, one of these executives came in for a yearly update. The client's chart held natal Jupiter in Libra in the 2nd House, one of the planets in a T-cross with Uranus and Pluto, all involving financial houses. The client was, at that time, a very senior vice-president at one of the nation's leading banks. During 1982, the transiting Saturn/Pluto conjunction would conjunct my client's natal Jupiter and set off the T-cross. Although the thought crossed my mind several times, I simply could not accept the idea that the bank was going to be in trouble, so I soft-pedaled the interpretation.

Along came 1982, and indeed the bank was revealed to be in so much trouble that it became the first of the major "bail-out" cases the government supported. The trouble was caused by the client's bank extending too much credit to another bank (actually a type of investment), so when the smaller bank was put out of business because of bad loans, the ripple effect hit the larger bank in its weakest spot. I immediately called my client to apologize for not emphasizing the danger enough. I learned never to think that any institution is impervious to ruin.

In the second case, I learned that the term *"cash flow"* *clearly applies to transiting Saturn through the 2nd House*. In early 1983, a self-made millionaire client of mine had transiting Saturn recently enter his 2nd House at the time he first consulted me. To expect that he would experience any great *personal* diminishment of his income during this transit was unlikely, unless he was completely irresponsible, and since he had built his own fortune he'd demonstrated his financial expertise. However, because he identified strongly with his business, when I suggested he may still need to "tighten the belt" in fiscal matters, he responded with the information that he was taking his company public and issuing stock for the first time. He said he was prepared to "run a tight ship" for several years, and as I told him when transiting Saturn would leave his 2nd House, he confirmed that that would be about the time his company could expect to get back to normal. Based on transiting Saturn entering his natal 3rd

House but then retrograding back into the 2nd House, I told him that although there would be some "lightening up" major matters of concern would still occupy his financial problem-solving abilities for the coming three years until Saturn finally left his 2nd House, and I asked for feedback.

Two-and-a-half years later when he returned for an update, transiting Pluto was in his 2nd House, beginning its square to his natal Pluto in the 11th House. I see Pluto in mergers and acquisitions, and in leveraged buy-outs (LBO). Since transiting Saturn was returning to his 2nd House within the "be careful" time period, he wanted my comments on his plans to acquire several more companies in an LBO. Saturn was trine natal Jupiter in his 10th House at this time, and would again trine after it became established in the 3rd House, so I judged that the transiting Pluto square natal Pluto from the 2nd to the 11th House would pay off big, as indeed it did. More time was needed to "free up" the natal 2nd House with the LBO, but he has officially become a billionaire.

For most of your business clients, however, slow transits through the 2nd House will affect the company's stocks, require the client to handle all his/her own personal resources differently, and may bring financial "perks" to the client through the employing company's changing attitudes toward bonuses or stock-option plans. Or, the client's "perks" may be reduced during the difficult financial times we are facing through the 1990s.

Many long-term successful businesses have been founded with Saturn transiting the 2nd House of the founder, but in my experience the founder in question always "knew the territory." People who are eager to start their own companies under such a transit need to pay attention to any gaps or lacks in their abilities or understanding of the field or market they hope to enter. The astrologer can best serve these clients by advising them to be ruthless with themselves in judging where they need additional strength before opening their own business. Remember that one invests time, energy, talent and money in establishing a business. All this rightly illustrates that the 2nd House is the 5th House from the 10th House!

3rd House – This house holds a double-whammy as it is the 6th House from the 10th as well as the 10th from the 6th. I can only assume that most people who consulted astrologers when the astrology books of the last 150 years were being written were not in business or not concerned about business matters since I don't recall ever reading any descriptions of the 3rd House that referred to business. The closest you might come is the statement that the 3rd House has to do with "everyday matters." Yes, indeed it does! Since most adults now work at jobs rather than the old male/female split between work and home, the 3rd House has really come into its own. It represents the *work you do for the company* as well as the *reputation you gain* through your job. Many charts give a clearer picture of the work a client does if you include the 3rd House along with the usual 2nd, 6th and 10th Houses.

The 3rd House still means local travel and communications, but judged by the client's standards, not the astrologer's. For a client who has never traveled very far from home, the 3rd House means the town or city s/he lives in, while for a client who has traveled more extensively, the 3rd House can involve statewide, regional or even national proportions. Be sure to ask the client what his/her perception of "local" encompasses, then apply the same criteria to local communications.

For instance, during a transit of Jupiter through the 3rd House, advertising, marketing, selling, publicity and word-of-mouth on a local level is highlighted and should bring the client more business benefit. Or legal issues may arise locally. Depending on how wide a geographic area involved, you can advise your client to look for a job, expect reward in the job they currently hold, increase profit by communications, or guard against legal snarls more effectively.

For a "job-holder" or 6th House type as opposed to a "career track" or 10th House type client, activation of the 3rd House can enhance *or reduce* one's worth as an employee since it is the reputation s/he has, based on his/her working record. So, when tough transits move through the 3rd House, the client needs to work harder or show more commitment to the job or company, else s/he runs the risk of being "dead-ended" or fired.

Companies often expand or contract their staffs when the 3rd House of a client's chart is activated by appropriate transits. Unless the client's 6th House is involved, there is no sure reason to expect that his/her job or department will be directly affected.

4th House – As the 7th House from the 10th, it represents the *clients or customers of the company* a client works for, but not necessarily those your client will deal with directly. This house can also show the company's *competitors* or other companies or individuals the employer may choose as a *partner*. In some cases, it shows the merger or takeover opponent.

It is also the 10th House from the 10th House of the 10th House! Wow! We're going to get dizzy running around the chart locating bosses! When your client is far removed from more direct contact with upper management, it is sometimes useful to indulge in such a runaround, but I've more often just used the 10th House to suggest what the company will do or how it will affect the client. This is obviously much easier and generally accurate enough.

Lawyers used or needed by the company show up

here, and this house also represents the company's standing among its peers.

Furthermore, this house shows circumstances pertaining to the *mate of the boss*. Whether or not you'll use it this way should depend on any questions you get from your client about such an individual, but it borders on a gray ethical area for you to speculate about a boss's spouse without a prompt from your client. Sometimes it's gray even if you do get such a question! Astrologers new to consulting are often carried away by the chart's ability to give information, so keep in mind that the privacy of an individual not directly important to a client shouldn't be breached. And in a case where the individual is important to your client, concern yourself only with the direct business situation.

5th House – As the 8th from the 10th House, it represents *taxes or insurance* the company must pay. It can also be used for information that points to possible *external financial sources,* such as loans or grants.

6th House – Being the 9th House from the 10th, it shows the company's *overall philosophy of business*. Increasingly in these days of global business, this house can indicate *potential international ties* for the company. In many charts, this house will reflect what the company may undertake in opening or closing any branches "elsewhere." The term *elsewhere* seems to work very well in describing any people or activity that isn't local. I've found that traditional astrological language is often too cumbersome or opaque for today's need for quick understanding.

The company's *legal affairs* and activities come under the jurisdiction of this house, and it also represents the *Board of Directors*.

7th House – Being the 10th House from the 10th, this house shows the company's *reputation* in the wider sense, its "larger public," if you like. It also shows the boss's boss, or *upper management*. I often use this house to indicate the CEO, the Chairman of the Board, or the Executive Committee.

8th House – Since it is the 11th House from the 10th, it indicates the company's *goals* or aims. Any *external supporters* or "friends" the company may have also show up here.

9th House – As the 12th House from the 10th, it depicts everything that goes on "behind the scenes" in the life of the company. Clients with planetary emphasis here often become active in the *preparation stages* of new projects undertaken by the company. Unseen, *internal stumbling blocks* the company may eventually have to deal with are also illustrated by this house.

When appropriate transits go through the 9th House, your client may do well to either expand his/her *education* for future business success or become more involved in the education or training of others. It describes any post-graduate work the company, organization or career track requires for the client to advance.

Planetary Influence

In forecasting, certain planets may be of more importance than others. Usually the slower-moving planets, from Jupiter out to Pluto, bring more emphasis than the faster-moving ones. However, eclipses that contact any natal planet or sensitive point by hard aspect or the retrograde periods of Mercury, Venus and Mars when they activate a primary business sector also impact the chart.

Solar eclipses may offer new opportunities, starting within a year or two after they occur, while *Lunar eclipses* usually show the necessity for letting go of attitudes and behavior that are outmoded. The three-month period that surrounds any set of eclipses is the most intense but usually doesn't accurately communicate the final picture. For six or seven weeks before and after eclipses, new opportunities that develop unexpectedly are probably not reliable. You can, however, point out to your client that if s/he wishes to make changes s/he can do so around the eclipses, provided the changes are in keeping with the symbology of the planets and houses activated by the eclipse and if s/he has done his/her "groundwork" sufficiently well. In any case, eclipse periods stir business waters very dramatically.

Stations of outer planets and retrograde periods of inner ones or major transiting mutual aspects between outer planets that occur during the three-month eclipse intensives further upset the equilibrium in the business world or within a company. Most of the panic calls I get from clients come during such times. In almost every situation, things calm down after the six or seven weeks following a set of eclipses.

Retrograde periods of Mercury, Venus and Mars are best used for what I call "fine tuning." The client can best utilize his/her time and energy by correcting any known weaknesses or soft spots in his/her work or attitude, or if s/he has responsibility for others in the work place, encourage such cleanup in the activities of the staff. Since business is ongoing despite such planetary events, emphasize the need for patience, consistent application and the value of repetition to effectively accomplish daily tasks.

Over the years I've noticed that many major changes come about under the ***retrograde motion of the outer planets contacting a natal or progressed position for the final time***. The ultimate disposition of events that occur at such times is often positive, so it seems that the idea of "fine tuning" on inner planet retrogrades applies to the outer planets as well, but in a larger context. With Uranus, Neptune and Pluto, this process may take several years, but if the client takes the appropriate action during the last retrograde, success seems assured by the time the planet moves forward to contact the natal or progressed position for the last time.

Another oddity is what I call *the midpoint in time*. This happens when a transiting planet is making the same aspect repeated times. Let's say the aspects occur in February, June and November of a given year. There are then two midpoints in time: one between February and June and the second between June and November. Even though the transiting planet is not *actually* making the aspect during the midpoint-in-time months, clients continually present feedback that circumstances appropriate to the nature of the planets involved often show themselves during these periods.

Jupiter brings *opportunity* and generally increases the effects of the house it is transiting and the planets it contacts. Overconfidence and overextending oneself or a situation are its usual pitfalls. However, if there are other more difficult planets at work at the same time as Jupiter, it can increase the negative effect of the other planets unless great care is taken. Sometimes difficult circumstances come about solely under Jupiter, but they are often easier to correct or recover from than those of other planets.

Saturn's most frequent negative effect in business is *delay*. When clients get frustrated because of such delays, it's often helpful if they concentrate on strengthening their talents and abilities or on filling in the gaps in their business knowledge. Sometimes the delay in accomplishing goals is directly attributable to such lacks or weaknesses. Of course, Saturn can also bring the successful culmination of projects and long-range goals. It only seems to do this, however, when there has been a great deal of concentrated, dedicated and sincere effort over a long period of time. Saturn can bring about improved conditions or opportunities that the client wanted but was denied so far in the past that s/he hardly remembers them!

Finally, Saturn can just simply say *no*—whether that no comes directly from a person or in the form of an opportunity or achievement denied or unrealized, the client needs to simply get on with life and find a new direction, field or company in which to accomplish new goals. Saturn usually denies because, in the long run, it is best. This is a very difficult concept for many people to accept, and often they become convinced that no amount of effort will ever produce the results they want, so they become part of the great number of people who simply go through the motions of life rather than mobilizing themselves to try again elsewhere.

Saturn presents challenges which, when successfully met, reward the individual—later, it's true—but with a type of recognition or a sense of satisfaction that s/he probably wouldn't have had at the earlier stage.

Uranus represents not only the potential for a new direction but it can be the primary indication for *diversifying*. Although it can certainly act in its well-known unpredictable style, the most frequent manifestation in business is a need to add something new to the present mix or to strike out in new directions.

When this urge is not recognized or is resisted, tension is produced. That's when the more difficult but familiar tendency of Uranus to "throw out the baby with the bath water" may take over. Most clients who broaden their scope with new information, techniques, products or services under the influence of Uranus benefit immediately in the reduction of negative tension that can lead to disruption or contribute to unhealthy physical conditions. "New" means new to the client, not necessarily especially new in the world.

Many people who have never had any direct dealings with computers or telecommunications equipment do so when transiting or progressed Uranus becomes powerful in their charts. One client of mine clung to an old rotary dial telephone because it was familiar and inexpensive. It also demanded her immediate attention every time it rang because she didn't have an answering machine or an answering service. Finally, so many of her clients complained about the interruptions that she acquired not only an answering machine but a speakerphone and a remote handset telephone. Now she feels more efficient and even enjoys using her new "toys." Perhaps most importantly, her clients have stopped complaining.

When Uranus is disruptive, it is doubtful that conditions will return to their previous state. Often the need for a change of position, company or field is necessary even though forced, such as is currently happening in many industrial fields. Workers in many industries are pursuing or should pursue retraining in different fields to promote job security in the future.

The influence of the three outer planets is often felt in major shifts in particular fields rather than just within one company.

Neptune is the one I call the "mess-up" planet to my clients. If there is anything that can go wrong, it will under the influence of Neptune. I've rarely encountered a client who has gone through a Neptune transit without some degree of agony. Frequently, the distress is prolonged and enervating.

Dissatisfaction with current conditions is the least unpleasant of Neptune's effects. Most frequently, *disillusionment* with the sabotage or jealousy of coworkers, *ineffective or unethical management*, or the *dissolving* or crumbling of expectations as well as of projects are the primary effects of a Neptune contact in the business world. Clients feel helpless or apathetic in the face of such circumstances, and this attitude can lead to removing the joy in other areas of life as well. Facing up to one's unrealistic expectations or outright illusions while not becoming cynical or losing heart to pursue better circumstances needs encouragement.

Ethics and standards don't seem to exist if we only believe what the news media present to us. In reality, however, many clients are concerned that the lax ethical climate in business can ultimately endanger their position as employers demonstrate little loyalty toward staff. Clients who employ or manage people are appalled at the lack of concern that employees show over doing a good job, or are disadvantaged by thievery.

Encouraging clients to never "cut corners" despite what goes on around them and explaining that the only way to create a climate of true integrity throughout life is for each of us to operate as "cleanly" as we can in any given area often comforts clients, employed as well as employers, who are frequently exposed to the poor ethics or working habits of others. Such circumstances will probably continue to be a serious issue as Neptune transits Capricorn through 1998.

Pluto, even before it was discovered, lent its name to a maligned and feared class of society—the plutocrats—those massively rich and powerful men who had built their wealth on the labors of workers without compensating or protecting them adequately. Not so different today, wouldn't you say? New fortunes seem to be made today by acquiring other companies, sometimes stripping their assets.

Pluto shows its hand in *mergers and acquisitions, leveraged buy-outs, and hostile takeovers* as well as more benign conditions, such as the opening or closing of branches, reorganizations, and "boom or bust" and "great oaks from little acorns grow" situations. *Power-wielding special-interest groups* such as unions and lobbies, as well as all levels of government, are also represented by Pluto.

Frequently, Pluto will connect with a natal factor three or more times. As yet, I haven't seen Pluto reverse its influence during such a cycle. So, the "boom or bust" indicators are present right at the beginning of a Pluto transit and continue throughout the cycle unless the client takes drastic action.

In a *"boom"* cycle, the only action a client needs to take is to be sure s/he is growing along with the company, department or individual job so as not to become obsolete soon after the growth slows. If your client owns a company or heads a department, the biggest challenge in "boom" times is to relinquish complete control and hire additional competent people to whom the client turns over much responsibility. Pluto is often as unable to do this as Saturn.

If the cycle starts with *"bust"* indicators, the biggest challenge to the client is to let go or make major downscale changes as soon as possible. Human nature often resists making a thoroughgoing change at the beginning of a bad cycle. Most often clients will "hang in there," hoping there will be a turnaround. But unless there's some major help from other planets, a Pluto "bust" cycle may wind up with the client holding an empty bag symbolically. For an employee, this may mean looking for a new job. For a company owner, it means finding a merger partner, cutting back ruthlessly, or closing the doors forever.

In the "great oaks from little acorns grow" scenario, we have a *new specialty* developing within a field as the most frequent manifestation. A recent example from the medical field: Some years ago, environmental allergies were so rare most medical practitioners denied their existence. Today, there is a growing medical specialty totally devoted to such conditions. Those doctors who had the courage to believe what their patients told them, and later what their own investigations showed them in the face of massive resistance from their colleagues, were in the vanguard of establishing this new specialty.

These opportunities can be recognized by a client in the following ways: 1) they find a new concept intriguing and most others deride it 2) in a few years they start meeting other people (the start of a special-interest group) who have the same or similar interests or points of view and 3) they still have to go it alone in their daily working life. Only once the new concept proves its worth in everyday reality by making money (Jupiter and Saturn again, our primary business planets) will there be a big enough "critical mass" to enable the new idea to sweep the country or the field the client operates within.

Since Pluto often puts one at the mercy of circumstances, the majority of clients simply have to adjust to the changes brought about in their working lives by the moves, both literal and figurative, that the company they work for makes during a Pluto cycle in the client's own chart. Often the situation is one where the client actually has no real power and must adjust or bust!

Special Charts
So far, we have considered only the client's natal chart. In many consultations that is quite enough, but when additional effort is called for there are two other types of charts that are useful, and in one case, necessary!

They are company charts and election charts.

Company Charts

If a client works for one of the Fortune 500 firms or for one of 750 other companies that have stock traded over the counter, two books by Carol Mull have noon charts for these companies.

Noon charts are calculated for noon standard time at the location in which the company was incorporated using the date of incorporation. Noon is used because the Sun will be somewhere around the Midheaven, the start of the primary business house.

I prefer to use a Sun conjunct Midheaven chart with the Sun in the 10th House. If you have a computer, you just keep running charts until you get one close enough if your calculation program doesn't have an option for setting the Sun at the Midheaven. Usually I do such a Sun conjunct Midheaven chart on the spot just after a client gives me the company's birth date.

Set up the chart by noting the latitude of the city of incorporation or the location of the company. Estimate the approximate degree and minute of the Sun at midday, and place it with the correct sign on the Midheaven. The other house cusps come directly from your Table of Houses for the proper latitude. Then, just estimate the other planets on the birthday and insert them where they belong.

You can use the same technique to set up speculative charts for a client's boss or the leaders of the company if your client gives you their birthdays. Use the latitude of the city where the business is located unless your client also tells you where the individual was born.

These charts can be compared to your client's for greater insight into his/her working relationships. The house cusps of these charts are responsive to transits even though what we are working with is speculative.

The company's birthday is usually the date of incorporation. Some companies haven't incorporated, however, so you use the date they opened for business, the date they were founded or, where appropriate, the date of reorganization, renaming, merger or acquisition.

If you have the time, doing a chart for the day and time your client started working at his/her current job can be very useful. Speculative charts of coworkers or of prospective employees can also be utilized, but in these cases put the Sun of the other person on the 6th House cusp and proceed as above in setting up the rest of the cusps and planets. In the case of a business partner when the birth time isn't known, set the partner's Sun on the cusp of the 7th House and proceed accordingly.

Election Charts

Covering this subject appropriately requires a book in itself! And since such books do exist, do learn the techniques of this method, for you can expand your value to your client immeasurably by having this option.

In most business consultations, time and money are major considerations, so election charts are not the general rule. However, I offer them to my business clients when they are opening or moving a business, signing a contract or lease, or entering a business partnership. In most cases when the client is simply anticipating a job change, the transits and progressions to the natal chart coupled with choosing a date in an appropriate New Moon cycle is sufficient because the starting time is almost always defined by the regular business hours of the company.

Donna Cunningham

Donna Cunningham has a Master's in Social Work from Columbia University and 25 years' experience counseling people in a variety of settings. In her private psychotherapy practice she has worked extensively with people who are recovering from addictions, with adult children of alcoholics, and with incest survivors. She has pursued astrology, metaphysics, healing, and other spiritual studies for 20 years.

Donna has gained recognition in the field of astrology for her eight books, her lectures and workshops at national and international conferences, and her private consultations. With her psychic co-author, Andrew Ramer, Donna has collaborated on two books about addiction: *The Spiritual Dimensions of Healing Addictions* and *Further Dimensions of Healing Addictions*, both released by Cassandra Press in 1988.

She is also the editor and publisher of *Shooting Star*, the independent flower essence quarterly integrating astrology and the remedies.

THE ADULT CHILD SYNDROME, CODEPENDENCY, AND THEIR IMPLI- CATIONS FOR ASTROLOGERS

Codependency is a major self-help buzz word, and groups for codependents and adult children of alcoholics (ACAs) are spreading throughout the country. People are talking a great deal about defining boundaries. Since you'll be hearing these terms from clients, you need to be familiar with them. I will discuss how these concepts apply to astrology clients, including chart patterns to look for. Case examples using the charts of some famous people are given. You'll also find out about resources to which you can refer your clients. In addition, I'll look at ways codependency or being an ACA yourself can influence your work.

What is Codependency?

Codependency is an *addiction to an addict or to some other person*. The obsession with trying to help or change that individual grows in strength until it takes over your life, giving you no peace. It doesn't change just because that person leaves; instead, it can become a pattern carried over to new relationships. Melody Beattie, in her best seller *Codependent No More*, defined it this way: "A codependent is one who has let another person's behavior affect him or her, and who is obsessed with controlling that person's behavior."[1]

The term *codependency* originally derived from the

233

field of chemical dependency and applied to families and significant others of alcoholics and addicts. Because of the way they grow up, almost all untreated adult children of alcoholics form codependent relationships with mates, lovers, family members, friends, and even bosses. In particular, they tend to get involved with one alcoholic or addictive personality after another. Alternately, they may stay away from codependency by staying away from committed relationships.

Rather than lavish all that energy on fixing *one* person, many ACAs work long, poorly paid hours in service fields like astrology where they may play the role of *rescuer*. There's nothing wrong with service, but when it's compulsive and driven by codependent needs it can ultimately be damaging to both practitioner and client.

ACAs aren't the only people who develop codependency. It can evolve at any stage of life when you love someone who has a severe physical or emotional problem. Parents aren't the only source—it could happen if a beloved brother started using drugs or a mate began drinking alcoholically. Grandchildren of alcoholics can also have the full-blown ACA syndrome, even when the parents are teetotalers. The grandparent passes it on to the parent, who passes it on to the child.

Many traits common to ACAs apply to members of severely dysfunctional families as well. It's been estimated (Lord knows by whom) that 95 *per cent* of all families are dysfunctional to some degree. I'm not talking about your average unfulfilling, emotionally illiterate, uncommunicative parents who don't validate your creativity or worth. I'm referring to families where there was physical or sexual abuse or where a parent was chronically and severely physically or mentally ill. It can happen where a parent died early or committed suicide, where a parent was a gambler or promiscuous, or where there were other severe or bizarre eruptions and disruptions. It could happen if your bedridden grandmother lived with you and her illness controlled the entire family, or if your sister was a child schizophrenic.

Beattie's book *Codependent No More* was on the *New York Times* best seller list for more than a year, so many people suffer from this problem. Robin Norwood's *Women Who Love Too Much* was on the list for more than two years, and Janet Woititz's *Adult Children of Alcoholics* was listed for over a year.

Codependency has been growing in recognition since Neptune entered Capricorn but gained widespread professional and popular recognition during the *Neptune/ Saturn conjunction*. Saturn represents boundaries and limits and Neptune represents the dissolving of them, so defining boundaries and learning to set limits became issues in the world at large. In particular, this seems to be an issue for the Neptune in Libra generation for whom that perfect relationship has been the Santa Claus that never came.

As recognition of codependency grows, so does knowledge of how to get free. There are many helpful books on recovery from codependency and the adult child syndrome. (See the book list at the end of this article, which you are free to reproduce and give to clients.) In the past several years, self-help groups, workshops, trained counselors, therapy groups, and even inpatient treatment programs have grown rapidly. In addition, approaches developed elsewhere, like assertiveness training and work with the inner child, can also be useful, so long as you keep in mind the part dysfunctional backgrounds and codependency play in the problem.

The Hidden ACAs in your Client Population

Statistics show that *one person in four* has been deeply affected by a relationship with an alcoholic. Therefore, at least 25 per cent of the people who come to you for readings are family members, lovers, or close friends of alcoholics. However, I suspect it is more than that for reasons we will presently discover. If you aren't finding this to be true of your own clients, it may be that they're not telling you this family secret out of shame. It's not the kind of information they readily volunteer, and they don't necessarily view you as having a need to know. After all, they're not coming to you about the firmly buried past but about the *future* and about when their relationships are going to get better. Until I came to know the chart patterns and began asking the crucial questions, very few of my clients told me about the alcoholics in their lives.

It isn't always simply a case of being secretive, either. One of the major traits of families of alcoholics or addicts is that everyone, beginning with the alcoholic, tends to *deny* the addiction. This protects the addict from having to give up the habit and protects the family from the pain and shame of seeing how destructive a problem it is. A Neptunian defense mechanism, denial means that they either don't recognize that an addiction exists or don't recognize that they're addicted to the addict. But many do see the addiction, and yet deny the extent of the damage. ACAs say things like "Yes, my Dad drank, but he stopped when I was 16, and it was so many years ago, it doesn't have any impact on my life today." As we'll see later, the residuals are considerable, especially in the ways they relate and work.

So, if clients deny the addiction or its impact in the consultation, and we don't recognize it, it's not addressed. Then there's no answer as to why their relationships are so crazy and addictive, why they're so isolated, why they just can't get along with their bosses, and why they're in so much pain. All they get is the momentary comfort of hearing "It's just your Neptune." And yet this momentary comfort carries a long-term sense of *helplessness*. You can't do anything about where Neptune is in your chart—*except die and be **reborn***.

Why ACAs are Drawn to Astrology

Many adult children of alcoholics or other addicts come to astrologers, psychics, and other readers looking for an answer to their inexplicable confusion, turmoil, and pain. A major reason they come to us is that when you grow up in a chaotic, unpredictable household, predictability has its appeal! Another reason they're drawn to us is that astrology and other such disciplines help ACAs solve that puzzling question of who they really are as opposed to roles their families conditioned them to play. Alice Miller, an important writer about treatment for ACAs, speaks of the path to health as finding the **True Self**, as opposed to who parents and others needed and expected one to be. In *The Drama of the Gifted Child*, Miller says that the alcoholic parent is narcissistic and may love the child, but only as an *extension of the self*. His/her love is given only on the condition that the child's True Self be buried to meet the parent's need for attention, admiration, and approval.[2] Astrology, numerology, and other such tools can be major arenas for exploring the True Self.

Our clientele may also have a higher proportion of ACAs than the general population because, I suspect, more ACAs believe in us than do other kinds of people. When you're a little kid and you have a grandiose parent whose brain is befuddled with alcohol, you get programmed with some remarkable ideas. (A kinder interpretation is that alcoholics are visionaries who stimulate offspring to look beyond everyday reality.) Like Alice in

Wonderland, you may be required to believe six impossible things before breakfast. So, it's not that much of a stretch to believe in astrology, past lives, absent healing, holes in your invisible aura, parallel realities or, for that matter, snake oil.

Finally, ACAs and people from dysfunctional backgrounds may have a special yearning for *spirituality*, unless they've been so wounded they wind up hating God. Those who had disturbed or addicted parents may have a strong need to find closeness with a Father/Mother/God who is loving, understanding, wise and all-powerful, and who cares deeply about them personally. And yes, it's profoundly comforting to know that this life, this crazy set of parents, this troubled history is not the only chance. Since we inevitably confuse the relationship with the Divine with the relationship with our parents, rarely is the spiritual path without potholes, detours, and false turns for ACAs. Often, the problem is not so much with the Divine but with the messengers to whom they transfer that need for an all-knowing, all-loving parent. They look for godlike qualities in astrologers and others who seem to be in touch with the Divine. When the messengers themselves are ACAs, the potential for distortion is compounded. As an example of such a messenger, the fundamentalist evangelist Jerry Falwell is an ACA, the son of a wealthy bootlegger who murdered his own brother and then became alcoholic out of guilt.[3]

Why Astrologers Should Know about Codependency

Astrologers need to learn about codependency for several reasons. First, it will help explain why so many of our clients repeatedly become involved in painful, crazy, abusive, addictive relationships. Second, *we're on the front line for referrals to treatment resources*. Many come to us who would not go elsewhere, even if they only come to ask when the alcoholic is going to straighten up. The codependent is used to being the helper and has difficulty asking for help. When you go to an astrologer, you aren't asking for help—oh, no—you're just curious as to what the future holds. Now that there are resources for codependents, astrologers need to be able to recognize the syndrome, educate clients about what's wrong, and suggest where they can go for help.

Most importantly, we need to *educate ourselves about the ACA syndrome and codependency because many of us are ourselves codependent without knowing it and, as we will see, it has an effect on the way we practice.* Talking to astrologers around the country and the world, I find that, like myself, a very high percentage, including many of the top speakers and writers, are ACAs or come from severely dysfunctional families. The reasons given earlier as to why ACA clients are attracted to these disciplines are also reasons we're attracted to study them. They become our path for understanding ourselves and other people. Even more, they're an outlet for the common ACA need to rescue and fix people, as we were never able to do for our parents.

Common Characteristics of Codependents and ACAs

In his important and readable book, *A Primer for Adult Children of Alcoholics*, psychiatrist Timmen Cermak discusses the major characteristics of codependents:[4]

1) Codependent people will hide or even change their identity and feelings in order to please and be close to others.

2) A sense of responsibility for meeting other people's needs comes first for codependents, even at the expense of their own needs.

3) Low self-esteem and very little sense of self to begin with is common to most codependents.

4) Compulsions and addictions drive codependents and keep them from having to confront their deeper feelings.

5) Just like alcoholics and other addictive personalities, codependents hide behind denial and have a distorted relationship to will power.

Cermak, who was the first president of the National Association for Children of Alcoholics, lists traits many ACAs share. Although not every ACA has all of them, these are common. They are *fearful* and especially fear their feelings, losing control, conflict, authority figures, and angry people. Although they're *fiercely self-critical* and suffer from low self-esteem, they're frightened of criticism from others, so they *constantly seek approval*. ACAs take on too much responsibility and feel guilty standing up for themselves. *Intimate relationships are a special area of difficulty*. Because they're afraid of being abandoned, they'll do almost anything to hold on to their relationships, which are often with addictive personalities or other unavailable people. They confuse love and pity, often attaching themselves to people who are victims or whom they can rescue. They can also place themselves repeatedly in the victim role.[5]

One statement in a list of traits circulated at ACA Twelve Step meetings is that "Even if we never picked up a drink, we took on all the characteristics of the disease of alcoholism." That is, ACAs who never drink can still act like alcoholics at times because, like all children, they pattern much of their behavior on parental models. Specifically, *grandiosity and defiance* are two main characteristics of alcoholics, and a great many New Age people are massively grandiose and defiant.

In their cosmic dimensions, studies like astrology encourage grandiosity. We may see ourselves as very, very special because of what we know, and may subtly or even unconsciously encourage clients to see us in the same way. We may even come to see ourselves as having a direct pipeline to the Divine. This arises from ACAs' need for a close tie to an all-loving Heavenly Father without the problems we experienced with our earthly father.

The defiant, rebel ACA often masks these traits by rigidly acting just the opposite. This doesn't mean they've overcome the conditioning from their alcoholic families but rather that they're controlled by having to act out the opposite pole. As Cermak and others in the field have remarked, ACAs are *reactors*, rather than actors. For instance, rather than showing their fear of authority figures, they may glory in defying authority. Rather than seeking approval from society, they may go out of their way to dress and act in ways that get negative attention. (In astrological terms, these are the Uranian types.)

Astrological Indicators of the ACA Syndrome

Let's take a look at chart signatures that go along with the ACA syndrome. No single aspect can be taken as a certainty, of course, so you must look for several confirmations. *Neptune*, naturally, is prominent, and often in the 1st, 4th, or 10th House, in aspect to the Sun or Moon, with Pisces in any of those spots, or highly aspected. A chart may also have many Pisces planets. The 12th House may figure strongly, often with the Sun or Moon there. An individual who has many of these signatures would be classified as "Neptunian."

It is frequently possible to distinguish which parent was alcoholic. When the Moon is aspected by Neptune, the mother is either an addictive personality or rendered severely dysfunctional by the situation. Sun/Neptune or

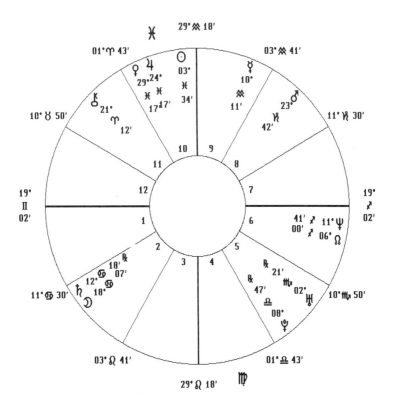

Drew Barrymore

Birth certificate information
given in Lois Rodden's specialized quarterly newsletter, "Data
News #15" (1/89), p. 4, as February 22, 1975, 11:51 A.M. PST,
Culver City, CA, 34N01,
118W25.

Placidus Houses

Mars/Neptune aspects hint at the males of the family. Saturn/Neptune aspects often show that the authority figures were unable to provide consistent structure, security, or discipline, with alcoholism only one of the possible reasons.

Neptune aspects also indicate *psychic abilities* in which we obliterate our boundaries and blend with others. Psychic abilities and boundary problems may just be two ways of defining the same phenomenon. As discussed in his book *The Medium, the Mystic, and the Physicist*, Lawrence LeShan found that healers were able to heal when they could let go of self and become one with the person in need.[6] The problem for many with psychic abilities is *shielding*—establishing boundaries so that people's thoughts, feelings, and needs do not bombard them.

Psychic merging is common in addictive and dysfunctional homes as the child or spouse uses psychic radar to monitor how the troubled person is doing to prevent an eruption. Thus, psychic gifts are common in ACAs—as a survival skill. Many intuitive astrologers are ACAs who use this gift in their work. We who are psychic need to examine ways in which we may be codependent or have difficulty with boundaries in our practice. Many who study but don't practice wisely hesitate. They know they haven't established firm boundaries and don't know how to set limits or to shield themselves psychically.

Chart Examples of ACAs

As an example of the Neptunian type of ACA, Drew Barrymore's horoscope is shown here. Part of the famous Barrymore theatrical clan, Drew began her career in the movies at the age of six in *E.T.* and has appeared in many films since. The Barrymores, including Drew's father, John Drew Barrymore, and her grandfather, John Barrymore, have been noted for alcohol problems. In fact,

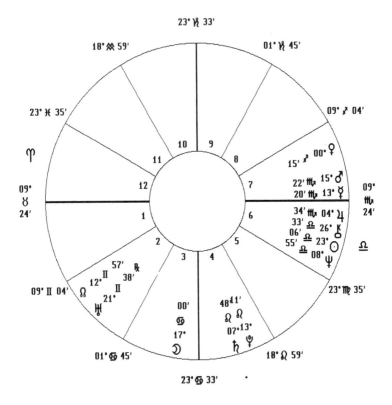

Suzanne Somers

As given in Lois Rodden's *Astro-Data II*. According to her birth certificate, she was born October 16, 1946, 6:11 P.M. PST, San Mateo, CA 37N34, 122W19.

Placidus Houses

Drew has called herself a fifth-generation alcoholic. Drew began drinking at nine, smoking pot at ten, and using cocaine at twelve. By 1989, her drug problem was serious enough that, at the age of 14, she went to rehab centers twice and tried to commit suicide.[7]

Neptune is angular in her chart in the 6th House of work square the Sun. This suggests that the pressures and terrors of fame at an early age may have contributed to the addiction. The father's side of the family and their addictions are shown by the Sun, Venus, and Jupiter in Pisces in the 10th House. Although the relationship is a difficult one, the mother does not drink and is the main stabilizing force, as seen by the Moon/Saturn conjunction in Cancer.

Strangely enough, *Pluto* is often co-prominent with Neptune and is also frequently found in the positions noted above. Thus, many ACAs would also be classified as "Plutonians." Here Pluto signifies the sober or less addicted parent who struggles mightily to keep the addiction and the addict under control. It also signifies the child's efforts to control his/her environment and keep it safe, efforts that continue into adulthood long after the original threats have passed. These same signatures, undiluted, often appear in the charts of grandchildren of alcoholics whose parents are not alcoholic. The ACA patterns of behavior and relating get passed on through the parents. Although a great many ACAs themselves have addictions, the strongly Plutonian may at least *resist* the parent's drug of choice in an effort to maintain control.

The chart of Suzanne Somers is shown here as an example of the Plutonian type of ACA. In her autobiography, *Keeping Secrets* (Warner Books, New York, 1988), she is quite open about her alcoholic family background. Pluto squares Suzanne's Ascendant, a potent aspect which is easy to miss in these charts. It is in the 4th House conjunct Saturn, the ruler of the 10th, a combination in

itself suggesting a difficult childhood and possibly abusive parents. (Drew Barrymore had a square. I've found
Pluto/Saturn aspects in the charts of several child stars.)
The conjunction squares angular Jupiter, Mercury, and
Mars in Scorpio, additional Plutonian energy. The Moon
again is in Cancer, which does not in itself suggest an
alcoholic background but may show that the issue of nurturing is a critical one for the individual. Neptune is quincunx the Ascendant but otherwise unaspected except for a
mild sextile to Saturn. Richard Idemon used to say that an
unaspected planet was like a "loose wire," often more
important in the native's life than would be expected.

Just in case your client files aren't full to overflowing with examples of adult children of alcoholics, the following section shows data for some famous ACAs whose
charts you may want to explore. Incidentally, I go along
with the Cancer rising version of Ronald Reagan's chart,
as reasoned out by Frances McEvoy. His father was an
alcoholic, and he looks most like an ACA in this chart. The
data was given in *Geocosmic News*, Fall '88, pp. 7–8, as
February 6, 1911, 2:00 P.M., Dixon, IL; 41N50, 89W29. Why
not put 12° Cancer on the Ascendant conjunct the U.S.
Sun, with Neptune even closer to the Ascendant?[8]

Who's Who of Famous ACAs

Carol Burnett: It is well known that both of Carol's
parents were alcoholic and she was raised by a grandmother. Her birth date as given in Lois Rodden's *Profiles of
Women*, p. 53, from the birth certificate is April 26, 1933,
4:00 A.M. CST, San Antonio, TX; 29N25, 98W30. (She herself gives the time as 4:15 A.M.)

James Cagney: Qualifiers were his father, who died
when Cagney was a child, and his maternal grandfather.
Astro-Data II, p. 276, gives July 17, 1900, 9:00 A.M. EST,
New York, NY; 40N45, 73W57 as his birth data. Although

the year has been questioned, this chart has a T-square with Neptune in the 10th, Saturn in Capricorn in the 4th, and Moon in Aries. His mother was a quick-tempered redhead who didn't hesitate to take a bullwhip to people. This family history is in *Cagney by Cagney*, Pocket Books, New York, 1976, pp. 16–17.

Lyndon B. Johnson: Qualifiers were his father and brother. Lois Rodden's *Astro-Data III*, p. 233, gives the data from his mother's diary as August 27, 1908 at sunrise, 4:18:20 A.M. LMT, in Gillespie County, TX; 30N04, 98W40. Family history is in Doris Kearns' *Lyndon Johnson and the American Dream*, Signet, New York, 1976, pp. 24–26.

Joan Kennedy: Qualifier was her mother as discussed by Joan in a speech at the Houston Council on Drug Abuse and Alcoholism in April 1987. Joan's birth certificate information is given in *Profiles of Women*, p. 184, as September 5, 1935, 6:10 A.M. EDT, New York, NY; 40N45, 73W57.

Jacqueline Kennedy Onassis: Qualifier was her father, Black Jack Bouvier. Her data is given in *Profiles of Women*, p. 159, as July 28, 1929, 2:30 P.M., Southampton, NY; 40N53, 72W23. Time variously given as EDT or EST, but EDT puts Neptune closely conjunct the MC trine her Aries Moon. Family history is in Bill Adler's *All in the First Family*, G.P. Putnam's Sons, New York, 1982, pp. 112–13.

Eleanor Roosevelt: Her father was an alcoholic and away most of the time, and when she was nine her mother died of diphtheria. Birth information is given in Lois Rodden's *Profiles of Women*, p. 214, based on a family birth record submitted by Joan Negus—October 11, 1884, 11:00 A.M. EST, New York, NY; 40N45, 73W57. Family history is discussed in Eleanor Roosevelt's (with Helen Ferris) *Your Teens and Mine*, Doubleday & Co., Inc., Garden City, NY, 1961, pp. 21–22.

Red Skelton: His father was a circus clown who died of drink two months before Red was born. Family history is discussed in Arthur Marx's *Red Skelton: An Unauthorized Biography*, E.P. Dutton, New York, 1979. Birth info given on p. 5 of Marx's book as July 18, 1913, 1:15 P.M. CST, Vincennes, IN; 38N41, 87W32. The year is given on his birth certificate, discharge papers, marriage license and passport as 1913, but he has also been known to say he was born in 1906. The 1906 chart makes little sense either astrologically or in light of family history, while the 1913 map appears very valid.

Lily Tomlin: Profiles of Women, p. 169, gives birth certificate information of September 1, 1939, 1:45 A.M. EST, Detroit, MI; 42N20, 83W03. This puts Neptune on the IC in a Grand Trine with Uranus and Mars.

Chart Signatures of Codependency

Astrologically, who are the codependents? Obviously, many of the same patterns as seen in ACA charts will be found, but there are additional indicators and interpretations. People with *Neptune aspects to the Moon* are often addicted to giving the nurturing they themselves never got. Those with *Neptune aspects to the Sun* may have their self-esteem and identity bound up in rescuing. People with *Neptune near the Ascendant* keenly feel the needs of everyone they meet. When *Neptune is near the Midheaven*, rescuing can be a career choice. People with *Neptune in the 7th House or aspecting Venus* are especially prone to committed but agonizing relationships with addicted people. Those with *Pisces planets* in any of these places can have similar tendencies. Note that many of these placements can also signify the addict or dysfunctional person. Such people can become vulnerable to addiction, even as they rescue. It can be a way of coping with the depletion and sorrow of rescuing.

While not all of us are codependent, we all have Neptune somewhere. We could become vulnerable to the syndrome, given the right predisposition, the proper transits, and a painful set of circumstances. (The child you adore starts using drugs, your beloved mother has a massive stroke, your spouse develops cancer.) Neptune's house and aspects in your chart show areas of confusion about where you leave off and other people begin—where your boundaries are blurred. In those areas, you may have trouble setting limits and can be taken advantage of or even victimized. Thus, *Neptune in the natal chart is often where we feel powerless, a victim or a martyr*. It is also the area where you would be most likely to get involved in codependency if the right set of circumstances triggered it. With Neptune in the 3rd House, you could be a lifelong sucker for siblings, some of whom may be alcoholic or addicted; in the 5th, with your love affairs or children; in the 8th, with sexual partners; in the 11th, with friends.

As a chart illustrating codependency, we couldn't do much better than the chart of CODA itself. CODA, or Codependency Anonymous, is a Twelve-Step program based on the principles of AA and Al-Anon. I have spoken to the founders—appropriately enough, a married couple—and they gave me the data on the first meeting. Ken and Mary R. say that they're sure the meeting started on time as that's a principle for the program. The chart shown here on the following page scans as valid for a group of this type.

The Sun is angular at the 29th degree of Libra and straddles the 7th House cusp in conjunction with Pluto in Scorpio in the 7th. Venus and Mercury in possessive and obsessive Scorpio are also in the 7th. Thus, partnership is both an obsession for group members and the focus of the healing effort. Pluto is in a tight square with Mars in Aquarius in the 10th, showing that a source of codependency can be a history of difficult relationships with erratic parental and authority figures, leading to difficulty

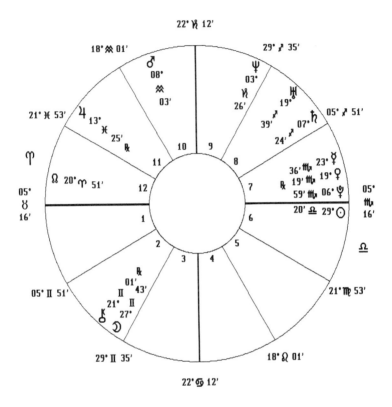

Codependency Anonymous

This is the chart of the first meeting of this group, held October 22, 1986 at 7:00 P.M. MDT in Glendale, AZ; 33N32, 112W11. It is printed with the permission of the founders, Ken and Mary R.

Placidus Houses

in managing conflict. The prominence of Pluto and the Scorpio placements illustrate the abandonment issues common to codependents and the need to manipulate, control and possess the partner in order to prevent abandonment.

Neptune's role is at first less obvious, but there is an out-of-sign opposition to the Moon in Gemini. Neptune trines the Ascendant and sextiles the Sun/Descendant/Pluto conjunction. Jupiter in Pisces in the 11th House shows that a group of others similarly afflicted can uplift the codependent and bring about growth and a spiritual awakening. (Jupiter is quintile Neptune as well.) Thus, Neptune is strong, but in this group it's dedicated to dissolving relationship addictions since the aspects are mostly positive ones. Even within the organization, however, there could be a need to be continually alert to the tendency for codependent relationships to form between members.

The Liza and Judy Show—A Case Study

As a case study in codependency, let's look at the charts for Judy Garland and her possibly equally talented daughter, Liza Minnelli. Their charts, based on birth certificate information given in *Profiles of Women*, are printed here. Judy's long struggles with alcohol, pills, and suicidal depression are a Hollywood legend. Liza herself was at the Betty Ford Clinic in 1984 to kick her cross-addictions to diet pills, tranquilizers, sleeping pills and booze.

Although Liza remains intensely loyal to her mother's memory, her childhood sounds like an ACA nightmare. By the age of ten, Liza was begging for food for herself and Judy and sneaking out of hotels and apartments to avoid paying bills and back rent. She was her mother's confidante, comforting Judy after her many suicide attempts.[9] In her teen years, the relationship between

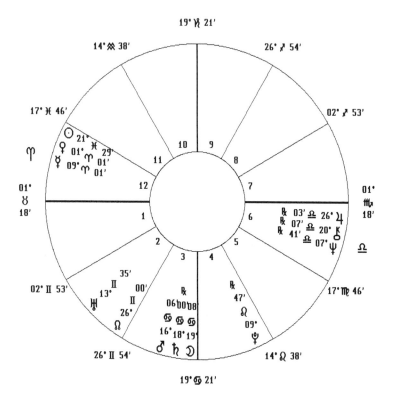

Liza Minnelli

Birth certificate data as given in
Lois Rodden's *Profiles of Women*,
p. 353: March 12, 1946, 7:48
A.M. PST, Los Angeles, CA;
34N04, 118W15.

Placidus Houses

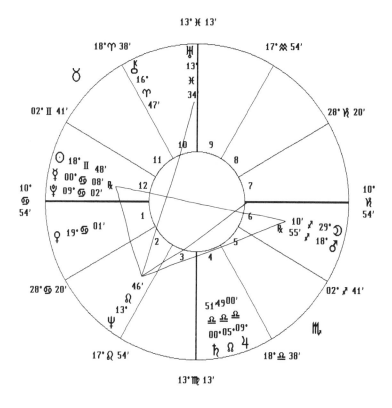

Judy Garland

Birth information as given in
Lois Rodden's *Profiles of Women*,
p. 84: June 10, 1922, 6:00 A.M.
CST, Grand Rapids, MN; 47N14,
93W31. (Birth certificate in
hand.)

Placidus Houses

them became more explosive, and Judy would periodically kick Liza out. In 1962, Liza left home for good at the age of 16, going to New York with $100 to pursue her show business career.

Liza's chart is a prime ACA profile. Her Sun in Pisces is in the 12th House. The trine from the Sun to her angular Moon/Mars/Saturn/IC conjunction in Cancer shows her closeness to her mother, but also the mutual dependency.[10] Liza's Venus and Mercury are also in the 12th opposite Neptune. Pluto in the 4th makes a wide square to Liza's Ascendant (8°)—but wouldn't you say it works?—plus a 3° sesquiquadrate to the 12th House Sun. Thus, Liza qualifies strongly as a Neptunian and less obviously as a Plutonian.

Judy's Neptune does not immediately register as a strong one, and yet she was both a sublime musician and actress and an addictive personality—all Neptunian pursuits. Then we note that her Neptune forms a Yod with her Pisces Uranus/MC conjunction and her Descendant. The strain of being constantly in the public eye and a sensation from her teens onward must have contributed to her addiction. We also discover that Neptune forms an odd-shaped triangle of a semi-square and a sesquiquadrate with her opposing Mercury and Sagittarius Moon (definitely over the rainbow!).

Like Liza, she has a strong 12th House containing the Sun, Mercury and Pluto, although Pluto is very closely conjunct the Ascendant. Both Judy and her daughter had a waif-like, lost quality, which can be attributed at times to 12th House placements. Once more we see the prominence of (ahem) Cancer with the Ascendant, Mercury, Pluto, and Venus. Pluto isn't exactly pallid conjuncting the Ascendant, widely conjunct both Venus and Mercury (a midpoint), trining the Uranus/MC conjunction, and squaring the nodes and Jupiter. And once more there's that child-star signature of a wide square to Saturn.

When you look at the connections between their charts, you will note that Judy's Venus at 19° Cancer is exactly conjunct Liza's Moon and IC, closely conjuncting Liza's Mars and Saturn as well. Liza's Neptune falls in Judy's 4th House conjunct Judy's Jupiter/North Node/ Saturn conjunction, suggesting confusion about exactly who the parent was. Liza's South Node on Judy's Moon indicates that nurturing her mother was an automatic re-action, possibly due to past-life connections. Judy's Neptune is widely conjunct Liza's Pluto. Even though these are generational placements, they do suggest a truth about the relationship, which was that Liza perennially had to keep the situation under control when Judy was falling apart. There are wide Sun/Uranus contacts on both sides. They not only show the stormy nature and the wildness shared by both women that the relationship may have sparked, but also that each supported the genius, charisma, and uniqueness of the other. The contacts also form a restless but lively T-square in Mutable signs involving Pisces, Gemini, and Sagittarius. The outlet is on Judy's Virgo IC, and the two traveled constantly during Liza's childhood, never successfully establishing a home.

Since both Judy and Liza have strong 12th House placements, then, as a mathematical and behavioral inevitability, so does the composite, shown on the following page. Self-destructive pursuits, such as addiction, the need for privacy, and the lost-child qualities, are present in both. The active 12th House in the composite chart suggests that the very fact of being together may have increased the tendency for each to be addictive. The Mercury/Venus conjunction points to a good and loving communication between the two, an understanding of each other that could not easily be verbalized to the world. Neptune in the 4th squares the Ascendant, further in-

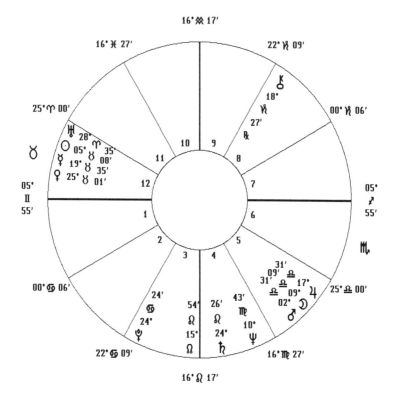

16' ♒ 17'

16' ♓ 27'

22' ♑ 09'

25' ♈ 00'

00' ♑ 06'

♅ 28' ♈ 35'
☉ 05' ♉ 08'
☿ 19' ♉ 35'
♀ 25' ♉ 01'

♂ 18' ♑
♑ 27' ℞

10   9

11   8

05' ♊ 55'

12   7

05' ♐ 55'

1   6

2   3   4   5

00' ♋ 06'

25' ♎ 00'

24' ♋
24' ♋
15' ♌ ♇

54' ♌
26' ♌
24' ♌ ♄

43' ♍
10' ♍ ♆

31' ♎
09' ♎ 31'
♎ 17'
09' ♎ 02' ♐ ♃
♂ ☽

22' ♋ 09'

16' ♍ 27'

16' ♌ 17'

**Composite Chart for Judy Garland and Liza
Minnelli for Los Angeles, CA**

creasing the Neptunian qualities, but also hinting that there must have been a strong psychic tie and mutual blending of boundaries. Pluto makes a 3° semi-square to the Ascendant as well. The difficult 4th House with Neptune and Saturn shows a painful struggle in finding a place to feel at home. The Moon, Mars, and Jupiter in Libra further testify to a loving, albeit often angry, connection. The fact that the trio is in the 5th House shows mutual support for their performing abilities.

Another famous codependent dyad which would be interesting to research astrologically is Liz Taylor and Richard Burton. Richard's father was an alcoholic, and Liz Taylor said in an interview that she came from an alcoholic family.[11] Unfortunately, the data on both of their charts has been held as questionable. Lois Rodden's *Astro-Data II* lists Richard's birth date as November 10, 1925, Pontrhydyfen, Wales; 52N17, 3W51, with a wide variety of times and rectifications listed. "Data News #12" (8/88), p. 1, gives the time from a close friend of Burton's as midafternoon, just before his siblings came in from school. As he was born at home, the twelfth of 13 siblings, the records are very scanty. *Profiles of Women*, p. 346, gives Liz's information as February 27, 1932, 7:56 P.M. GMT, London, England; 51N31, 0W06, from her mother. "Data News #10" (4/88), p. 1, says that she has given it as 2:00 P.M., "the same as James Dean." Either chart for Liz scans as ACA. Perhaps someone will be able to rectify these charts through the composite and significant dates in their tempestuous history together.

How an ACA Background Can Affect Your Practice

As I discussed the astrological profiles of the ACA and codependency syndromes, did you find some of your chart involved? You are not alone—a great many of us in the field of astrology, myself included, are ACAs. It is up to us as individuals, of course, to recognize and work on how the dysfunctional background affects our personal lives. My immediate concern here is to explore how it can affect your astrological practice.

Let me begin by saying that many of us have worked very hard to transform ourselves through a variety of healing tools. Thus, we are generally able to offer valid service. By now, many of us have already done some work on our ACA issues. And yet, unless we remain conscious and vigilant, we may still be triggered into ACA and codependent patterns when clients' problems are similar to those of family members or others we love—or to our own. I myself attended ACA groups and later Al-Anon for several years and thought I made some good quality recovery. Yet, when reading the material on codependency, I was dismayed to see my blind spots.

Although most astrologers have no counseling background, whether we recognize or like it or not, we're in essence counseling from the minute the client walks in our door. Most ACA astrologers and most of their ACA clients are in ignorance and denial about the effects of growing up in an alcoholic or dysfunctional background. Yet, when not dealt with consciously, the personality traits identified with the adult child syndrome can profoundly affect the ways we deal with clients.

The following exploration of traits of untreated ACA therapists was developed by Cermak in *A Primer for Adult Children of Alcoholics* and is used with his permission.[12] My comments about how they may manifest in readings or healing work are interspersed.

Cermak says that untreated ACA professionals can be recognized by the way they *encourage one to be angry for their own purposes*. They often push a client to take action before s/he is ready. (Although clients may come to you about a life concern like marital separation, they aren't necessarily ready to make a move.) They *intellectualize,* rather than encourage one to express his/her feelings. (For instance, if you suddenly find yourself inundating the client with jargon and technical material, ask yourself if the emotional content of the session is making you discomfited.) They are *uncomfortable with silence.* (When the client pauses for reflection, do you rush in with a metaphysical lecture or information about their fixed stars, asteroids, and so on?) Untreated ACAs resist exploring Twelve-Step programs and are certain that they've already dealt with all their codependency issues.

Reading other writers like Claudia Black, Alice Miller, and Janet Woititz listed in the bibliography led me to consider additional ways the ACA syndrome and untreated codependency can cause difficulty in chart readings. For instance, Alice Miller says *narcissistic practitioners,* as many ACAs can be, have a great need for approval, understanding and validation from clients. There is a need for the client to meet one's expectations and to present material that fits one's concepts and belief systems.[13]

The codependent practitioner easily becomes defensive and *needs validation and stroking from clients.* Do you get upset if a client questions your interpretation or doesn't tell you how right on target the reading is? Many of us are overly attached to client's approval and admiration. We feel we have to know it all and have the right answers. We do tap dances to dazzle and amaze. We may also be overly attached to being right in our predictions and interpretations—at the cost of a true dialogue with the client. We can get depressed after the interpretation if we don't get enough positive feedback. Then we question ourselves, our work, and our worth.

Boundary problems show up in readings as *over-identification* in its various forms. The client's problem becomes your problem or, conversely, your own difficulties get confused with the client's. You may feel pain or anxiety about giving clients other than what they want to hear, even though the transits or progressions are anything but positive. There may be problems in setting limits, e.g., taking too many phone calls from a client who becomes excessively dependent or allowing your consultations to go on for hours. Fuzzy boundaries can also result in feeling drained after a session. (This may mean you're doing healing without conscious awareness and need to channel divine energy rather than your own energy.)

The common ACA *need to fix people* may have motivated us to do consulting in the first place. That need may lead us to want to rescue clients who are addicted or in difficulty. We may try very, very hard to solve every problem in the client's life through three-hour sessions. Where we are overly responsible, we may take on too much of our clients' problems or spend too many hours preparing. For instance, astrologers may think they have to do several years' worth of transits, progressions, harmonic charts, midpoints, and fixed stars. Furthermore, the pervasive trait of low self-esteem may result in not charging or charging too little.

Untreated ACAs and codependents also tend to be *extremely controlling*, although they can be subtle and gifted at manipulation. (Keeping things under control was a survival skill at home.) When clients don't respond by doing what ACA astrologers recommend or don't believe that this is *the* answer, ACAs can sometimes become agitated, enraged, or vindictive. They may respond by invoking their divine connection, scaring clients about their Pluto transits, or threatening clients with cancer if they don't straighten out their way of thinking. Similarly, there can be agitation and even rage when clients don't change in the way the ACA thinks they should.

There are two main issues clients come to us

about—career and relationships. Unfortunately, two primary characteristics of untreated ACAs are *authority problems and distorted relationships*. If we haven't addressed these issues in our own lives and are in denial, it's a matter of the blind leading the blind. If we have difficulty with intimacy or anger, can we teach clients how to have healthy relationships or be positive role models for them?

Let's suppose you're still living out the victim role and have a history of being betrayed in relationships. You bring your ACA mindset to the chart session, so when clients ask about difficult relationships you counsel them to watch out for betrayal.

Similarly, out of unresolved anger toward our own parents we may encourage clients in anger against their parents or bosses. If we're grandiose, we may encourage clients in grandiose career plans, rather than taking a grounded and realistic approach to vocational astrology. Many ACAs live on the edge financially because of improper grounding in their unstable families, and the financial path in career astrology is anything but sure. Many of us have serious difficulty working for anyone else, and that's part of the attraction of being self-employed. With difficult 8th or 2nd House transits, we may ignore the fact that a client has gone deeply into debt with credit cards and bill-payer loans.[14]

Traits like *low self-esteem* explain why some ACAs study astrology for many years and never feel they're good enough to do interpretations. Many don't practice or practice infrequently because they don't feel they *can* fix people, and yet expect themselves to. Or they don't practice because they feel it's too much of a responsibility. Given the grandness of our tools, they may expect themselves to be all-knowing and feel self-hate if they're not as grand as their sources of knowledge.

Finally, ACAs are *especially susceptible to addictions*

and compulsive behaviors. In our field, more of us than we like to recognize are alcoholic or suffer from some form of addiction. We practice individual and collective denial about it, but it's an occupational hazard. It's a way of dealing with the weighty responsibility, sense of isolation, endless giving out of energy, and psychic bombardment that chart consultations entail. We also may want to stuff feelings that get stirred up in a session when we deal with major life issues in such a concentrated form. If your role models used substances or compulsions to deal with stress and keep feelings at bay, you tend to live what you learned.

The Adult Child Syndrome and the Politics of Groups
    The combination of grandiosity and defiance, as you can imagine, plays holy heck with the politics of astrology organizations and other New Age groups. Many of the traits Cermak mentions also play into group dynamics. They include the leaders' need to be in control, the members' fear of conflict and of angry people, inability to take criticism, the tendency to see things in a black-and-white perspective, the need for agreement and approval, and the tendency to feel like a victim. Put a large number of defiant, grandiose, unrecovered and in-denial ACAs together, and you're likely to see some bizarre group behavior. You may find feuds, splintering, casting out those who dare to question, and crowds who are oohing and aahing over the emperor's non-existent new clothes. (We will get public respect when we deserve it.)
    When such groups predominantly consist of ACAs, it's not unusual for top positions to be filled by the equivalent of alcoholic parents. That is, even if they never pick up a drink, leaders have been known to behave alcoholically. *Strong denial and a high tolerance for bizarre behavior* are ACA characteristics that can be carried over into group

life. Thus, members may indulge and overlook even the most astonishingly dysfunctional behavior from leaders. The members' need to create a happy, close family-type experience is a powerful one. The painful isolation they've suffered and the lifelong sense of being different and not belonging makes the group so precious to its ACA members that they tend to deny dysfunctionality so as not to threaten the sense of finally belonging. With these blinders on, everyone and everything is WOOONNN-DERFUL.

If you should be so unwise as to point out that the emperor is not, in fact, wearing any clothes, they may turn on you as though you'd done something indecent. "Oh," they say, "but he's sooooo spiritual." The group may ostracize you, and they certainly won't ask you back to speak. *Truth is an unwelcome commodity in places where denial is king.*

Further characteristics of alcoholic families that may be replicated in groups made up largely of ACAs are codependency and fuzzy boundaries. Many ACAs (myself included) elect to stay out of even healthy groups and out of group politics because of family histories that wildly violated personal boundaries. Far more likely than the average astrology group to violate members' boundaries are cult-type organizations, to which ACAs are more vulnerable than the average person. A close-knit spiritual group can be a priceless gift; a group which insists that you give up your individuality to belong is destructive. A group mind intent on invading boundaries can do great damage to an individual whose boundaries are shaky in the first place. Cults which profess to be spiritual are notorious for this, but even a more loosely organized group can at times lose respect for individual members' rights, beliefs, and feelings.

The coming conjunction of Uranus and Neptune in

264 / *Astrological Counseling*

Capricorn bespeaks exciting new discoveries and directions for the New Age movement as a whole. However, it
does not, in my view, augur well for our organizations.
The politics are likely to become more insane before they
get saner. Many will be disillusioned with groups, and
groups that do not meet the needs of their members will
dissolve. The hope for sanity is the hope that more and
more ACA members will come to recognize the syndrome
in themselves and their groups. It would be helpful if
some of the traditions the Twelve-Step programs aspire to
were adjusted for use in these groups. Just for starters,
there is one that says "Our leaders are but trusted ser-
vants; they do not govern."

How Current Conditions Intensify the Need
for Recovery

Current world conditions, as signified astrologically by the lineup of outer planets in Capricorn, are inten-
sifying the demands on all service professions. People are
extremely needy and confused, feeling helpless and powerless because of the vast social changes just on the horizon. The forces of chaos are very strong just now. As a
result, people are looking to astrologers and other service
professions for guidance and answers. Many of us are
burned out from clients' excessive demands, or what feels
like excessive demands. Learning to set limits is becoming
crucial. We need to master limit-setting so that we don't
get so burned out that we stop the work.

We also need to assess which clients' demands are
legitimate and which are not before we act. Alcoholics and
chronically dysfunctional people can project feelings of
helplessness and bottomless need so powerfully that the
psychically sensitive pick them up and react. To bolster
low self-esteem, rescuers need to be needed, so they hook
into the helplessness and *keep people helpless* by enabling

them to continue dysfunctional patterns. We need to learn how crippling rescuing is so we don't do it with clients. We cannot keep on enabling, rescuing, and answering the non-genuine need, or we will not survive.

However, we're also being forced to function at the outer limits of our capabilities and to stretch ourselves to a higher level of professionality, and that's stressful. You'd be in physical pain if your limit was a mile a day and then you ran a ten-mile marathon. If you then proceeded to run ten miles every day, it would eventually become your new limit. Likewise, as we continue to be stretched past our limits as service workers, those new levels of functioning will ultimately become ours.

Even where the needs are legitimate, there's so much more pressure that we can grow weary. It's important to rest, relax, and take care of ourselves emotionally, spiritually, physically, and fiscally. One important way of taking care of ourselves is to recognize and let go of codependency in our personal and professional lives. I hope this discussion has been a beginning of that recognition. If we astrologers who have the syndrome use the tools that are developing—the books, the groups, and other self-help aids—and if we tell our ACA and codependent clients about them as well, we'll all gradually get free.

Tools for Recovery for ACAs and Codependents

I. Books for Adult Children of Alcoholics

Ackerman, Robert J. Ph.D. *Perfect Daughters: Adult Daughters of Alcoholics*. Deerfield Beach, FL: Health Communications, Inc., 1989.

Black, Claudia. *It Will Never Happen to Me*. New York: Ballantine, 1987.

Bradshaw, John. *Healing the Shame that Binds You*. Deerfield Beach, FL: Health Communications, Inc., 1989.

Cermak, Timmen L. M.D. *A Primer for Adult Children of Alcoholics*. 2nd ed. Deerfield Beach, FL: Health Communciations, Inc., 1989.

Miller, Alice. *The Drama of the Gifted Child: The Search for the True Self*. New York: Basic Books, Inc., 1981.

Wegscheider, Sharon. *Another Chance: Hope and Health for the Alcoholic Family*. Science and Behavior Books, Inc. (701 Welch Road, Palo Alto, CA 94306), 1981.

Woititz, Janet. *Adult Children of Alcoholics*. Deerfield Beach, FL: Health Communications, Inc., 1983.

_____. *Struggle for Intimacy*. Deerfield Beach, FL: Health Communications, Inc., 1985.

Changes: The Magazine for and about Adult Children of Alcoholics. Six issues a year, $18/year. Health Communications, Inc.

II. Books about Codependency

Beattie, Melody. *Beyond Codependency—And Getting Better All the Time*. New York: Harper/Hazelden, 1989.

_____. *Codependent No More*. New York: Harper/Hazelden, 1987.

Co-Dependency (a collection of essays). Deerfield Beach, FL: Health Communications, Inc., 1988.

Diamond, Jed, LCSW. *Looking for Love in all the Wrong Places: Overcoming Romantic and Sexual Addictions*. New York: G. P. Putnam's Sons, 1988.

Hayes, Jody. *Smart Love*. Los Angeles, CA: Jeremy P. Tarcher, Inc., 1989.

Norwood, Robin. *Women Who Love Too Much*. New York: Pocket Books, 1986.

Resources for Recovery from Codependency

National Offices of Anonymous Programs (ask for local groups):

CODA (Codependency Anonymous)
Box 33577
Phoenix, AZ 85067–3588
(602) 277–7991

ACA Central Service
Torrance, CA
(213) 534–1815

Al-Anon Family Groups
Box 182
New York, NY 10159–0182

Major Sources of Recovery Materials (call for catalogs):

Compcare Publishers
1–800–328–3330

European Distributor:
Recovery Tools, Ltd.
31 Craven Street
London WC2 5NP, England
Phone: 83–8868

Hazelden
1–800–328–9000

Health Communications
1–800–851–9100

Seminars and Workshops Around the Country

Health Communications
1–800–851–9100

Life Cycle Learning
1–800–962–9992

COMPUTER BULLETIN BOARD: Free access to information for ACAs, codependents, and others interested in recovery. Call (703) 821–2925, computer setting 8N1.

ACA OR CODEPENDENCY INPATIENT TREATMENT UNITS: See listings in *Changes* magazine for programs around the country.

Notes

1. Melody Beattie, *Codependent No More*, Harper/Hazelden, New York, 1987, p. 31.
2. Miller, Alice. *The Drama of the Gifted Child: The Search for the True Self* (previously called *Prisoners of Childhood*), Basic Books, Inc., New York, 1981, p. 14.
3. Lois Rodden's "Data News #5" (8/87), p. 2, gives the birth information from his twin brother as about noon, EST, 8/11/33, Lynchburg, VA; 37N25, 79W09. Family history discussed in Falwell's autobiography *Strength for the Journey*, Simon and Schuster, Inc., New York, 1987. The chart is not presented here because this time doesn't seem exact.
4. Timmen L. Cermak, M.D., *A Primer for Adult Children of Alcoholics*. 2nd ed. Health Publications, Inc., Deerfield Beach, FL, 1989, pp. 19–23.
5. *Ibid.*, pp. 34–37.
6. Ballantine Books, New York, 1982.

7. Family and recent history discussed in "Falling Down and Getting Back Up Again" by Jeannie Park and Robin Micheli, *People*, 1/29/90, pp. 57–61.

8. Reagan tells his family history in his autobiography (co-author Richard G. Hubler) which has the perfect ACA title of *Where's the Rest of Me?*, Karz Publishers, New York, 1981, p. 12.

9. Family history discussed in Alan W. Petrucelli's *Liza! Liza! An Unauthorized Biography of Liza Minnelli*, Karz-Cohl Publications, Inc., New York, 1983.

10. As a 12th House Cancer Sun, I seem to have had a personal blind spot to the role of Cancer planets in ACA charts until writing this article!

11. The Burton family history was discussed in Paul Ferris's *Richard Burton*, Coward, McCann, & Geoghehan, New York, 1981, pp. 17–19. Liz was quoted in *USA Today*, 2/29/84, p. 2D, as saying, "I'm a very addictive person. It is a disease. It is in my family."

12. Cermak, pp. 69–70.

13. Miller, p. 24.

14. An astrological aside: Pluto, rather than Neptune, appears to be the predominant theme for people who are addicted to their credit cards and to ruinous debt. It may show up in the 2nd or 8th Houses or form important aspects to planets in these houses, or Scorpio placements may be there. Here the issue seems to be spite and revenge. Many incest survivors have debt compulsions.

Eileen Nauman

A medical astrologer since 1974, Eileen works behind the scenes with doctors and other health practitioners from around the world as a consultant on hard-to-diagnose or undiagnosable cases.

As a lay homeopath with over 180 hours of training in Homeopathy, she teaches courses and speaks on the use of this alternative medicine. An international speaker, Eileen offers two-day and five-day medical astrology workshops to health professionals as well as beginning through professional astrologers.

She has taken courses pertaining to medicine from Kent State University and has served as a firefighter for three years with an EMT background. Presently, she divides her time between teaching, speaking and acting as a consultant to doctors. She can be reached at P.O. Box 2513, Cottonwood, AZ 86326.

MEDICAL ASTROLOGY COUNSELING

Medical astrology requires a different approach to counseling than natal astrology.The medical astrologer is usually not a licensed medical practitioner, such as an M.D., N.D., D.C. or D.O., since most medical astrologers evolve out of the field. This in itself is not good or bad, but becomes a critical point to clients who come to the medical astrologer seeking health-oriented advice.

Medical astrologers are rare, and most people don't even know we exist. Those who do seek us out are generally one of three types: Either they are *chronically ill* and have made the "rounds" of the accepted medical establishment and have found no relief from their problems; they are *health-oriented individuals* who wish to maintain good health and are seeking advice to accomplish this; or they have been *abused by the accepted medical establishment* and refuse to ever seek advice from such practitioners again.

Two out of the three types pose serious problems for the medical astrologer—the chronically ill individual who is desperate and the one who has literally come to hate the accepted medical establishment.

The chronically ill person is usually at the end of his/her rope, emotionally, mentally and financially as well as physically. Despairing, s/he is willing to seek any kind of alternative treatment, which makes him/her particularly vulnerable and willing to accept anything the medical astrologer says.

Those who have developed disgust or even hatred of standard medical practices are apt to be better educated about themselves, their bodies and their problems than the other types. This person is *ready* to accept responsibility for his/her health, realizing that the doctor or health practitioner is really (and only) a part of the "team" to get him/her on the road to health. This individual takes part in the dialogue regarding his/her health problem, wanting questions answered in a straightforward manner, not wishing to hear "medicalese"—a hodgepodge of medical words that make no sense at all to the layperson. S/he also expects to be consulted and respected for personal opinions about his/her body.

Just because you, the astrologer, may be able to look at a natal chart and glean health information from it doesn't necessarily make you a medical astrologer. What does qualify you for such a label?

As an astrological counselor who is serious about undertaking a medical astrological practice, you have accepted the most complex type of challenge offered in astrology. You must not only be a top-notch astrologer, but you should have an extensive background in nutrition/diet, a thorough understanding of physiology and anatomy, and literally be prepared to become a "clearinghouse" of health information.

At no time, even with this education and background, can the medical astrologer *ever* classify him/herself as a medical doctor or a doctor of medical astrology, or in any way let the client think that you fulfill any of these roles. Medical astrologers walk a narrow line that, if overstepped one iota, falls into the realm of PRACTICING MEDICINE WITHOUT A LICENSE, a federal offense punishable with a hefty fine, not to mention a prison term.

Hypothetically, a client could sue the medical astrologer for MEDICAL MALPRACTICE just as quickly as an M.D. is sued. As you can see, medical astrology is a most dangerous form of practice. Very sick people come to you, desperate for a last chance to halt their invasive illness, and willing to believe anything you utter. Remember, what you say comes from your background or education in the *health* field. The more you know about nutrition, diet, the human body and other related fields, the better service you can provide to your clients. The less you know, the less the client receives, which has a direct (and usually instantaneous) impact on his/her health.

In no other astrological field does your knowledge (or lack of it) have such a direct and immediate effect on an individual. This is a complex area, one demanding a number of disciplines, and it is most difficult in terms of potential problems with the AMA and federal government. This is not a field for the faint of heart or the foolhardy. It is a field for a dedicated healer who happens to employ astrology as a focus or mandala to help those who seek assistance in getting well.

Astrologically, we recognize that the human being is *holistic*, that all parts make up the whole. We are who we are because of our conditioning, our parents, our society, an amalgam of mental attitudes that were molded and shaped since birth, emotions that went through the same fires of experience, plus a spiritual counterpart that tries to bring through only the finest and most positive energy to make us what we are: human beings. All of these things affect the physical body, the fourth and last component of the holistic concept. Most medical astrologers are holistic in their approach to health because we include the spiritual, the mental, the emotional, as well as the physical of the person who seeks our counsel.

Allopathy Versus Homeopathy

Recently, the allopathic medical establishment in the United States has had to come to grips with this concept. Let me define *allopathy*: It is a system of treating disease by producing conditions different from or incompatible with the effect of the disease. In other words, if a person has a fever, an allopathic doctor treats it with an *anti*-fever drug such as aspirin, which is known to reduce fever. If one has an infection, the allopath treats it with an *anti*biotic (infection drug), such as penicillin. Allopathy accounts for 95 per cent of the medical practice in the United States. The doctors who use it are taught to zero in on a specific symptom and eradicate it with the use of large doses of a drug(s). The side effects, as many people are now coming to realize, can be horrendous.

The type of medicine practiced in 75 per cent of the rest of the world is *homeopathy*. It is a system of medicine that prescribes minute doses of such medicine as would produce in a healthy person the symptoms of the diseases treated. In other words, *like cures like*. A homeopathic doctor, first of all, is holistic, recognizing from the outset that the human being is a combination of spiritual, mental, emotional and physical formation. Secondly, the patient *is* a part of the healing procedure and plays a powerful and responsible part in his/her own healing process. Lastly, homeopathy, unlike allopathy, *cures* and *heals*. It has no adverse side effects, *nor will it suppress the illness*, as does allopathic treatment.

For example, following allopathic philosophy, if you have a headache the doctor prescribes aspirin to suppress the pain. The aspirin doesn't heal or cure the cause of the headache. Two or three hours later after the first dose of aspirin, the headache may come back, proving that all this drug does is suppress the symptoms, but it doesn't cure the problem.

On the other hand, if you went to a homeopathic doctor, s/he would ignore your label of "headache" and ask you questions about your spiritual, mental, emotional and physical state, gathering a vast amount of extra information from which an assessment could be made of what is needed to cure and heal your headache. In homeopathy there is no describing and defining a particular disease because it is made up of many symptoms. These symptoms will be found in a *Materia Medica* that has 2,000 remedies from the *Homeopathic Pharmacopeia*. The doctor then gives you a minute dose of a potent remedy. Your headache goes away, but this time it is healed and cured, not suppressed.

The proper medical astrologer is holistic, just like the homeopath. In my opinion, homeopathy is a much healthier way of approaching a client's illness. Happily, there are homeopathic doctors (M.D.'s, N.D.'s, D.C.'s, D.O.'s) here in the United States. As a responsible medical astrologer, you can recommend to your client the National Center of Homeopathy, 1500 Massachusetts Ave. NW, Suite 42, Washington, D.C. 20005–1808, 202–223–6182. They offer a directory available for purchase which lists homeopathic practitioners by area.

As a medical astrologer, your goal is not to prescribe for the client (which is against the law) but rather to become a clearing-house of information in addition to *educating* your client about possible choices. You can become the hub of a wheel, educating yourself in many systems of medicine and approaches to healing that are available to the clients who seek you out.

It is very important not to misrepresent what you are and what you do. When a client accepts you as a medical astrologer, it is not the same as if s/he accepts you as his/her "doctor." Nothing could be further from the truth. *In essence, you are a healer using the tool of astrology as a focus on health-related problems.* Your responsibility is to send this individual (after informing him/her of the many choices s/he has) in a direction s/he has chosen and is comfortable with to seek competent medical help.

A medical astrologer does *not* tell a client to take a vitamin, mineral, herb, homeopathic remedy, or anything else. The medical astrologer educates the client about these things, then leaves the responsibility of choice up to the person. One's health is one's own responsibility. Gradually, people in this country are coming to view and accept this vital concept. *Your health is your responsibility.* It is your right to ask questions of your health practitioner about his/her diagnoses, what s/he is prescribing, what it will do, if there are any side effects, etc.

Unfortunately, the allopathic community in the United States has, since its inception in the late 1800s, set itself up to be godlike and empirical, refusing to allow the patient to become part of the healing process. In the 1980s we experienced a tremendous backlash from this unhealthy thinking with medical malpractice suits rising at a skyrocketing rate. Doctors are not gods, nor do they know everything, nor are they always correct in their diagnoses, let alone in prescribing drugs. Neither are medical astrologers.

Anyone who has ever seen a doctor has been misdiagnosed at one time or another. Doctors are human. They have our best interests at heart (we hope), but they are fallible. And their mistakes can be costly in terms of human life. That is why medical malpractice suits continue to be prevalent. A medical astrologer can, and probably will, make mistakes, too. Many of these will be made out of ignorance and lack of education in the health/medical field. Some will be made regardless of knowledge. Why? Because we are all human beings and we don't know everything there is to know about healthiness.

A medical astrologer is not better or any worse than any doctor when it comes to counseling a sick person. The sad, scary and potentially legal situation is that if we make a mistake it can harm our client just as much as if an M.D. had made it. In no other astrological practice is so much demanded of the astrologer. Let me share with you what I do as a medical astrologer.

What Are You?

1. When a client calls to seek my services, I inform him/her of exactly what I do and cannot do. I give my qualifications: college courses in biology, physiology/anatomy and math from Kent State University. I am a lay homeopath with 180 hours of instruction from M.D.'s on homeopathy from the National Center of Homeopathy. I treat only first aid and acute cases homeopathically; I turn over chronic cases directly to a homeopathic doctor. I have written a book, *The American Book of Nutrition and Medical Astrology* (Astro Computing Services), which is based on seven years of research and was two-and-a-half years in the writing. The book has sold 15,000 copies and is now in print in Dutch. I make it clear to the prospective client that I am *not* an M.D.

2. I explain to the client that I am a "clearing-house" of information along certain lines, as mentioned above; I have a knowledge of vitamins, minerals and nutrition—and I am *self-taught*. I do not have a degree in nutrition, etc. I do practice as a lay homeopath, but most often I suggest that the client call NCH (National Center of Homeopathy) to locate a homeopathic doctor in his/her area. In other words, I do not misrepresent myself in any way to my client.

3. If the person accepts this, I tell him/her that I will not diagnose using the astrological chart. Rather, I will

educate him/her about certain *potential* discrepancies that I discover using medical astrology, discussing these with him/her. I will not tell the client to take a specific vitamin, mineral, herb, or homeopathic remedy or to pursue a certain kind of diet. To do so is practicing medicine without a license. Further, *I will never tell a client when s/he is going to die.* It has been my experience that a person can "opt out" of this lifetime anywhere along his/her life path. It is impossible through use of the horoscope for a medical astrologer, or any other kind of astrologer, to say when a person will choose which time to leave this plane.

I also do not make decisions for other people. An example: A woman called and wanted me to decide whether or not her son should be put in a mental hospital or stay at home with her as his caretaker. As a medical astrologer, remember it is not your responsibility to make a decision on something of this magnitude—ever. Turn these questions over to professionals—to doctors or therapists, who can make a better evaluation than you can.

4. I am paid for my consultation to educate the client about the vast array of possible health/healing "tools" that are available if s/he chooses not to utilize or go through generally accepted medical options. This information is given before the client ever consults with me. I let him/her decide if this is what s/he wants or is looking for. At all times, I put the responsibility for his/her health back into his/her hands where it belongs. I make no decisions for the client. Do not say "I know I can help you." How do you know that? Do you know that an ill person, if s/he is not ready to let go of his/her illness, won't get well, no matter what kind of medical treatment s/he chooses? With many people, this is an unconscious concept. So they come to you, saying they want to get well, but in reality they may not be ready to take that big step or turn around. No medical astrologer (indeed, no doctor)

knows ahead of time if a person is honestly ready to get healthy. Say instead, "I can help lead you to an informed decision regarding what you want to do about your health." This puts the responsibility back into the hands of the client and relieves you of having to "perform" upon demand for a person who may still want to give away his/her responsibility to the medical establishment.

How Can You Help?

A good medical astrologer offers lists of licensed health practitioners, directories, services offered by the city, county and state, phone numbers and names to the client when s/he comes for consultation. For instance, the national directory of Massotherapists, Homeopathy or Orthomolecular Physicians (allopathic M.D.'s who practice holistic healing with vitamins, minerals, etc., and sometimes use drugless therapy) is one such resource. I have names of hands-on healers—reflexologists, polarity therapists, Reiki healers, Native American medicine women, rolfing therapists, psychotherapists, psychologists, the Rape Crisis Counseling Center, and so on—at my desk and available to my clients.

A medical astrologer must have myriad amounts of information available to give the client the widest possible selection of healing modality that s/he feels is correct. It is not the medical astrologer's decision who the client should see. Rather, it is your responsibility to simply make the client aware and allow him/her to make a choice. We know our own health and sickness feelings best. The client is capable of knowing which tool is best for him/her. The medical astrologer does not.

How to Counsel as a Medical Astrologer

1. A week before the consultation, I send the client a MedScan Questionnaire. This is a 15-page medical ques-

tionnaire designed to elicit information from the natal chart. On the front of the first page is a release form saying:

Date:

MEMORANDUM

TO: (name of medical astrologer)

To establish and clarify my purpose in coming to you for a consultation, I want to clearly state that my interest is in learning a helpful path to follow and a beneficial nutritional program. I wish to change my present habits and establish new ones, as well as a new way of living, to build good health. I understand it is my personal decision to follow or not to follow your nutritional program outlined in the MedScan.

I thoroughly understand that this program does not replace any additional or present professional counseling with any other doctor I may wish to consult; that your analysis and nutritional counseling is an adjunctive analysis which can be coordinated with any advice or treatments by other doctors or practitioners who are licensed by State and Federal laws; and also that the decision to follow or reject the MedScan program is left to my own discretion.

Again, I wish to state that I clearly understand that this analysis and consultation is not meant to take the place of any other form of analysis, counseling or diagnosing by my regular physician or any other licensed doctor or practitioner.

Respectfully yours,

Signature, Address, Telephone

The other reason for the MedScan Questionnaire is purely research oriented. I can use the information on it to further the budding science of medical astrology. All questionnaires are, of course, treated with complete privacy, the case never discussed unless with the client's permission.

2. After clearly stating your credentials so the client understands them, the appointment is made. I allow clients to tape the session. Although tapes are not admissible court evidence, they may at some time be used against you. The decision to tape or not to tape is an individual one.

3. I provide handouts with lists of referrals as discussed above to give to the client. I also have brochures on what homeopathy is, the Bach Flower Remedies, etc.

4. When the client comes to my office, I make him/her comfortable. I prefer a round table rather than a desk where the client sits opposite me. Psychologically, this is like an opposition in the horoscope instead of a conjunction. I prefer to teamwork with my client, so I sit next to him/her. I have been hired as part of his/her healing team, and I view our time together as a tactical and strategic session viewing the possible arsenal of "weapons" or tools with which s/he can get well.

I usually offer my client herb tea, coffee or cold water since I like a relaxed "coffee klatch" kind of atmosphere, rather than a stiff, professional milieu. Most clients have had years of that in the medical establishment. I try to be warm, responsive and put him/her at ease. A smile, a brief touch of the hand on his/her arm or shoulder is healing, too.

My attire is comfortable. I do not wear a white smock or parade around in a nurse's uniform. My certification from NCH is on the wall should the client wish to verify my credentials. There is also a copy of my book available. I invite my client to check me out. I feel it is a mistake to dress up like Madam Zora the Reader—no bizarre outfits for me, no gobs of makeup, just my own natural healthy look, which speaks for itself.

Your client will always inspect you closely to see if *you* look healthy! If you are obese or seem ill, this may work against the client placing trust in you. You are a medical astrologer and know about healing, you are supposed to look the part. The client expects you to take your own advice: Medical astrologer, heal thyself.

5. My first question is "Why have you come to see me?" Open-ended questions are a must in this business. I do not say "I understand from our phone conversation that you have chronic headaches." Lay homeopaths are taught not to particularize; let the client tell in his/her own words what the major complaint is. If you paraphrase for your client, you will get less useful information, and what is really a pressing problem may be put aside because the client thinks it is unimportant.

The first half-hour of any session, as the information pours from the client's mouth *uninterrupted,* is the most vital. Let your client tell you what ails him/her. If s/he stops, you should ask, "Is there anything else?" Keep prompting until you're satisfied you understand the chief complaint. Take copious notes.

6. From the client's information, I can assess whether the condition is *acute* or *chronic*. *Acute* means the illness is momentary or of a few days' duration. *Chronic* refers to an illness that has been troublesome for a much longer time. Someone who has appendicitis and doesn't realize it may come to you complaining of a "stomachache." If that stomachache has persisted for three or more days, it is your responsibility to suggest that s/he be examined immediately by a doctor. This must be done without throwing him/her into a panic, of course. You may

suspect an ulcer, appendicitis, gallbladder dysfunction, twisted intestine—the list is endless—and the lesson here is that you do not really know what you're dealing with. Any illness or discomfort has passed the acute stage after one, two, or at the outside, three days.

As a medical astrologer, you may see an indication in the natal chart or through progressions and transits of possible appendicitis, but do not tell your client that. What if you are wrong? Think of the fear and panic you are creating for the person. What you can say is this: "Astrologically, it looks as if there could be some abdominal involvement, but you should see a doctor for a diagnosis."

If the person doesn't know what "abdomen" means or where it is located (and this does happen), you explain by standing up and pointing to the region on your own body, telling him/her about all the organs in that part of the body, and that you cannot pinpoint exactly what is causing the problem but the astrological chart indicates that a potential problem exists in this area of the body.

A large part of being a medical astrologer is interpreting the "medicalese" that the client has been confronted with for years by physicians, making it simple and understandable. In order to do this, you must have a thorough, working knowledge of physiology and anatomy, especially if, as I do, you work with doctors. I don't speak astrology to the M.D.'s who consult with me; I speak medicalese. So to be a competent medical astrologer, you must become an interpreter with the multilevel skills to speak to each group in their particular language. But you must also be able to define it in lay terms so that your client understands it as well.

7. If the person suffers from a chronic illness (cancer, multiple sclerosis, arthritis, AIDS, etc.), I check out the horoscope and verify that these potentials are mirrored in

the chart. I then tell the client that s/he has a serious chronic problem and can either get rid of it or put it into a state of remission if s/he so desires. It is not the prerogative of the healer to take hope away from the client, but to instill it. A medical astrologer should always give hope—not promises. I offer the person my referral list of licensed health practitioners, and we discuss the ones who are of interest to him/her. S/he then makes a choice and leaves with a request to call or write and let me know what the practitioner diagnosed, the course of healing decided upon, etc.

8. Often, the medical astrologer works in a 12th House (hidden) capacity. Over the last decade, I have quite an expanded list of doctors to whom I refer clients with health problems. These doctors know that this person has been referred by a medical astrologer. If I don't know the practitioner and am not sure what his/her reaction will be to my client because a medical astrologer sent him/her, I tell my client to say nothing about me. Why? Because the point is not to put the client in the middle by having the practitioner take umbrage with the person who is coming for help because s/he sought the advice of someone perceived of as a "quack." The medical astrologer is not only unsung, but often unheard of, and 90 per cent of the time, unseen. The reason you do what you do is to help the client in his/her choice of healing methods.

Helpful Hints

1. Don't ever say "I think you ought to take (name a vitamin, mineral, herb, homeopathic remedy, diet, food or anything!)." That is prescribing and is a no-no. Rather, say "Why don't you read about vitamin A and see what you think about it? Here are the deficiency symptoms. If you manifest any of these, why not check it out with a doctor to

see how much you should take, the type and how often?"

2. Never say "I think you have cancer (or any other disease, acute or chronic)." This is diagnosing, and a sure way to incur legal problems. Medical astrology is in its infancy, and we know too little to tell a client what illness s/he will attract according to his/her horoscope. If you suspect a chronic condition, send him/her to a licensed practitioner to make that assessment. This judgment is not yours to make. It is a negative approach that may frighten the client. You could be wrong in how you judge the chart medically, just as doctors are sometimes wrong in their diagnoses. Suggest that the person get two opinions (at least) to discover what the problem is. Do not assign a label to the difficulty before the physician does.

3. Don't say "I think a macrobiotic diet is best for you." Or any other kind of diet, for that matter. Even though the chart may indicate the person should be on grain/rice-type fare, you could say it better this way: "Why don't you read about the macrobiotic diet and see what you think about it?" If the person has colitis, for example, the last thing s/he needs is a diet high in grains only! As a medical astrologer, you will probably have favorite books on diets that you could recommend to your clients. Or direct them to the library or a health food store to buy a copy.

4. When the client returns after reading the book and thinks it is the right thing for him/her, providing s/he has no present health problems (especially of the intestinal variety), you can discuss what to do. You should recommend dieting of any kind under a doctor's guidance with yearly checkups. Do not tell the client what to do. S/he must make his/her own decision.

5. Don't ever badmouth a physician to a client. As a

medical astrologer, I hear surgery and doctor horror stories from my clients. It is a travesty, but medical malpractice suits are providing some retribution for these people. It is certainly not your place to defame a health practitioner—rather, the list of health professionals that you give your clients should be those with whom you are familiar, who have a leaning toward holistic health practices. Professionally, you should keep your opinions of all health practitioners to yourself. If word got out, the doctor could sue you for libel. Think about it. Be 12th House; see everything, but *say* very little.

As a medical astrologer, you can provide key services that can benefit nearly any ill person. If you are a lay homeopath, all the better. You can also serve as a willing, sympathetic and knowledgeable listener. Nowadays, many patients feel like cattle being herded through a doctor's office with little doctor/patient contact. Healing is an amalgam of words, touch, prescription, but most importantly, it is another human being who is there in any health crisis. Sometimes, just listening will help heal certain acute conditions. Don't dismiss the art of listening, touching, and allowing your client to cry or express his/her fears.

A Case History

The following incident depicts the many roles the medical astrologer may play. I received a phone call from a client who lives on the East Coast. "Ann" was referred to me by another astrologer who was pleased with the results of a MedScan done a year prior.

Ann had experienced a number of female/reproductive problems, including rectal bleeding at age nine, which had cleared up but come back with a vengeance in her early 20s. She had irregular periods throughout her life and a seemingly incurable, painful vaginal/yeast infection, bladder infections, allergies and chronic fatigue. Ann had been through the allopathic medical world without success. If anything, she was worse, not better. Having been on antibiotics frequently, she was concerned that they were doing more harm than good. This had gone on for a decade.

I listened quietly while she listed her frustrating problems and lack of success via the normal medical routes. After a viral illness in 1987, she was prescribed a broad spectrum antibiotic for three weeks. Suddenly her vaginal problem was much worse. Her faith in allopathic medicine was at a low ebb, and she was desperately searching for any alternative form of healing that was available, even to the point of contacting a medical astrologer.

She was a typical "last ditch stand" client who was at the end of her rope, in pain and discomfort 24 hours a day. Ann was taking vitamins and minerals; they had helped, but she wasn't "cured."

I offer three services to doctors, health professionals and the public: the best dates to have surgery, a computerized, completely individualized MedScan, and a personal MedScan workup done by me rather than a computer, which includes progressions as well as referral for a year. I use a sliding fee scale for the elderly and those on fixed incomes.

The computerized MedScan covers vitamins and minerals plus deficiency symptoms in detail. To my mind, Ann didn't need the MedScan or surgery dates. She mentioned that she was seeing a homeopath. I was enthused. I knew the gentleman, a brilliant homeopath, but he was, in my opinion, erratic and somewhat anti-feminist. I urged her to continue seeing him, and if she wasn't satisfied with him or the results of his treatment, to call me back. I told her I felt homeopathy could play a role in her recovery and

288 / Astrological Counseling

that the vitamins and minerals prescribed were good, but only an adjunct on her path to health. She agreed.

Four weeks later, Ann called again, having found the male homeopath to be quite off the mark in his comments about her condition. Reluctantly, she had taken the remedy he suggested and nothing had happened. Having taken homeopathic remedies before, Ann had discovered that her body usually reacted to them immediately. This time she had no reaction and was disappointed, so she decided to discontinue his treatment.

At this point, I tried to persuade her to go to a homeopathic M.D. (the other gentleman had no degree in a health-related field) and gave her the phone number for the NHC. For $5.00 she could purchase the list of the U.S. Directory of Homeopathic Doctors and choose one. But she wanted me to personally work on her case because she felt she could trust me. I had displayed a great deal of homeopathic knowledge and she was comfortable pursuing my assistance. I agreed, but reluctantly, since I felt she should be seeing a homeopathic M.D.

Ann was born August 24, 1957 at 6:30 a.m. CST in Chicago, Illinois; 41N52, 87W39. She has the Sun in Virgo conjunct Pluto in the 12th House, with Mars widely conjunct both. In my experience, a Pluto conjunction in the 12th can often indicate early sexual abuse. Her Virgo conjunction squares Saturn, suggesting difficulties with a male (father, brother, uncle, cousin).

Physiologically, she has Neptune in Scorpio widely square Uranus, ruler of her 6th House of health, which can indicate a weak reproductive area plagued with viral or bacterial infections. Saturn ruling the 5th House and with challenging aspects reinforces this. Ann told me of a two-year vaginal infection that was getting worse, and she feared it was becoming chronic. Scorpio rules the bladder, and she had experienced repeated bladder infections.

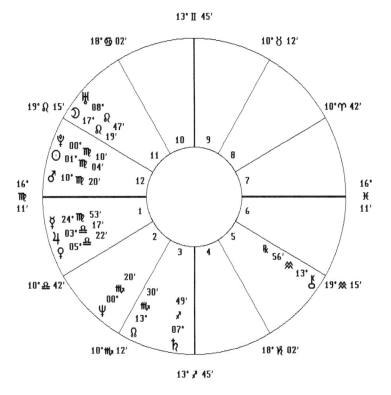

13° ♊ 45'

18° ♋ 02'   10° ♉ 12'

19° ♌ 15'   10° ♈ 42'

⛢ 08°
☽ 17' ♌
       ♌ 47'
         19'
♇ 00° ♍ 10'
☉ 01° ♍ 04'
♂ 10° ♍ 20'

16°
♍
11'   16°
                                                                 ♓
                                                                 11'

☿ 24° ♍ 53'
        17'
♃ 03° ♎ 22'
♀ 05°

10° ♎ 42'

               20'
            ♏ 00°
                    30'
                 ♏ 13'
                            49'
            ☊   ♐ 07°
               ℞ 56'
              ♒ 13'
                      ☿
            19° ♒ 15'

10° ♏ 12'   18° ♑ 02'

13° ♐ 45'

"Ann"

August 24, 1957   6:30 A.M. CST

41N52   87W39

Chicago, Illinois

Placidus Houses

These too reflect the Sun/Pluto contact.

Working out her MedScan, I did the progressions, using the 90-degree dial, the Uranian planets with average solar arc directions. This all pinpointed sexual abuse at a very early age. I know from 20 years' experience that many other cases where women had chronic reproductive ailments (endometriosis, breast cancer, uterine cancer, ovarian cancer, cervical cancer, yeast infections, bladder infections, irregular menses) often indicated sexual abuse—whether or not they remembered it.

Any professional astrologer can tell you that you draw people to you who are much like you—not only with the same physical ailments, but shared life experiences. With a Mars/Pluto conjunction in Leo in the 12th House, I suffered sexual abuse from ages 2-5; I was raped when I was 24. At 35, I finally went into therapy for the rape and discovered my earlier abuse which I had completely blocked and of which I had no memory recall. This denial of an occurrence so heinous is quite normal. It took four years of therapy to work through and clarify myself.

Interestingly, in all my years as a medical astrologer I had hundreds of women clients who had either been raped, beaten as a child or adult, or been sexually abused as a child. I was drawing what I had experienced—but had no inkling that the same thing had happened to me until I was in therapy.

I wrote to Ann at length of my findings and suggestions. I still thought she should be under the care of a homeopathic M.D. and wondered how she would react to my letter and "bottom line" that her basic 'health problems were emotionally related to early childhood sexual abuse. Her instant reply recounted that a few months earlier she had gone into therapy and that during the second session the therapist said she felt Ann had been sexually abused as a young child. Ann has absolutely *no recall* before kindergarten. I was unaware of this. A few days before my letter arrived, a hands-on healer told her the same thing. We talked for an hour, sharing experiences, discussing that she should stick with her therapist and what could be expected from the therapy.

Ann felt heartened and supported that my medical astrology appraisal of her situation confirmed what other professionals had determined. She confided that from age 14-17 her mother (who, in Ann's opinion, was sick) had "mentally" abused her by detailing many explicit sexual experiences she had had with Ann's father and various lovers. Her father also had problems, in Ann's opinion, and their relationship had strong erotic overtones, but she can't ever remember him sexually abusing her.

Ann continues in therapy, digging for the truth about her blocked-out past and her boiling, inflamed emotions that reflect physically in the reproductive/sexual area of her body. She has requested that I treat her homeopathically until I feel it is beyond my scope of experience, and I have agreed to do this. The outcome is that Ann is recovering through a many-pronged plan. She continues in therapy to cleanse her subconscious. She continues with her vitamin and mineral support plan, and the homeopathic remedy will start to cure her reproductive ailments. She understands that these problems can come back if she doesn't actively pursue therapy.

Finally she has the support of a medical astrologer whom she trusts and believes in. A healer, whether a medical astrologer or any healing professional, plays a significant part in a client's road to wellness. It could be in providing nothing more than moral support or the offering of useful information about certain kinds of treatment from other health professionals. The medical astrological counselor can offer all of the above and truly be a healer.

STAY IN TOUCH

On the following pages you will find listed, with their current prices, some of the books and tapes now available on related subjects. Your book dealer stocks most of these, and will stock new titles in the Llewellyn series as they become available. We urge your patronage.

However, to obtain our full catalog, to keep informed of new titles as they are released and to benefit from informative articles and helpful news, you are invited to write for our bi-monthly news magazine/catalog. A sample copy is free, and it will continue coming to you at no cost as long as you are an active mail customer. Or you may keep it coming for a full year with a donation of just $2.00 in U.S.A. ($7.00 for Canada & Mexico, $20.00 overseas, first class mail). Many bookstores also have *The Llewellyn New Times* available to their customers. Ask for it.

Stay in touch! In *The Llewellyn New Times'* pages you will find news and reviews of new books, tapes and services, announcements of meetings and seminars, articles helpful to our readers, news of authors, advertising of products and services, and much more.

The Llewellyn New Times
P.O. Box 64383-Dept. 385, St. Paul, MN 55164-0383, U.S.A.
• • •
TO ORDER BOOKS AND TAPES

If your book dealer does not have the books and tapes described on the following pages readily available, you may order them direct from the publisher by sending full price in U.S. funds, plus $2.00 for postage and handling for the first book, and 50 cents for each additional book. There are no postage and handling charges for orders over $50. UPS Delivery: We ship UPS whenever possible. Delivery guaranteed. Provide your street address as UPS does not deliver to P.O. Boxes. UPS to Canada requires a $50 minimum order. Allow 4-6 weeks for delivery. Orders outside the U.S.A. and Canada: Airmail—add retail price of book; add $5 for each non-book item (tapes, etc.); add $1 per item for surface mail.

FOR GROUP STUDY AND PURCHASE

Because there is a great deal of interest in group discussion and study of the subject matter of this book, we feel that we should encourage the adoption and use of this particular book by such groups by offering a special "quantity" price to group leaders or "agents."

Our Special Quantity Price for a minimum order of five copies of *Astrological Counseling* is $44.85 cash-with-order. This price includes postage and handling within the U.S. Minnesota residents must add 6% sales tax. For additional quantities, please order in multiples of five. For Canadian and foreign orders, add postage and handling charges as above. Credit card (VISA, Master Card, American Express) orders are accepted. Charge card orders only may be phoned free ($15.00 minimum order) within the U.S.A. or Canada by dialing 1-800-THE-MOON. Customer service calls dial 1-612-291-1970. Mail orders to:

LLEWELLYN PUBLICATIONS
P.O. Box 64383-Dept. 385 / St. Paul, MN 55164-0383, U.S.A.

PLANETS: THE ASTROLOGICAL TOOLS
Edited by Joan McEvers
This is the second in the astrological anthology series edited by Joan McEvers. Take off through the solar system with 10 professional astrologers as they bring their insights to the symbolism and influences of the planets.

- Toni Glover Sedgwick: The Sun as the life force and our ego
- Joanne Wickenburg: The Moon as our emotional signal to change
- Erin Sullivan-Seale: Mercury as the multi-faceted god, followed with an in-depth explanation of its retrogradation
- Robert Glasscock: Venus as your inner value system
- Johanna Mitchell: Mars as your energizing inner warrior
- Don Borkowski: Jupiter as expansion and preservation
- Gina Ceaglio: Saturn as a source of freedom through self-discipline
- Bil Tierney: Uranus as the original, growth-producing planet
- Karma Welch: Neptune as selfless giving and love
- Joan Negus: Pluto as a powerful personal force

0–87542–381–7, 380 pgs., 5 1/4 x 8, charts, softcover $12.95

FINANCIAL ASTROLOGY FOR THE 1990s
Edited by Joan McEvers
Favorably reviewed in the *Wall Street Journal* by financial expert Stanley W. Angrist! Nine respected astrologers share their wisdom and good fortune with you.

- Michael Munkasey: A Primer on Market Forecasting
- Pat Esclavon Hardy: Charting the U.S. and the NYSE
- Jeanne Long: New Concepts for Commodities Trading Combining Astrology & Technical Analysis
- Georgia Stathis: The Real Estate Process
- Mary B. Downing: An Investor's Guide to Financial Astrology
- Judy Johns: The Gann Technique
- Carol S. Mull: Predicting the Dow
- Bill Meridian: The Effect of Planetary Stations on U.S. Stock Prices
- Georgia Stathis: Delineating the Corporation
- Robert Cole: The Predictable Economy

0–87542–382–5, 368 pgs., 5 1/4 x 8, illus., softcover $14.95

THE HOUSES: POWER PLACES OF THE HOROSCOPE
Edited by Joan McEvers

This volume combines the talents of 11 renowned astrologers in the fourth book of Llewellyn's anthology series. Each house, an area of activity within the horoscope, is explained with clarity and depth by the following authors:

- Peter Damian: The 1st House and the Rising Sign and Planets
- Ken Negus: The 7th House of Partnership
- Noel Tyl: The 2nd House of Self-Worth and the 8th House of Values and Others
- Spencer Grendahl: The 3rd House of Exploration and Communication
- Dona Shaw: The 9th House of Truth and Abstract Thinking
- Gloria Star: The 4th House of the Subconscious Matrix
- Marwayne Leipzig: The 10th House of the Life's Imprint
- Lina Accurso: The 5th House of Love
- Sara Corbin Looms: The 11th House of Tomorrow
- Michael Munkasey: The 6th House of Attitude and Service
- Joan McEvers: The 12th House of Strength, Peace, Tranquillity

0–87542–383–3, 400 pgs., 5 1/4 x 8, charts, softcover   **$12.95**

THE ASTROLOGY OF THE MACROCOSM
Edited by Joan McEvers

Joan has done it again! This fifth volume of Llewellyn's anthology series meets the challenges and explores the possibilities of Mundane Astrology with chapters by 11 competent astrologers. Topics include:

- Jimm Erickson: A Philosophy of Mundane Astrology
- Judy Johns: The Ingress Chart
- Jim Lewis: Astro*Carto*Graphy—Bringing Mundane Astrology Down to Earth
- Richard Nolle: The SuperMoon Alignment
- Chris McRae: The Geodetic Equivalent Method of Prediction
- Nicholas Campion: The Age of Aquarius—A Modern Myth
- Nancy Soller: Weather Watching with an Ephemeris
- Marc Penfield: The Mystery of the Romanovs
- Steve Cozzi: The Astrological Quatrains of Michel Nostradamus
- Diana K. Rosenberg: Stalking the Wild Earthquake
- Caroline W. Casey: Dreams and Disasters—Patterns of Cultural and Mythological Evolution into the 21st Century

0–87542–384–1, 420 pgs., 5 1/4 x 8, charts, softcover   **$19.95**